The Shaping of Modern
Hereford

The Shaping of Modern
Hereford

by

Graham Roberts

Logaston Press

LOGASTON PRESS
Little Logaston, Logaston,
Woonton, Almeley, Herefordshire HR3 6QH

First published by Logaston Press 2001
Reprinted (with revised chapter IX) 2002
Copyright © text Graham Roberts 2001
Copyright © illustrations, see credits in Acknowledgments 2001

ISBN 1 873827 67 9

Set in Times by Logaston Press
and printed in Great Britain by
Bath Press Group

Contents

Acknowledgments

I have drawn extensively from the great wealth of research, information and scholarship of previous authors and wish to acknowledge the debt which I owe, notably to those mentioned in the Preface. They have supplied much of the essential motivation for the exertions involved, none more so perhaps than Mrs. Lobel who breaks off so tantalisingly at the end of the 18th century at what is arguably the most significant time in the whole of Hereford's enthralling history. I have also been fortunate in being able to call upon just over a quarter of a century of close involvement and absorbing interest in the continuing changes that have so dramatically occurred in the city. My work has brought me into contact with countless numbers of citizens from all walks of life, 'Whitefaces' as well as adoptees such as myself.

Naming names is a most worrying process, for inevitably there has to be a limit. But this book, and many other existing and forthcoming works about the people, activities and character of the county and its environs would not have appeared without the infectious enthusiasm of Andy Johnson of Logaston Press and it has been my turn to appreciate and acknowledge his great fund of ideas, editorial skills and flair. Nor can I fail to make special mention of Basil Butcher whose encyclopaedic memory spanned nearly half the period I covered. We both knew Herbert Powell, an 'Old Herefordian' like him, and Kenneth Lee, both of whose deep knowledge of city and county and sense of history informed their respective roles as a leading local architect and the city council's chief planning assistant. Their valuable input to this story has been shared over the years (without them necessarily knowing it) by many of my former colleagues, especially Roger Thomas, Peter Meiklejohn, Paul Bainbridge, David Nicholson, David Berry, David King, Anne Sandford, Howard Pilkington and numerous others. I have also been helped and encouraged by several former mayors or city aldermen and councillors, particularly Derek Davies, Kit Gundy, George Hyde, John Newman, Robin Price, David Short, Dick Vowles, Ivor Williams and Frank Warr. For some specialised aspects I have been able to call upon a very wide range of sources, most especially at the Reference Library, Woolhope Club Library and Herefordshire Record Office.

Countless local people have helped, with or without cajolery, to speak about events in the more recent life of Hereford. Yet not all that recent, for nonagenarian Jane Marpole rivalled even Basil Butcher by how far back she could go when I asked her! After domestic service for the Revd. Gustavus Bosanquet at Newstead House, Venns Lane, she left to get married when she was 21—and some 75 years later was being cared for at the nursing home there, full of vivid memories. I am grateful to Colonel John Blashford-Snell, Dr. Mike Deakin, Fay Farmer, Lt. Col. Tom Hill, Bill Morris, Jan Morris, Lionel Read Q.C., Charles Renton, Dr. John Ross, Jenny Watkins, Terry Watts, Bryan White and a host of others for particular contributions or timely encouragement. Most of all I thank Wendy, my wife, for all the long evenings alone looking after our family during my interminable absences at meetings (sometimes gathering material for future deployment here!), and afterwards in generous measures of forbearance and help.

I have several people to thank for providing and permitting the use of illustrations as follows: Herefordshire Council Libraries and Information Services for those on pp.6, 7, 10 (top left and bottom left), 11, 12, 14, 42, 49 (top), 77(bottom right), 78 (top left), 91, 96 (bottom), 134 (bottom), 148 (top), 171 (top), 193 (top), and 195; Ron Shoesmith pp.3, 49 (lower), 52, 64, 86, 98 and 153; Derek Evans pp.57 (top left, centre right, and lower), 60, 63 (top), 65 (top), 77 (top left), 78 (top right), 154 and 197 (bottom); Donovan Wilson pp. *iii*, 16, 56, 61, 62 (lower right) and 70; Richard Hammonds pp.4, 72 (top left) and 157; Logaston Press pp.34 (lower), 39 (both), 138 (top right and centre left) and 139 (top right and bottom right); *Hereford Times* pp.59 and 97; Herefordshire Hospitals NHS Trust p.129; V&A p.148 (bottom); Mr. A.J. Hubbard p.23; W.H. Bustin & Son p.15; Woolhope Club Library p.110; Barry Griffiths p.191 (top); Foster/Skeffington p.76; Basil Butcher p.79; Henry Wiggins/Inco Alloys p.100; Derek Foxton p.123 (bottom); Ken Hoverd p.166; Herefordshire Light Infantry Regimental Museum p.173. Many of the other recent photographs, and some of those of the past, are my own.

Preface

Since its origins in the early 8th century, the role and significance of Hereford has known continual change in shape and fortune due to military, ecclesiastical, economic and many other circumstances. But nothing has approached the scale met during the final two hundred years of the 20th century since the city emerged from its prolonged medieval guise and, rather later than most communities, started to exhibit the first effects of the Industrial Revolution.

By its nature this is not a definitive social, economic or physical history of this recent period, that may come with the planned new *Victoria County History of Herefordshire*. Yet there is already a wealth of material available from antiquarians, archaeologists, historians, town planners, cartographers, visitors—and from the county's citizens. This is nowhere more fully demonstrated than in the *Transactions of the Woolhope Naturalists' Field Club* of Herefordshire, which was established in 1851. There is much more besides. Most of the books and papers are available in the Broad Street Reference Library or the Hereford Record Office, whilst recently published titles include *The Royal Charters*, *The Mappa Mundi*, *The Civil War in Hereford* and *Herefordshire under Arms* through to *The Hereford and Gloucester Canal* and *The Pubs of Hereford City*. There is an insatiable appetite for old photographs, postcards and other illustrations of 'Hereford Past and Present' and this has been particularly well satisfied. There have occasionally been reprints of old 'classics' that have been long out of print, such as John Price's *Historic Account of the City of Hereford* of 1796, John Duncumb's *Collections towards the History and Antiquities of the County of Hereford* of 1804, Ella Mary Leather's *The Folklore of Herefordshire* of 1912 and William Collins' *Historic Landmarks of Hereford*, which was first published in 1915. It is helpful to be able to read these fascinating books in conjunction with a range of authoritative new works by local authors such as David Whitehead, Jim and Muriel Tonkin, Anne Sandford, Betty Grist and Derek Foxton. Probably the most prolific of them all is Ron Shoesmith, the longest serving of a succession of archaeologists whose scrupulous and painstaking excavations and thorough recording practices and presentation of results have added so greatly to knowledge of the material history of the city. I have been fortunate in having Ron's guidance with several aspects of this book.

Urban archaeology was in its infancy during the early 1960s, but in 1965, the Council for British Archaeology undertook research which led to the publication of a list of 324 towns in England, Scotland and Wales the historic qualities of which required careful treatment in any planning or redevelopment proposals. Of these, 51 were considered to be of special importance, and thus regarded as 'so splendid and so precious that ultimate responsibility for them should be a national concern'. The City of Hereford was one of them. It has to be said that archaeologists were among those who had been slow to react to the situation arising from the vigorous programmes of redevelopment schemes in historic towns in the 1950s and 1960s, partly because of the costs of disentangling the intricate strata of centuries of active occupation with only minimal help from government. It was providential, therefore, that when extensive works were about to start in the centre of Hereford there was on hand a company of archaeologists of the calibre of Frank Noble, Margaret Gray, Stan Stanford, Philip Rahtz and Ron Shoesmith. As city surveyor for over a quarter of a century of this critical period I was able to gain an invaluable historical perspective from them and their associates for my particular role in the planning and shaping of Hereford. I am grateful for this, for there is abundant evidence in many historic towns and cities, their fabric violated and 'raped' during the 1950s, '60s and '70s, that their councillors an officials could have done with such guidance.

In the mid-1960s the International Commission for the History of Towns became concerned with the production of a series of studies comprising a ground record and historical commentary on each of eight long-established British Towns, covering the processes of their development until the end of the 18th century when their medieval character was transformed by the industrial revolution. Hereford was considered to be eminently suitable for the first volume of maps and essays by virtue of its very early place on the map of England and Wales and its prominence in history books. It was also one of the most extensively mapped towns of any, having first appeared in the late 13th century at the very edge of an illustrated representation of a round flat world. This was the Mappa Mundi, drawn by Richard of Haldingham and Lafford. The first known detailed map of the city was 'performed' in 1610 by the Tudor cartographer, John Speede, and in 1757, Isaac Taylor produced one of the finest of all urban maps of that or any other period. Coincidentally this portrayed the topography, 'texture' and a number of the chief buildings in considerable and accurate detail near the end of pre-industrial Hereford.

The historical commentary for *Historic Towns: Hereford*, the fifth study of the initial volume of the British section of town plans, published in 1969, was provided by Mrs. M.D. Lobel of Oxford. Colonel W.H. Johns of the Lovell Johns - Cook Hammond and Kell Organisation acted as topographical mapping editor and both were able to contribute their considerable academic and technical resources as they worked in close collaboration with the Hereford Research Committee, a team of local advisers and contributors. Under the chairmanship of Frank Noble, the members were Miss R.E. Hickling, Mrs. J. O'Donnell, Mr. H.J. Powell, Mr. I.M. Slocombe and officers of the highways and planning sections of my department. Much special help was provided by Mr. J.F.W. Sherwood, city librarian and curator.

Changes to the face of the city during the past two centuries have been well covered by the mapmakers, commencing with H. Price, who published his map in 1802 (republished with additions to 1852 by W.H. Vale), G. Cole and J. Roper also around 1802 and Lieut. R. Dawson of the Royal Engineers in 1831. In 1858 Timothy Curley, another engineer, produced the most comprehensive of all plans of Hereford as a preliminary for the many changes with which he was associated. These were indicated in some detail in 1867 in a Plan of the City of Hereford embracing all the Recent Developments, published by Joseph Jones and Son. This gave a clear picture of the state of development of the Victorian city at that time. By then the Ordnance Survey had become increasingly involved in cartography and has since become responsible for producing and regularly updating most of the present-day range of maps.

Foreword

My early life was spent at Holy Trinity Vicarage, which, during World War Two, became a centre of activity and was the local Air Raid Precaution Headquarters. Sand-bag blast walls were built across the front of the house, an Anderson bomb-shelter was installed and the study became the control-room. Nearby a regiment of Indian Cavalry with horses was camped on the racecourse. At night a band of portly gentlemen armed with shotguns and pitchforks patrolled the parish on bicycles. The Home Guard, as it was named, was led by our churchwarden, the redoubtable Captain Faulkner. For a small boy it was very exciting and I wished I could grow up quickly and rush off to fight, but, if the posters that adorned the walls were anything to go by, it was likely that the Germans would come to me anyway.

Mother spent much of her time helping welfare organisations and ran the parish whilst Pa was abroad with the Herefordshire Regiment and the 53rd Welsh Division. Early education at Miss Gibson's School for Girls and Young Boys at Broomy Hill became a nightmare when we lads were forced to go through 'wedding ceremonies' every break-time with the older pupils. However, I can claim to have 'married' the daughters of a number of Hereford's leading families!

By 1942 the vicarage was being used to house 20 attractive nurses and Mother, seeking to add a little sparkle to their lives, invited the Commanding Officer of a nearby American Air Force unit to send along some of his men for Sunday afternoon tea. It was my duty to welcome them at the front door and as such, receive the copious quantities of candy that our gallant allies carried. The scarcity of chocolate made this a highly-prized trade good. Tea was served in the drawing-room and soon the airmen were fascinating the ladies with tales of America. One huge sergeant named Tex came from Texas, where, he informed us, everything was larger, faster, stronger and better than anywhere else in the whole wide world. He was a very big man and I feared for Mother's bone china tea cup, which was completely encompassed by his vast hand. I noted that no one contradicted Tex. When the hot crumpets, a special treat, were produced the door rattled. Brutus had a passion for crumpets and had learned to open doors by seizing the door knobs in his great jaws. Tex was in full flow when it swung open to reveal the awesome sight of a massive St. Bernard, strings of saliva hanging from his cavernous mouth.

'Gawd, what a dog,' cried the Texan.

'Oh, that's only the pup, wait until you see his mother,' said my Mama, refilling the tea cups.

Meanwhile my faith in the Home Guard had diminished and, unable to play a more active part in the war other that run messages for the ARP, I decided to raise a small private army to defend the parish. Recruiting was easy. Before the war Mother had laid in a plentiful stock of tinned pineapple and other mouth-watering delights. These, plus our fruit orchards, and the abundance of cuddly pets, attracted hordes of children. From this host I was able to select some 30 loyal followers of both sexes. We had our headquarters in an old stable, shared with a pet fox, and from there would sally forth against the enemy, which, in the absence of German paratroopers, was provided by a rival organization of uncouth lads, whose main occupation was to raid the apple crop. Epic battles involving dozens of children raged back and forth across the countryside. Our weapons included catapults, grenades, Molotov cocktails and even a ballista (copied from a history book) to hurl evil-smelling dead cats.

By the time I was 14, the need to defend Hereford from Hitler had long receded and my schooling was making serious inroads into the conduct of the campaign. Father, believing that I was a useless waster, encouraged me to do something positive to help at home. With reluctance, I agreed to rise before dawn on Wednesdays and ring the church bell for mid-week communion. The searing cold in the un-heated vicarage bit through me as I stumbled through the snow to open the heavy vestry door and tug the aged bell-rope. Even a nip of the sideboard brandy failed to fortify me and I knew that, if I were to survive, I must find a better solution.

It came to me like a vision—indeed, it may have been divine providence that showed the way. The great bell was within view of my bedroom window and a round of .300 rook rifle fired from my bed would produce a ring to waken the dead. Twenty shots and we had filled five pews, but, alas, the resultant ricochets may have had more to do with it. As the last of the faithful scampered into the cover of the church porch, Father, in a biblical rage, reminded me that it was a house of peace.

However, I had the happiest childhood in Hereford. Reading Graham Roberts' text, memories of learning to swim in the Edgar Street baths, canoeing on the Wye (ever fearful of polio), skittles matches at Holy Trinity Institute, the race days, the back row of the Odeon cinema, all the fun of the May Fair and trying to impress my first girl friend with dinner at the Green Dragon, flood back.

Of course there were more sombre occasions and I still enjoy my visits to the great cathedral and seeing the treasured Mappa Mundi and chained library.

Hereford is a friendly city with a fascinating history and Graham Roberts' thorough research has brought alive 200 years of its past in a most readable style.

What is more, it is a mine of information about the people, their habits and homes, events and even the costs that have shaped Hereford's history since 1800. We read of the impact on the city of Britain's changing fortunes, the political wrangles and the problems of disease.

I believe this is a most valuable work for scholars, citizens and all interested in the development of a great cathedral city.

John Blashford-Snell
Expedition Base
Motcombe

Chapter I
Setting the Scene

Markets have been in existence for as long as people have met to barter or exchange goods, and wherever there was such business traders soon appeared on the scene to set out stalls or pitches. Fairs were known in prehistoric societies and there would have been markets of a kind during the Bronze and Iron Ages but it was above all the Romans, with their extensive road system and need to fund and supply an army, who encouraged trade and the circulation of goods upon which taxes could be levied. Markets continued where Saxons built their strongholds, and the Church its monasteries and bishops' palaces. It would be surprising if, from its earliest days, Saxon Hereford did not become a significant trading centre and possess a market. Indeed, during the reign of Edward the Elder (899-924) growing levels of trade across the country led to a royal decree regulating all buying and selling, and stipulating that all activities should occur in open market places. Documentary evidence suggests that there could well have been a market in Hereford in 958 and there is no doubt that the trading character of the city was well established by the arrival of the Normans.

At the beginning of the second millennium, in the days of King Ethelred, Hereford had become one of the principal centres of Saxon England. Then, just over half way through the 11th century, the city was ravaged by the Welsh with a degree of savagery and destructiveness which sadly is still all too familiar in parts of the world at the end of the millennium. Yet, by the time William the Conqueror undertook an inventory of his human and productive resources in the Domesday Survey of 1086, the city had established a new level of prosperity and precedence. It was classified as one of just 16 shire towns ranking as cities, its dignity stemming not only from its bishop's seat, but also from the long established customs, privileges and duties applying to its burgesses.

William fitzOsbern, of Breteuil-sur-Iton in Normandy, was one of William the Conqueror's closest companions and soon after 1066 he was created earl of Hereford and placed in charge of affairs in the city and much of the border territory between Chepstow and Ludlow. The state of Hereford Castle called for his urgent attention, whilst space required for rebuilding of the Norman cathedral across the east/west route (King Street/Castle Street) meant the removal of the bishop's market site from the crossroads. William chose a spacious site north of the gate to the Saxon burh on flat, well drained land owned by bishop Walter of Lorraine. Compared with the former market site it was huge and shaped, bounded as it was by present day High Town, Commercial Street and Union Street, like a great wedge—possibly modelled on that which William knew at home in Breteuil. A reading of the *Domesday Book* written some 20 years later suggests that Earl William had rather pressed the bishop to exchange 'the land in which the market is now' for property at Eaton Bishop and Lydney. William did not remain in Hereford for long (and was killed in 1071), but the measures he took or initiated contributed great economic benefit, leading to rapid expansion during the remainder of the century and for a considerable time afterwards.

The holding of markets and fairs had always been the principal and most coveted privilege of any medieval town and all were controlled by the king through the granting of charters.

In 1189 Hereford obtained one such in exchange for hard cash. The standing and prosperity of the city was demonstrated by, for those days, the hefty payment of £40, an amount which it was considered the citizens could afford each year, and for ever. In exchange the city secured priceless opportunities to conduct its own affairs, and successive city authorities have budgeted for this amount for over 800 years. However, the charter also imposed a new duty—that of refortifying the town. At its strategic position within the buffer territory dividing the English from the Welsh, Hereford time and again figured in violent conflicts. Indeed, without this continuous military involvement the course of its own history would have been completely different. As it was, the Welsh had been driven back beyond the Black Mountains after their assault of 1055, and the creation of the Norman Marcher Lordships as a buffer along the Welsh border had reduced the urgency for defensive measures. It took until the end of the 13th century before the new walls, bastions and gates were substantially constructed, by which time they embraced a modest area of just 93 acres, centred on the great market place.

The origins of Hereford's May Fair can be traced to a charter granted in 1121 by Henry I to the bishop, probably as a source of revenue for works at the cathedral. Although the word 'fair' has its roots in the Latin *feria*, signifying a festive holiday, it was at the time much more to do with business and trade. The event started on the eve of the feast day of St. Ethelbert on 20 May and lasted for three days, during which time the bishop claimed the keys and government of the city and all the tolls. The fair was subsequently extended to nine days (later reduced once more to three) and remained an important source of revenue for the see, and a centuries-long source of wrangling with city authorities, until an Act of 1838 enabled the municipality to buy out the rights. In compensation the bishop was granted 12½ bushels of best wheat or its monetary equivalent every year and this tradition has been maintained at the opening of each subsequent May Fair.

In addition, there came to be five other fairs. The first was held on the first Tuesday after 2 February; the Wednesday in Easter Week a fair where cattle, sheep, pigs, horses, hops and pedlary were sold; and 1 July saw a fair renowned for its wool. A particularly large fair fell on 20 October, when, in later years, farmers and dealers travelled considerable distances to Hereford to buy and sell Hereford cattle. Typically some 1,000 head were sold, and many horses also changed hands. This was also the occasion when hops and butter, cheese, and most other country produce were purchased in preparation for the winter. However, a final such opportunity arose on the Wednesday after St. Andrew's Day (30 November), after which there was every chance that the countryside would soon become swamped or blocked by snow.

During these fairs the wool was disposed of in the market-house, hops at the market-house and the Old Gaol, cattle in Broad Street and King Street, horses in St. Owen Street and butter and cheese near St. Peter's Church. The many domestic and other needs of the farming and village communities were also keenly served by the small shopkeepers, solicitors, bankers and, of course, by many innkeepers. In addition the fairs were visited by itinerant traders from far afield bearing colourful materials, sparkling metalware, pungent spices and all manner of unfamiliar goods; they also provided a wide range of entertainments.

The fairs also traded in farm labour and in common with other local towns Hereford held a hiring fair. Dressed in their best clothes, labourers brought a token or badge of their trade with them to High Town: the kitchen maid her mop (hence the name 'mop' fair in some places), a shepherd perhaps a piece of wool in his hat, a horseman or waggoner plaited straw pinned to his lapel, and hard bargaining took place with farmers before terms were settled, usually until the following May. The contract was generally settled by the giving and receiving of the 'farmer's bond' or 'earnest money', typically a shilling. These hiring fairs were active until the turn of the 19th century.

Markets and fairs were a fundamental part of the business economy and appeal of the city, but also formed the highlights of many citizens' lives, not only because of the provision of most necessities of life and welcome entertainment but, importantly, as social opportunities for keeping up with news from beyond their own confined parochial boundaries. The state of congestion can well be imagined as animals filled the streets, farmers parked their horses and carts and people from the countryside flocked in and out.

At the west end of High Town was the High Cross, a feature of many medieval markets stemming from the time when traders gathered beneath their churchyard crosses, until a law of 1285 required them to move away on grounds of unseemliness. It would probably have taken the form of a stepped stone pedestal surmounted by a shaft, rather like that at Whitecross. Always at a focal position in the market, the cross was seen, perhaps rather optimistically, as bestowing a measure of spiritual security on traders' activities. It would in any case be a

gathering place for all those in town for the gossip, to exchange local news, sort out the affairs of the world, compare prices and engage in all the countless activities that take place in a busy market. In addition the steps served as a useful platform for orators, for the delivery of sermons and proclamations, promulgation of new laws and even banns of marriage. And they had another, quite macabre, function when from time to time they were used to exhibit the severed heads of those executed for their misdeeds or, in times of conflict, for being on the losing side.

Owain ap Maredudd ap Tudur (Anglicised as Owen Tudor), a minor squire from Anglesey, was one to suffer this fate. Captured by the Yorkists in 1461 at the battle of Mortimers Cross, he was executed at Hereford and his head placed on the

The shrine of St. Thomas Cantilupe in Hereford Cathedral which, along with the shrine of St. Ethelbert, brought many pilgrims— and hence wealth—to medieval Hereford

top step of the cross, lit by 100 candles. Many years before, he had served in the household of Katherine de Valois, ardent young widow of Henry V and despite constraints placed upon the dowager queen as the mother of Henry VI, who was not yet a teenager, and his own inferior status as an obscure commoner, they married secretly without statutory royal permission. Edmund, their eldest son, married Margaret Beaufort, a descendant of John of Gaunt, and their only son was born at Pembroke Castle in 1457. Through his mother's royal ancestry—and one quarter Welsh, one quarter French and half English—he was to become Henry VII, the first Tudor monarch, at Bosworth in 1485. The long enmity between English and Welsh was ended, subsequently endorsed by the Act of Union, and resulted in a major waning in Hereford's frontier role and economy. His heir, Arthur, Prince of Wales, was born in 1486 and when only 15 married the 16 year-old Princess Catherine of Aragon. With profound consequences for State and Church (not least in Hereford) and in Europe, he died on honeymoon at Ludlow Castle six months later. In 1509 his younger brother, Owen's other princely great-grandson, became King Henry VIII and most controversially

married Catherine, Arthur's widow. This move led to a major quarrel with Rome and thence repudiation of all papal authority in England. A conservative Hereford did not support Henry's consequent 're-formation' of the Church: in 1526 this accounted for his fierce response in authorising the destruction of two fulling and two corn mills on the Wye belonging to the dean and chapter. The devastating impact on wool and corn trades, and on employment, caused lasting additional damage to the economy of the city.

The Tudor dynasty continued past the date of Hereford's Charter of Incorporation in 1597, ending with the death of Elizabeth I in 1603. Owen Tudor, the line's progenitor, lies almost forgotten in Hereford somewhere at Greyfriars, within the site of the former Franciscan friary. As a rare tribute to his seminal role in the history of England and Wales, the Mayor of Hereford unveiled a granite plaque in 1998, close to the place in High Town where the head 'that had lain in the lap of a queen'—as he stoically observed to his executioner—had been so cruelly displayed. (Had normal patronymic rules been followed, Owain would have been called Owen Meredith [in English] after his father and not his grandfather, Tudor, and the dynasty called The Merediths!)

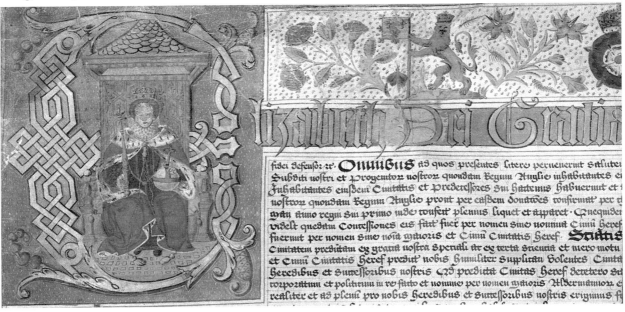

Part of Elizabeth I's charter granted to the city of Hereford in 1597

The Reformation also led to the tailing off of the highly lucrative pilgrim tourist industry associated with belief in the healing powers of Saint Ethelbert and Saint Thomas Cantilupe of Hereford, centred on their shrines at the cathedral. Much human distress and material devastation resulted and just over a century later, in the 1640s, this was compounded when the whole country was plunged into civil war.

Even after these serious economic setbacks, the market area was at times said to be almost impassable because of piles of merchandise on offer, and at the end of the 16th century there was enough money available to build quite the most magnificent market-house and guild-hall. Elizabeth's charter confirmed the right for the corporation to hold the city in return for £40 per annum—the same amount required in 1189 by Richard I. Within four highly decorative sheets of parchment, written in close set Court Latin, it created a corporate body in place of the former community of privileged members. This governing body was to consist of a common council of 31 members, including the mayor and aldermen, who were intended to meet for the transaction of business in the guild-hall, once it was built. The charter also granted authority for the new corporation to hold three weekly markets and two annual fairs: in this way the queen exercised her prerogative to grant a 'franchise' conferring a right to hold 'a concourse of buyers and sellers' for the disposal of commodities, either at a market or a fair. Unwelcome competition between neighbouring market towns was prevented by this form of royal management and Hereford's franchise still entitles the city to protection against any rival market within a distance of 6^2/$_3$ miles as the crow flies. (This was the statutory distance between markets in the 14th century, based on the 20 miles a man could reasonably walk in a day divided by three, allowing him to get to market, time to do business and then return home).

The earliest mention in the city archives of the guild-hall is in 1596, and it is thought to have taken up to three years to complete. There is no record of who designed it, although the name of

The east elevation of the market-hall and guild-hall as envisaged by John Clayton (1846)

the talented and highly regarded Hereford craftsman, John Abel (1577-1674), has been suggested. At little over 20 years of age, it is more likely that, at most, he only assisted as an apprentice. A magnificent half-timbered building of three storeys, it was erected towards the western end of High Town. Supported on 27 walnut piers arranged in three rows, the first floor was used for magistrates' chambers and courts (leased to the county for assizes and quarter sessions) and for meetings, and the second provided chambers for 14 craft guilds—each with their arms and other devices above their doors. The open space between the pillars was used for the market-place, whilst the city council seemed, in fact,

Butchers' Row in High Town, 1815 by David Cox

generally to meet at the Tolsey, at the Commercial Street end of High Town. This was a plain building of stone from where the market was administered, tolls collected and law and order maintained. It would usually be the venue for the Court of Pie Powder (a corruption of *pieds poudres*, meaning 'dusty footed' travellers) where of necessity judgements were rapidly delivered. Acting rather in the role of an all-in-one trading standards, weights and measures authority and summary seat of justice, such courts were of very long standing and would also have been held in a

much earlier Tolsey known to have existed in 1339, when there is a documentary record of it having been broken into and robbed.

In time the rest of High Town became crammed with timbered buildings, with Cooken Row on the northern side separated by Golden Alley from the Old House and Butchers' Row, or Butchery to the south.

There was another cross at St. Peter's Square, the 'low' cross, at a place which had served as a market since the church was erected by Walter de Lacy prior to Domesday. Documents in Town

High Town in 1838, with the market-hall and guild-hall as it could have appeared in 1600, as depicted by G.R. Lewis

Hall archives confirm the existence of 'Saynte Peter's Crosse in Hongry Strete' standing at 'an ancient market place for butter and cheese' and also refer to stocks. Further reference to the market is in a petition of 1589, which asked for the removal of the fruit and iron markets from the High Causey to St. Peter's Cross. Documents also record a 'Markett House at St. Peter's Crosse', but only the market cross is shown on John Speede's map of 1610, and there was pressure for a new one in 1676. By 1757 the cross had gone and, just within St. Owen Street, Isaac Taylor instead depicted a 'Machine' used for weighing goods housed in a 'cumbersome brick building'. This had also served as a guardhouse, and was replaced by a neat octagon white stone structure that remained until the 1860s. It became redundant with the opening of the new markets and a lamp was erected in its place.

Further charters were granted until 1697 and by 1800 merchandise was being traded at three weekly markets at Hereford. Butter, poultry, garden produce and other necessaries were sold on Wednesdays and cattle, sheep and pigs were offered on Fridays in what is now Aubrey Street. This was apparently the venue for a butcher's auction of his wife in 1802: it seems that the lot raised £1 4s. and a bowl of punch. In an issue of *The Hereford Times* in 1876 a nonagenarian lady referred to similar scenes witnessed, 'going from Barton to the other [east] side of town having to pass the bottom of the pig market [Aubrey Street]'. Once she had seen a woman with her hat in her hand and a rope around her neck. A man was holding the other end and eventually sold his wife for 1s., with her consent, being willing to throw in the rope into the bargain!

On Saturdays a plentiful supply of almost all the necessities of life was available. Butter, poultry and similar farm produce were sold in High Town, wheat and all sorts of grain in the market-house, meat in Bye Street (Commercial

Street) and garden produce near St. Peter's Church and in Cabbage Lane (Church Street). Everything was in the open, the only covered space being between the 27 pillars on the open ground floor of the market-house and at the Booth Hall. Here the chief commodity had long been leather for the shoemakers. This was later joined by flannels and other woollen goods with the arrival of the Welsh clothiers, or frysemen, and items such as salt butter also started to appear.

Despite continuing activity in the markets, the decline of the pilgrim trade, the loss of the corn and fulling mills and the ending of trade generated by having a busy royal castle, reduced the local economy to tatters. The city lapsed into the condition of an isolated, unimportant market town. Despite this it seemed to have been a pleasant enough place to Celia Fiennes, who in 1696, found 'a pretty little town of timber buildings, where the streets are well pitched and handsome as to breadth and length'. Yet in 1700, T. Cox wrote 'the buildings are mean and old, and but thinly inhabited, there not being any staple trade to enrich it, or invite people to go and settle

in it ... Gloves were the most important manufacture but this is too poor a trade to make a place to flourish'. And in 1724, Daniel Defoe, the author of *Robinson Crusoe* and described as the keenest observer of economic growth of his time, was to refer to 'truly an old, mean built and very dirty city'. This opinion was shared at the time by the writer John Macky, who described 'the dirtiest old city I have seen in England'.

What none of them described, nor could they fully appreciate, were the parlous consequences of acute overcrowding caused by an ever growing population. For more than five centuries, much of the increase had been concentrated into the 93 acres enclosed by the 13th-century walled defences, but the problems of primitive healthcare, poor hygiene, appalling housing and the lack of any basic 'amenities' would have been very difficult to grasp during a fleeting visit. In any case they were not at all remarkable at that juncture in 18th-century Britain.

A more graphic indication came in 1757 when Isaac Taylor published his map of the city. Drawn with great detail and accuracy and embellished with artistic vignettes and drawings of the town-

The Bucks' view of Hereford in 1732, showing the city hemmed in by its walls, with the 'sally walk' on the outside

The view in 1757 of the city from Broomy Hill that frames Taylor's map

such as the 'stews' off Bewell Street. By modern standards the state of hygiene and sanitation must have been beyond description and in consequence of which the health and vitality of the resident population was low, infant mortality high and life expectancy very short.

Something had to be done, and after the passing of Hereford's own Lamp Act in 1774, town commissioners were appointed and saw to a measure of paving, cleaning and lighting of the streets and lanes and to the removal of nuisances and annoyances. This was at least a start and they produced more results than had ever been managed or thought of by the city council, with which the commissioners nevertheless worked in reasonable harmony.

By the first national decennial census of 1801 the population of the city had risen from the 5,592 recorded by Taylor to a purported 6,828, a modest increase of 1,200 in 44 years, and in the next ten years it was to rise by a further 500. Nevertheless, by the turn of the century a transformation had already commenced in the city

scape and some of the principal buildings, it depicts very thoroughly the town's character and extent at that time. In essence it differed little from the Hereford of 1610, as drawn then in another style by John Speede. In his time the walled city had started to show the signs of overcrowding and a consequent outward movement and by 1757 some 467 dwellings were straggled in ribbon development along the roads leading radially from the centre. Within the walls, there was the cathedral and its close, the bishop's palace and gardens, the site of a large castle, three churches, a substantial market place and much commercial development— as well as 812 dwellings with 3,816 inhabitants. This was an average occupancy rate of almost 4.7, contrasting strongly with late 20th-century levels of nearer 2.5. Many places between the market area and the six gates were severely congested and poorly built. Run down buildings overhung the streets and even worse were the houses in the courtyards. These had been created by infilling,

and of the river, bridge, bishop's palace and cathedral

Bysters Gate

centre. One of the first tasks of the commissioners had been to let in some light and air to reduce the dangers of epidemics, and among the first obstacles to be dealt with were the six city gates. These were demolished between 1782 and 1799, an operation which achieved the added purpose of improving the entrances into the city.

Caswall's cutlery store and the last house to be demolished in Butchers' Row, by G.R. Lewis

It did not meet with universal approval (and nowadays Conservation Area rules would have prevented this and any other such demolition schemes in the absence of adequate plans guaranteeing an enhancement of the city centre!). In addition the High Cross and bull ring in High Town and the Tolsey in Bye Street had been taken down, the entrance into the city at Wye Bridge had been widened and improved and the streets were considered, by the standards of the day, to be 'well paved and lighted'. The entrance into Widemarsh Street from the High Town had been widened by taking down the adjoining houses, as had the northern end of Broad Street at Norgate. Further improvements were 'in agitation'.

It had been thought necessary in 1792 to ease the pillars of the great market-house and guild-hall in High Town of part of their load and the upper storey, which had housed the trade guilds, was removed and the remaining building very

Four of the original support columns with moulded beams and carved capitals from the guild-hall reused in a summer house at Holmer Park by Charles Watkins, brewer and miller

10

High Town in the mid-19th century, after the market-hall and guild-hall had had its upper storey removed

badly 'refurbished' in tasteless plaster. Despite many further repairs, the whole building became a dreadful eyesore throughout much of the 19th century. The county functions moved in 1817 and the remains were finally demolished in 1862, the materials being sold to Mr. William Davies of Widemarsh Street for £200. Some columns, bases, spandrels, brackets and beams remain at Holmer Hall, Lyde House and Whitfield Court, south-west of Hereford.

To the east was the range of buildings called Butchers' Row. It was considered that their speedy removal was called for because:

not only the situation and irregular appearance of these houses recommend this measure, but also their appropriation, which is a real nuisance; the

circumstance of cattle being slaughtered in the centre of the city, to the great annoyance of the inhabitants, being an evil of a very serious nature.

They duly came down, and by 1837 there remained only the Old House, built in 1621, which subsequently served as a butcher's, saddler's, haberdasher's and fish shop, bank and from 1929, a public museum. Also to escape the demolition crews were houses on the west side of the narrow Cabbage-lane, subsequently Boots Passage, which it was thought would be susceptible of considerable improvement—enabling a handsome avenue to be made from the High Town to the cathedral'. It was also felt that the end of Bye-street (now Commercial Street) 'which is next the country, and the entrance into

11

High Town, looking west, with open air butter stalls, as depicted in 1803 by J. Varley

Eigne-street [now Eign Gate] from the centre of the city would be improved by removing the projecting houses'. These ambitions were not realised either.

In the anxiety to give the city a 'modern' appearance, many edifices were to acquire 'the same regular appearance as those in other parts of the kingdom'. Unfortunately this was largely managed, though most interiors were mercifully untouched. Early examples of this process can be seen in St. Owen Street and Bridge Street and also in places such as St. John Street, St. Martin's Street and High Town. A mid-19th-century portrayal of High Town (see.p.11) shows how the medieval character of the area had been replaced completely by one that was at the time described as 'tidy and proper'. In fact the centre of Hereford was being rebuilt almost completely. Larger buildings of an entirely new character and appropriation were regularly starting to appear along a medieval street system which, in spite of it all, remained largely unaltered in pattern.

Chapter II
Commerce

Markets

At the City Arms Hotel in 1809 a public meeting resolved: 'that the present markets of this city being detached from each other and exposed to the weather at all seasons of the year ought to be removed or altered'. It was further decided that 'the Red Streak Inn and adjoining premises, now the property of the Corporation, and the extensive yard etc., lately belonging to the New Inn, and since contracted for by the said Corporation, afford, from their contiguity to each other, and from their central situation in the city, a most desirable site for an entirely new range of markets, on the extensive plan submitted to this meeting'. Thirdly: 'that such markets be constructed without delay and that the sum of £3,000 be immediately raised'.

No time was lost and the first markets on the present Butter Market site were opened at the beginning of the October Fair in 1810. The entrance was through the present archway, without the classical figures or clock tower. The new butter and poultry market under a handsome iron and glass roof 'for the sale of poultry, butcher's meat, fish, vegetables and all other commodities usually sold in such markets ... together with new hop and wool warehouses' was opened in 1860, producers displaying their goods on benches and rows of tables. After a fire in 1922 the interior was reconstructed, stalls newly set out along the walls, and from 1925 the market maintained its popu-larity for the rest of the century enhanced, (or maybe not) by a subsequent controversial suspended ceiling. This certainly 'modernised' the interior and made for improved comfort and lighting, but some traders and customers regretted a loss of intrinsic market atmosphere when the old roof structure disappeared from view. The personality had in any case changed over the years as stalls and tables, which had been a showcase for produce grown in and around the city, were gradually taken over by professional marketeers and Peacocks, a leading national discount fashion chain. Apart from a small range of seasonal fruit, vegetables and plants or perhaps an occasional rod-caught salmon or pike at the fish stall, most supplies are from distant wholesalers. Some effort was made to provide trestle tables allowing the equivalent capacity of a pannier basket, for the sale of farm or home produce, but these were not over popular and tended instead to be taken up by volunteer members of charity organisations offering mainly 'car boot sale' type merchandise.

A market for home-made and home-grown produce in Hereford is provided by the Women's Institute, situated close to the old St. Peter's Square market place. The WI markets have been run since 1919 on strictly businesslike lines and are subject to the statutory regulations governing weights and measures, labelling of goods, health and hygiene and other such matters. As part of the market tradition, the stalls at St. Peter's Church

*The Butter Market, High Town, opened in 1860.
It suffered a fire in 1922—and a later suspended ceiling!*

Hall are very popular among both producers and customers and the cakes and breads, savories, eggs, honey, flowers, fruits, vegetables, plants and hand crafted goods sell very quickly. The organisers have been able to convince the city council that they are not violating its market franchise, for reasons largely to do with selling their own produce and thus not falling within the normal market definition as a 'concourse of buyers and sellers'.

This exemption has not been recognised in the case of the many car boot sales which started to appear in the 1980s, mainly on Sundays and it was necessary for Town Hall lawyers to suggest ways whereby these could be accepted whilst protecting and asserting the city council's monopoly Markets Franchise, the result of historic trade protection practices. An indulgent policy emerged under which no objection would

be raised, or legal action taken, provided that the events were held for verified charitable purposes, had adequate car parking, barred professional traders and complied with all appropriate environmental health legislation. Subsequent indications in columns of newspaper advertisements, and at the sales, were that these rules were widely observed only in the breach!

In 2000 'Herefordshire Food Links' and the council reintroduced Farmers' Markets to High Town. Once again local organic meats, poultry, eggs, fruit and vegetables are on sale in William fitzOsbern's 11th-century market place. Unfamiliar to our ancestors would have been the ostrich meat, wines, potted plants and other produce also usually available, once a month, on the 20 or so stalls—all to be 'grown, reared, caught, brewed, pickled, baked, smoked or processed' within 30 miles of the market.

Livestock

Until the middle of the 19th century the streets of Hereford were blocked not by through traffic but by cattle being sold 'by hand', chiefly in Broad Street, King Street and Aubrey Street. Congestion was not the only ill effect, for the bacteria-carrying dust from the excrement of livestock and all the transport horses must have caused many respiratory problems. Although home living conditions no doubt accounted for many of the deaths caused by tuberculosis and other diseases of the lungs, it is significant that these ailments were responsible for more than twice as many deaths as those attributed to the widespread epidemic and contagious diseases of the mid-19th century. As it was, respiratory disease produced almost 8 of the 27 annual mortality rate per thousand which imposed the need for a Board of Health Inquiry in 1853 (as against 3.5 for typhoid, typhus and the many zymotic diseases of that unhealthy period). Significantly it was shown by studies in cities elsewhere that TB rates plummeted in the 1920s after road surfaces were improved and horses eventually replaced by motor vehicles.

There was at times also a noise problem, as suffered by the music correspondent of *The Times* in September, 1852 when attending the Three Choirs Festival. He found that:

Selling Hereford Cattle 'by hand'
in Broad Street

The passage to the cathedral from St. Nicholas Square through King Street was rendered anything but agreeable by a large concourse of kines and beeves brought to the Hereford market for sale - bellowing vociferously and obstructing the way; the neighing of a solitary horse and the bleating of a stray sheep, not to omit the loud bell and louder voice of the 'cryer' completed the concert of 'livestock' which jarred discordantly with the solemn peals of the organ reverberating from within the cathedral.

Mild efforts had been made in the early 19th century to relieve some of the difficulties from a burgeoning market and these were renewed in 1852 on account of the approach of the railways, which would surely lead to even more business. At a public meeting at the market-hall Mr. William James, a leading auctioneer, stated:

the absolute necessity of providing more convenient and commodious markets, as it was allowed by men from all parts in the country, that Hereford had the best provincial market in the kingdom, but much to its demerit, the very worst accommodation.

It was proposed that new markets be erected on a site close to the pig market (Aubrey Street) at a cost of £8,500, but the money could not be raised and so nothing happened. However, the topic was soon brought up again when accounts appeared of new markets at Leominster, Abergavenny, Shrewsbury, Newport and other rival centres where, for a moderate toll, every description of livestock could be carefully stalled and tied 'so that the knocking about and damage consequent in those places where the cattle are exposed in the public streets are entirely prevented'. This was sufficient incentive for the city authorities to take positive action and they appointed Timothy Curley, a consulting engineer, to make plans and estimates for the construction of a new cattle market. In January, 1854, having rejected the Aubrey Street site as too small, circumscribed, costly and remote from the coming railway system, he suggested a new site, owned by Mr. William Leather, lying between Widemarsh Street and Moorfield Place. This had all the necessary qualities, with an area of between 3 and 4 acres compared with the 1.25 acres of the old site and was served by four main roads and close to the all-important railway lines. It was also less expensive and Curley's estimate of £6,500, with a nett probable annual income of £500 were accepted as part of an unprecedented improvement package. All necessary powers were obtained in the Hereford Improvement Act of 1854 which, with a subsequent Act of 1872 and the Hereford Corporation Act of 1936 still comprise the council's statutory authority for market matters. Little time was wasted, for at a meeting of the city council on 16 October 1856 an Order was made that the new market should be opened at Newmarket Street on Friday, 17 October. As from that day the market ceased in the streets, although animals continued to be walked in and out of the market for another hundred years.

However, some market activity was to remain in Broad Street, for in the following year a grand corn exchange—a structure of brick with a Bath stone front, and a portico supported on columns surmounted by a tower with an illuminated clock, was erected by subscription at a cost of £3,580. Opened for business in January 1858, the building was enlarged in 1911 by the addition of a public hall and theatre at a cost of £5,000 to become the Kemble Theatre. This survived until 1963 when it was demolished to make way for a less than worthy substitute.

The new livestock market was heralded as 'The foundation of the city's future prosperity' and after the arrival of the railway it grew apace. The site allowed for expansion and the nucleus of 1856 grew as new facilities were added in 1888, and by the end of the 19th century the animal 'throughput' had reached over 150,000 a year. Horse and poultry sales were started, and in 1914 a rail service was provided across Edgar Street by arrangement with the Great Western Railway.

A 'centenary' reconstruction scheme in 1956 provided a new store cattle section, the Langford Sale Ring with room for some 800 producers and buyers, a new pig market and two new lairages, which all helped to account for an annual throughput which had risen to almost 270,000 animals. Just over ten years later the long awaited inner relief road works were to take up land on the western side of the market for the widening of Edgar Street, and compensation moneys were added to city council resources to produce a further development of the 12.5 acre site to fit in with the new road pattern. The £200,000 scheme provided for new offices, a poultry market, furniture sale and showroom, agricultural implement showroom, sheep penning extensions, alterations to the pig market and auction offices, a weighbridge and new roadways. A café replaced the Dean Leigh Temperance Canteen, built in 1915 as an alternative for (and perhaps the salvation of) thirsty drovers during the extended licencing hours of the nearby inns. A new open cattle section and sale ring were built and brought into

Hereford Market in 1956, showing the electricity generating station at the bottom, to the right of centre

The open stalls market in 1966, with the Dean Leigh Temperance Canteen

use in 1979 and the new facilities produced record turnover figures during subsequent years. Sales, held on approximately 260 days each year, regularly reached an annual throughput of almost 440,000, (in one year made up of 74,549 cattle; 24,503 calves; 320,409 sheep; 18,014 pigs and 1,797 horses and ponies), despite strong competition from neighbouring markets such as those at Ross and Gloucester, and a growing tendency for off-market deals. Business became more difficult for all markets in the 1990s as agriculture moved into recession, and was not helped by the B.S.E. crisis and tuberculosis affecting beef and dairy cattle. In 2000, of a total annual 'throughput' of 325,000 beasts there were just 7,400 cattle and 6,000 calves, most of the remaining 94% being fat and store sheep and cull ewes, with a very few rams and pigs.

Although not very popular with people operating in the livestock section of the market because of the disturbance caused, the Wednesday market and cheapjack stalls were very well attended by Herefordians, farming families and many coming from some distance, not least from Central and South Wales, sometimes in coach loads. Up to 130 stallholders regularly attended, any vacant stalls being rapidly snapped up by 'casuals' queueing hopefully outside the superintendent's office early each Wednesday. As the market area and much of its car parking capacity were generally not used at weekends a Saturday market was tried and quickly proved a success, complicated only during the very busy autumn sheep and Fayre Oaks mountain pony sales. Initially special steps were taken to try and restore a tradition attracting individual producers, but by that time any interest did not last and, as on Wednesdays and at the Butter Market, the majority of stalls were eventually taken up by professional market traders.

The market lies just outside the medieval wall line and inner relief road but is close enough to enable market visitors to reach all parts of the city centre on foot. Studies in the 1960s revealed a total market catchment area containing 230,000 people from Herefordshire, the West Midlands, and Mid and South Wales, showing a strong interaction between the market and the central shops and business area which was of great significance for the economy of Hereford. In 1997 this was estimated by consultants to be worth £2.35 million, but they could offer no other benefits to compensate for disadvantages such as increased traffic congestion and loading and unloading delays, and advised relocation to make way for a multi-million pound redevelopment scheme. What they could not quantify was the likely effect of a move from the central position on the market character and 'atmosphere' which had previously set Hereford apart from ordinary towns of its size throughout more than 1,000 years. 'The foundation of the city's future prosperity' when it was moved to Newmarket Street in 1856, the cattle market with its associated agricultural businesses has flourished and grown well into the 20th century. Eventually the motor age and the late 1960s inner relief road brought about changes, with the dispersal of tractor, implement and farm suppliers, ironmongers and corn merchants to more spacious premises outside the city centre, animal health scares and the introduction of new buying and selling practices. The kind and variety of central shops changed, whilst farmers conducted more of their business from home by telephone and e-mail rather than at the market, and most regular farm and household needs are now met by edge-of-centre and fringe supermarkets, DIY stores and retail warehouses.

Yet, just as one writer put it in 1905, there are still, in 2000: 'streams of wheeled traffic on market days ... a spectacle of congested animation' — a feature of any successful market-place. Although there has been a fall recently in annual animal 'throughput', the 1,800 or so car and lorry spaces are still usually almost filled: the heavy pedestrian movement across, or beneath, Newmarket Street argues for the continuing 'pull' of the city centre. Without outside revenue of this kind, it is unlikely that, on their own, the citizens of Hereford would be able to support the present amount and range of shopping, business and leisure facilities. It is by no means certain that moving the cattle market to the outskirts would bring any benefits to the city centre, which is in great need of all the help it can get if it is to retain its viability and improve its appeal.

At the end of 2000 Hereford cattle market was at the centre of much 'kite flying'. One faction urged that a new south Hereford site might be the key to the success of any by-pass initiative, another that it should 'stay put' as part of a development brief for the Edgar Street area. From February 2001 the market was closed for many months because of foot and mouth disease, and in August new proposals emerged (see p.204).

Shops

Alongside a continuing and lucrative pilgrim industry and considerable provisioning needs for its castle and many others on the Welsh borders, Hereford's commercial activity brought increasing rewards in the 12th century, attracting in the process a substantial and prosperous Jewish community to the area near Bysters Gate. The highest point of medieval development was reached by the 13th century. This activity was concentrated within a modest area of 93 acres centred on the market-place, to the extent that almost before the defensive wall was completed the city was becoming congested.

Initially the market was conducted from flimsy stalls and booths, but in the course of time more permanent structures evolved, the stalls developed into shops and upper storeys were added and used as living quarters.

Eventually, market infilling and encroachment occurred within the main market triangle and the area between Bewell Street and Eign Gate, and this produced narrow streets and rows of shops such as Cooken Row and the Butchery. In no market town can it all be better or more accurately illustrated than by Taylor's plan in 1757.

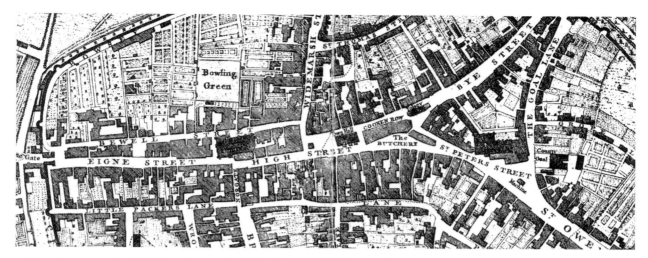

The city centre in 1757 as shown in Taylor's map. Within High Town there were the market-house and guild-hall, High Cross, pillory and maypole. The Tolsey was in Bye Street

What he could not portray was the effect of the congestion and poor state of buildings between the market area and the city gates. Run down timber buildings overhung the streets in many places and conditions in the courtyards and rows were indescribable. By 1837 most of the buildings in the centre of High Town had been removed, leaving only the forlorn two-storey remnant of the market-house and the Old House of 1621, later restored and furnished as a Jacobean period museum.

By 1851, when the city population was put at 12,128, there were eight ironmongers, including Philip Morris of Widemarsh Street, and R.M. Harding of Commercial Street and Union Street, founded respectively in 1845 and 1850, where 'scythes, reap-hooks, sheep-shears, bill-hooks, spades, mattocks and hoes' might be displayed. For 'bee-hives, butter-firkins, churns, milking stools and pails, hay-rakes, field-flagons and seed-lips' there were at least 10 coopers; for 'cart ropes and plough harness' some 9 saddlers and harness makers, soon to be joined by C.F. Jennings of Eign Street; 7 wheelwrights and machinists for 'carts, wheel-barrows and mill-gear'; 13 chemists for 'horse-embrocations'; and 10 curriers, leather glovers and breeches makers for 'hedging-gloves, roofers' knee-caps, ploughmen's leggings and villagers' pattens and clogs'.

There were about 72 boot and shoemakers, 58 assorted small shopkeepers, 54 milliners and dress makers, 44 tailors, 36 grocers, tea and provision dealers along with a similar number of butchers, 27 bakers and flour dealers, 17 maltsters, 16 blacksmiths, 15 linen and woollen drapers, silk mercers and hosiers, likewise 15 straw bonnet makers, 8 hatters, 6 millwrights and machinists, 5 corn millers and 3 tanners. One of the tailors, hatters, hosiers and outfitters was William Pritchard of Nos. 1 and 2 Commercial Street who had opened in 1836 and soon built up a solid business among the clergy, gentry, farming, sporting and professional classes. In those days there was a big livery trade for coachmen, footmen and butlers, all normally with two outfits a year, for hunting, shooting and fishing wear, and skilled cutters and tailors also undertook special orders for military uniforms, clerical outfits and Benedictine sacerdotal garments. Edward, William's great-great-grandson, is still trading in the city at the beginning of the 21st century, but did not adopt the approach of the five travelling drapers based in Hereford in 1851—last representatives of a breed—who (often on foot with their packs) sold cloth and clothing door to door out in the country. Three travelling tea dealers worked from bases in Commercial Street and St. Peter's Street in a similar fashion.

Part of the appeal and continuing importance of the city arose from its role as an administrative centre and a place for the delivery of professional services. There was evidently much business to be gained from farmers and others rich enough to pay for professional services: there were 27 insurance agents, 11 assorted 'agents', 7 accountants, 7 land surveyors, 5 bankers, 2 architects and surveyors, 9 surgeons, 7 physicians, 2 surgeon dentists, 2 veterinary surgeons—and 28 solicitors should any of them perform badly! And, for leisure and recreational needs, there were 12 booksellers, stationers and newspaper agents, 5 wine and spirit merchants and large piano forte and music warehouses. Established in 1830, Heins and Co. claimed to possess the largest and finest supplies of musical instruments in the provinces and West of England at their showrooms in Broad Street and Beethoven Hall in Berrington Street.

One by one Hereford traders of the 18th century pulled down their grand and often richly carved timber houses and substituted buildings with plain red brick shop fronts. All this helped to give Hereford the 'modern' look which other towns had acquired and for which its citizens earnestly craved. In High Town a typical example was No. 18, later to be combined with Nos. 16 and 17 and rebuilt in a Classic design to become Alban House, the emporium of Augustus C. Edwards and Sons. Established in 1865 as a silk mercer, draper, milliner, costumier, etc., of a 'superior class', its avowed object was to enable customers 'to obtain at their own doors, and at all times, those advantages in purchasing seasons' goods, and fashionable novelties which at that time were regarded as the peculiar privilege of residents in the Metropolis only'. Mr. Edwards himself exercised a constant personal superinten-

Augustus Edwards' emporium at 16 to 18 High Town, now occupied by a mobile phone shop and River Island (see opposite)

dence to ensure that his favoured clientele were kept *au fait* with all the latest fashions, whether in French or British fabrics, oriental silks or furs and skins such as seal, beaver, otter, musquash, lynx, wallaby and skunk.

At the end of almost a century and a half, after many other appropriations, adaptations and alterations, Alban House returned to the fashion trade in the very different hands of the River Island Clothing Company. One visible improvement has occurred in the design of the shopfront, which has paid regard to the window and pilaster grid of the 19th-century first and second storey facade. As an important feature of the 'streetscape', this is greatly to be preferred to the commoner approach where, due to commercial pressures for as much frontage exposure as possible, upper storeys appear to be 'supported' by an uninterrupted expanse of plate-glass shopfronts. Some of the original half-timbering has been exposed and restored at the rear of the building.

Another striking example of how good design can succeed in both visual and trading respects occurred when W.H. Smith moved to 25 and 26 High Town. William Smith had originally started his business in 1848 when he opened the

first of his many railway bookstalls established during the Victorian era, including one at Hereford station. Between 1906 and 1909 Smiths had a shop at Stonebow House in Commercial Road and then moved to 46 Commercial Street. By March 1991 they had become short of space and moved to 25 High Town. The building had been a grocer's shop for many years, owned in 1867 by George Cooke. George J. Mason Ltd. had continued the grocery business from 1922 and by the 1970s were the last large grocers in Hereford to provide a delivery service. In 1980, International Stores moved across High Town from No.12 (formerly Gurneys and now Dorothy Perkins and Game) to take over No. 25 and also expanded into Frederick Ltd., the costumiers at No. 26. Their two buildings were quite different, No. 25 dating from around 1860 with a fine neo-classical two-storey facade in Bath stone, a narrow passage bay to the east and the remainder in three symmetrical bays. The facade of No. 26 has been rebuilt as a facsimile of the late 18th-century wall fronting a late 16th-century three-bay timber-framed rich merchant's house (which

River Island

W.H. Smiths

Once entered from Bewell Street, the Cellar Bar beneath the Pippin at 3 Widemarsh Street (now B/A/S/L/E/R fashion shop)

was probably older by some 50 years than the Old House). Under the management of W.H. Smith, the individual elements of the two facades have been restored to emphasise their quite separate nature. New ground floor arched openings similar to the originals were constructed, the main bedrooms became offices and the ceiling of the first floor chamber was made visible from within the new ground level shop floor. No longer accessible to the public are the old cellars, common with many others beneath buildings facing High Town—notably at No. 22, a listed building with a 4-centred arched tunnel-vaulted cellar dating from about 1500.

The history of 27 High Town also starts in the 16th century when a new, three-storey timber-framed building was erected, making use of elements of the existing medieval cellar. Panelling and wall paintings of the 17th century have been cleaned and exposed but can only be seen by arrangement with the proprietors, Clinton Cards. This property had previously a long association with drapers, such as Wooley and

Watkins, Knight, Stoate and Co. and, for much of the 20th century, Wakefield Knight. One Herefordian remembered leaving school, aged 14, in the mid-1940s to work there: 'It was a very old shop with a cellar and three flights of stairs. The ground floor was haberdashery and fancy goods and at the back were the dress materials. Ladies' fashions, underwear and millinery were on the first floor and the rest of the rooms stored

The framing above Clinton Cards at 27 High Town

22

stock. We also had a work room where, for a small charge, customer alterations were done. Some staff lived on the premises. There was a house at the back of the shop with living quarters where we could have our tea breaks and lunch'.

Living with his impoverished mother at Bosbury, another 14 year-old boy was also about to leave school in 1922 for the inevitable farm job when, instead, the local minister helped to secure him a job at Wakefield Knights. He took to it 'like a duck to water' and at the age of 17 had become a buyer. By the time of his 21st birthday he, with his fiancée Jessie—whom he had met at Wakefield Knights—set up a small drapery shop of their own at 41 Commercial Street, then at the 'wrong end' of town, quite near the old prison and workhouse. They took £48 (by 2000 worth about £1,800) on their first day, and ignoring the 'Jeremiahs' of that slump era, they also rented no.42 six months later. Married on Boxing Day, 1929, Mr. and Mrs. W.A. Chadd lived over the shop for many years, 'Bob', as he came to be called, regularly setting off for the local markets laden with goods.

The business prospered, and by 1983 ten separate shops had been built into two main blocks on either side of the street. Thanks to all the hard work and enterprise of the family and their committed employees, Commercial Street is no longer regarded as a secondary shopping area. But at the end of the century its fortunes still rely heavily on the presence of Chadds with the second and third generations at the helm, now one of fewer than 30 successful family firms of its kind in Britain.

The only other remaining 'family owned' department store in Hereford had been Greenlands. It was sold for £350,000 to Marks and Spencer and closed in 1968. The resulting shop rebuilding left 2 High Street to the west (previously a fruit merchant and afterwards a jeweller) squashed as a small greeting card shop between the large new edifice and the new Littlewoods chain store.

George Greenland came to Hereford from Newbury in Berkshire in 1856 and flourished with

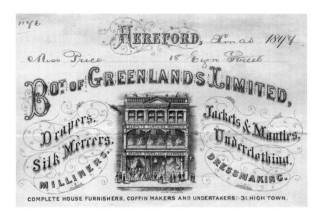

Bill heading from Greenlands

a Mr. Barratt in a drapery business at 1 High Street for almost 20 years. He suffered the double disaster of the death of his partner and, soon afterwards in 1878, a fire (one of three suffered by Greenlands), when he had to move temporarily to Widemarsh Street with serious loss of trade. When George Greenland died in 1901 the business passed to four of his five sons—George, Harry, Frank and Alfred (William became a solicitor)—and extended to High Town, High Street, Church Street and Commercial Road.

It was regarded as a great privilege to work at Greenlands: after a gruelling interview by formidable-looking directors, successful 14 year-olds were told to change into long trousers and were admitted as apprentices, after which they worked long hours for three years without payment. As with many of their competitors, including Augustus ('Disgusting' as he was jokingly called by the less respectful) Edwards, Kings of London House, and Gardners, the majority of the shop girls lived-in under strict discipline in the warren of rooms above the shop.

Much of the furniture they sold was produced at their own furniture factory in Foley Street, where they were particularly proud of their patented Oak Stair Rods and Oak Stair Eyes, distributed throughout the country. The various departments of Greenlands embraced not only furniture and furnishing but also house decoration, lighting, heating, structural work, auctioneering, estate agency, furniture storage and

H	O	P	E		A	N	D		L	I	V	E
(1)	(2)	(3)	(4)		(5)	(6)	(7)		(8)	(9)	(10)	

The price 'code' used at Greenlands

removing, undertaking, drapery, dressmaking and many lesser departments such as china, fancy goods, books and toys.

The majority of customers had accounts and were not aware of the prices of items which they bought. These were coded to the letters of the words 'Hope and live' (the last letter was not used). Thus an item charged at 2s. 11d. would appear as 'o/hs' —the second and first letters— with 's' indicating a repeat. Due to the size of the shop, money travelled by tube to the cashier along the Lamson Paragon Vacuum System in a brass container, rather than on overhead wires to a cashier seated in a distant cubicle, who returned the change 'humming on wires'. (Overhead systems operated at Gurneys, George Masons and, until the late 1960s, at Philip Morris in Widemarsh Street.) For many years older customers remembered special features of the shop such as the revolving doors (acquired from The Mitre Hotel after it closed), the arcades providing valuable extra display space, and the mechanical singing bird. At no time was the store more alluring for children of all ages than Christmas, involving an exciting progress along thick carpets, past elegant stands, to the toy department and The Grotto— and a chat with Santa Claus.

The present Greenlands furniture shop in Widemarsh Street is run by Colin, great-grandson of George Greenland.

Multiples

As independent traders, Augustus C. Edwards and Greenlands built up considerable business empires to become large department stores, as did Chadds later, but apart from W.H. Smith, national chains did not appear in Hereford to any great extent until after the First World War. However Marks and Spencer opened as a Penny Bazaar at 20 Eign Street in 1908 and moved to 13 High Street in 1928. Boots Cash Chemists, established by Jesse Boot in 1877 from his family's herbalist shop in Nottingham, opened in High Town, to be joined by more multiples in the 1930s. At the end of the Second World War, however, the chain stores were still in a minority.

This was set to change and by the 1960s the former pattern of sporadic small scale developments and refurbishments was being replaced by one of larger developments. The redevelopment of the very prominent Greenlands site with a massive new Marks and Spencer store was an extreme and challenging example. Marks and Spencer wished to erect a building which took account of retailers' requirements of the 1960s, with an internal layout allowing the free circulation of customers, economic handling, presentation and storage of merchandise and the crucial financial return per square foot of floorspace. These and other factors, including modern ceiling heights, optimum footway display frontage and the company 'house style', combined to produce external elevations requiring architectural skill and sensitivity in any situation, let alone at a key location in the central conservation area of a historic city. There were many hours of discussion and argument between the various interests and, as in most things, it was not possible to arrive at designs which satisfied every view. As one design and aesthetic feature, activity on the ground level shop floor was originally intended to be visible from 'Boots' Passage' but subsequent arguments about loss of valuable sales and display area and viability persuaded a sceptical planning authority to delete the requirement. The monotonous outcome of this decision has long been exposed on the long flank wall of the store between High Town and the cathedral. Not all storage could be accommodated within the main shop site and further space and a loading bay were constructed on the south side of East Street, linked by a service tunnel beneath the road. As with other significant building schemes along the line of the Saxon defences, every opportunity was sought by archaeologists to discover more about Hereford's early years during the deep excavation works, and whilst given access to the subway at the rear of the building, regrettably they were not allowed on to the remainder of the site in this instance.

*The old Littlewoods (behind the road sign) in 1965 awaiting redevelopment,
with 3 High Street two doors to its left*

Soon after Marks and Spencer moved, Boots forsook long established premises at 28 High Town (and 'Boots' Passage') and took their place at 12-13 High Street. They subsequently extended towards All Saints Church into Nos. 10 and 11 and in 1999 underwent a complete refurbishment.

Standing opposite them was the recently built Littlewoods store with its own, rather quaint, history. Littlewoods Restaurant had occupied 5 High Street for several years prior to the mid-1960s when plans were drawn up for a much larger store occupying the sites of a number of their neighbours. One of these at 3 High Street had been the home and business of wealthy merchants for much of its previous 350 years. The timber-framed premises had been occupied successively by Webb and Bosley, Bosley and Marchant, Marchant and Matthews and finally, Marchant and Son, grocers and wine and spirit merchants which, like many other such shops of the time, always seemed to send out an alluring aroma of

spices and roasting coffee. By 1964 the building had been greatly altered at ground floor level, but much of the first and second floors and attics were intact. A scheme for the new Littlewoods store covering this and adjacent properties was finally approved, on condition that part of the fine facade of the old building was incorporated in the new development. And so, in the winter of 1964/65, 3 High Street was demolished, except for one small part which was moved on rollers into High Town, enveloped in polythene for several months and then returned and hoisted up above ground floor level. There it remains, largely unnoticed and unappreciated—standing as a monument to one of the most bizarre examples of 1960s urban conservation!

On 21 November, 1960, Herefordshire's first 'supermarket' opened in Commercial Street next to the Odeon Cinema. Heralded as 'a miracle of planning extending over two floors', the new mainly self-service Maypole dealt with food on

3 High Street ready to be temporarily moved into High Town, for later reinstatement within the Littlewoods store

Advert for R.M. Harding & Sons

the ground floor, reinforced by an assisted counter-service for items such as meat and bacon which at the time did not lend themselves to pre-packaging. As for the first floor, it was 'an Aladdin's Cave, just waiting to be explored', offering anything from (appropriately) lamps and other hardware to toiletries, nylons and under-wear. Those who could not bear to enter this new style store, representing a trading technique which would come to change their shopping habits for ever, could telephone their orders for free home delivery. However, it did not survive the onslaught of the larger supermarkets and by

2000 the premises were the home of Etam, one of many clothing shops.

Despite frenzied searches by other new self-service grocery firms, no other property of any size seemed obviously available in Hereford, until Tesco made overtures to Hardings at 48 Commercial Street. This shop had been founded in 1850 by Mr. R.M. Harding, when he took over and converted the Crown and Sceptre inn. Containing yet another 'Aladdin's Cave' of every imaginable tool, device, implement and house-hold article, the staff rarely failed to produce what was wanted, often triumphantly achieved after much enthusiastic rummaging in ancient and worn drawers or boxes. It was still possible to buy the exact number of nuts, bolts or screws needed and not have to acquire a whole plastic packet of them. And 'If we didn't have it, we'd get it' was the confident offer by the black-aproned assistants. The goods were lavishly displayed on two floors, the condition of which had reached the state that in some places it was possible to watch activity on the ground floor from above though gaps in the flooring! As well as its Commercial Street frontage, the shop ran along Union Passage (once known as Crown Passage and then as Harding's Passage) to connect with Union Street and the stables for the horse and cart, and later for the lorries and vans.

In 1965 the main shop in Commercial Street was demolished, to be followed by the Bye Gate Inn, formerly the Coach and Horses, and work started on Hereford's first purpose-built supermarket, unfortunately far from being an improvement to the 'street scene' in that part of the Conservation Area.

Supermarkets

When supermarkets arrived in Britain, some ten years or more after they had become established in the USA, they brought about the start of a comprehensive revolution in grocery retailing. Regional companies, such as Saverite and Quicksave in Commercial Road, managed to trade successfully on 'pile it high, sell it cheap' principles—but none made the impact of John Edward Cohen. His retailing career started at a small grocery stall in the east end of London in 1919 and by 1931 he had founded Tesco Stores Ltd. (the title devised from the first three letters of his tea suppliers, T.E. Stockwell, and the first two letters of his own name). By the start of the Second World War, Tescos had opened 100 small food stores and in 1956, after further acquisitions, produced Britain's first 'supermarket'. (By 1998 the company ran 639 stores in Britain and many more overseas, reporting an annual turnover of £16,175 million and operating profit of £882 million).

Tescos launch in Hereford was fairly modest, taking up a grocery sales area of less than 6,000 sq. ft., but the return per square foot was reputed to be among the best in their region. The boost in trade in other shops in Commercial Street, plainly caused by the drawing power of the new store, was also very marked. This success was to continue through the 1970s, whilst floorspace requirements for food stores steadily advanced to 8,000 - 10,000 sq. ft., thence to 25,000 sq. ft. or more. Despite desperate searches by several of the big supermarket firms no suitable property of this size could be found anywhere near Hereford's prime central locations. Meanwhile floor space at the Commercial Street Tescos rapidly became uncomfortably cramped.

In 1978, partly to provide space for modern retailing needs, but also to compensate for the 110,000 sq. ft. of outdated shops, showrooms and other capacity lost to the relief roadworks, Hereford City Council and Hereford and Worcester County Council jointly approved a Development Brief. This allocated additional shopping floorspace in two areas considered to be 'ripe for development'. One was described as Sector A/B and lay between Newmarket Street and Bewell Street, where central area developers, including Taylor-Woodrow Industrial Estates Limited, had already registered an interest with West Country Brewers, owners of the brewery site. The other was Sector C, between Blueschool Street and Maylord Street.

Sector A/B, at the north-western corner of the walled city, had served many uses since the 12th century and by the 18th and 19th centuries was the site of Bewell House and its gardens, the Hereford Brewery, British Canners and Weaver's Hospital. It also contained two bowling greens, the larger one said to date from 1484—possibly making it the oldest in the country. The eastern limit of the site extended to the rear of properties in Widemarsh Street properties, a severed Wall Street and Bewell Street forming the other boundaries.

At first it was thought that Sector C, based on Maylord Street, would be more suitable for immediate redevelopment. During the 1960s the city council had started to acquire property to the east of Widemarsh Street with a view to its eventual commercial redevelopment and integration with existing shopping areas in High Town, Commercial Street and Widemarsh Street. By 1968, over 70% of the potentially developable land had been bought. By then the city owned the former Enterprise Garage, the White Lion public house, *The Hereford Times* offices and printing works and a number of other Maylord Street properties. The city council circularised potential developers with particulars of how it visualised the future of Sector C, but the proposed terms received a chilly response from them all. Then, in March, 1971, Taylor-Woodrow, one of the list of developers, warmed to further approaches and eventually put forward their scheme for the sector. This comprised a traffic-free precinct with a supermarket, department store, 18 shop units, a post office, improvements to the Butter Market Hall, parking for about 700 cars and rear servicing for many of the High Town, Commercial Street and Widemarsh Street shops.

After some amendment the city accepted the proposals in principle and voted to exercise compulsory purchase powers for any further land necessary to implement them—subject to agreement on content, financial and other terms.

Meanwhile there had been a quickening of interest in Sector A/B on the part of Parking Management Ltd., who produced a scheme for a supermarket, warehouse, shop, discotheque and loading facilities. In 1972 this was followed by a plan for just the brewery site, providing a supermarket of between 30,000 and 35,000 sq. ft. and a 484 space car park. However, the planning authority insisted that the land could not be developed in isolation prior to the remainder of the sector becoming available for a comprehensive scheme. In early 1973, Whitbread-Flowers as owners, revealed that they had contracted to dispose of their brewery site to Pagebar Properties Ltd., developers who were said to have in mind

Aerial photo with the outline of Sector A/B superimposed, showing the former Hereford Brewery, Bewell House, British Canners, the ancient bowling green and All Saints Church

Hereford from the north-west if the Pagebar development had gone ahead on what is now the Tesco site. The ancient bowling green was to be moved and raised to face the roundabout

just the sort of comprehensive scheme that was needed. After acquiring interests in other sites in Sector A/B, they submitted planning and listed building consent applications in November, 1973.

The proposal was for 'Development of Shopping (206,000 sq. ft. and allied storage), enclosed Mall, Maisonettes, Multi storey car park (for 1,051 cars), Hotel, Offices (50,000 sq. ft.), Liberal Club, Bowling Green and Clubhouse and access and egress for pedestrians and vehicles'. In July, 1974, however, an amended application was made for 'Shopping (314,500 sq. ft. retail and storage space, including a department store), enclosed mall, basement car parking (790 spaces), hotel (80 bedroom, or 28 residential units and approximately 20,000 sq. ft. of recreational/entertainment facilities), bank, offices (40,000 sq. ft.), Liberal Club and access/egress for pedestrians and vehicles and related works'. A further amendment later omitted the department store, reducing the new retail floor space to

201,000 sq. ft. and placing 27,149 sq. ft. of shop floor space into a second phase.

In the meantime, in June, 1974, a planning and listed building consent application had been submitted jointly by the city council and Taylor-Woodrow in respect of Sector C. This was for shopping (74,500 sq. ft. including replacement of three existing shops and work at the Butter Market Hall), storage, a supermarket (31,000 sq. ft., said to be reserved for Sainsburys), a post office, a public library, offices (5,500 sq. ft.) and a multi-storey car park.

Each proposal involved a great deal more commercial change than any experienced at one time in the long history of the city and decisions were beyond the powers of the local planning authorities and so were 'called in' for decision by the Secretary of State for the Environment, then Anthony Crosland. This led to the setting up of a public inquiry which was to last for 22 days at the end of 1974 and beginning of 1975.

Before the opening, however, the city council and Taylor-Woodrow were persuaded by the county planning authority to withdraw their application from the inquiry on the grounds that, because of the proposed scale, a local plan, involving detailed studies and further public consultation, should be prepared first. Had they not done so, the county council would have opposed the scheme before the inspector. That left the Pagebar Investments applications to be opposed by both city and county councils with representatives of the Hereford Civic Trust, Woolhope Club, Chamber of Commerce and Hereford Archaeological Committee, as well as private individuals.

Had Pagebar and the city council/Taylor-Woodrow consortium been able to suppress their vested commercial interests in securing maximum retail floorspace to fund their schemes, both could have joined with the county planning authority in preparing an agreed design brief covering both their sectors. This could have formed a foundation for any planning applications, but it was not to be. It took until August, 1975, for the Minister to digest and consider the inspector's report before supporting Mr. Dahl's recommendation that the Pagebar application should be refused, citing as the main reason that 'development on the scale proposed would have a detrimental effect on the existing Town Centre'. The outline plans also suggested that it was 'unlikely to blend well with the historic town'. In conclusion the Minister felt that any further approach should be on the basis of Sectors A/B and C being 'looked at as a whole'.

In consequence both Pagebar and Taylor-Woodrow withdrew from the scene and the city and county councils got down to further discussions. In 1976 an 'Issues and Choices' report was published and widely distributed for comment prior to the drawing together of a draft plan. Out of this a development brief was approved in April, 1978, which provided detailed guidance for any prospective developer.

The land at Sector A/B was duly put on the market and it was no surprise when Tesco expressed an interest, or that Sainsbury also entered the bidding. Sainsbury had been in the grocery trade for much longer than Tesco, having been established in 1869 by John James Sainsbury and Mary Ann Staples, with the modest aim of providing a shop for each of their six sons to manage. From the start they had established their own special trading culture and built up exceptional loyalty from their customers. The leading supermarket chain, their closest store to Hereford was in Worcester. It would be a while, however, before Sainsbury moved to Hereford, for it was Tesco who gained the prize albeit, it was said, by a very small financial margin. It was clear that the development was generally welcomed as a benefit which Hereford people wanted, and thought vital that a modern supermarket, with its associated car park and pedestrian links, should form an integral part of city centre shopping and not be placed on remoter land where its drawing power would not contribute to the viability of other shops and businesses.

During the ensuing months there might have been times when Tesco and their advisers could have wished it otherwise. Commercially, all they needed for their store was a large shed, roughly the size of a football pitch and about 6m high, with a good expanse of servicing and car parking. But this would clearly not be appropriate within the historic core of a city 'so splendid and precious that ultimate responsibility for [it] should be a national concern'.

Many months elapsed as successive attempts were made to reach general agreement on plans which would respect the character and 'grain' of the older buildings in the rest of the Conservation Area, not least in getting away from the all too familiar 'Essex Barn, with Clocktower' approach then and even now widely favoured by supermarket designers. Much attention was paid to ways of blending the new 30,500 sq. ft. supermarket, its storage and other facilities with the great variety of styles and scales in that quarter of the city centre. The huge proportions were broken down by the application of familiar architectural techniques, such as the colours and textures of bricks, tiles and other materials. Of the 270 new car parking spaces, many were located out of sight beneath the store and the visual impact of those at ground level was relieved by walls, trees, shrubs and other forms of landscaping.

The brick paving was extended to a small bus station and taxi rank and to footpaths connecting with Widemarsh Street, Sector C, Newmarket Street and the subway leading to the cattle market and its large car parks. Bewell Street was resurfaced with paving bricks and a property in Eign Gate was acquired in order to provide a pedestrian link to shops in that street and to the Victoria Street subway. At the western end, Bewell House was renovated, conserved and used for offices, and the former line of the medieval city defences (buried beneath the relief road at that point) was reflected by a sandstone masonry wall almost as high as the original fortification.

It would have been a miracle if everyone had approved of the development and, not unexpectedly, there were caustic comments from some quarters, one wag making references in *The Hereford Times* to the Disneyland look of the new design. However, as the first of two major redevelopment challenges at the very heart of the ancient city it was generally felt that the scheme had settled in to its prominent historic setting with reasonable style and effectiveness.

Following the opening of the Tesco store in the summer of 1983, it was not long before Sainsbury scouts were again in evidence and negotiations with the British Rail Property Board led to proposals for another supermarket on part of the 'brownfield' former Barton railway land to the west of the city centre. One of the principal considerations was road access and traffic generation, notably in Ryeland Street and Barton Road. Negotiations led to a requirement that Sainsbury would bear the cost of lowering the hump-backed bridge over the old railway lines on the A438 Whitecross Road and the road widening work, the installation of traffic and pedestrian-operated light signals and other measures associated with their project. Removal of the bridge involved construction of an underpass to serve an extension to the Great Western Way, the footpath and cycle way following the line of the old railway from south of the river towards Widemarsh

Common, with a new length between the Broomy Hill/Barton Road link and the Whitecross Road underpass. The store opened in August 1988 and, despite protests from local garages, a subsequent phase added a petrol station at the northern end of the car park. By the end of the 1990s, Sainsbury was drawing up plans to extend their store further westward over more of the former railway yard to take in the site of the local authority Grimmer Road Highways and Housing Depot.

Safeway was the third supermarket of the 'Big Five' to become established in Hereford. Like Sainsbury it had the British Rail Property Board to thank for the opportunity, this time near Barrs Court station on the site of the city's first gas works and Canal Wharf timber yards, saw mill and pits. The land, used more recently for engineering works, was also close to the former Monkmoor Mill, once served by the Tan, Stonebow and Scut Mill Brook. In the 1980s it was part of an area known as Sector F, lying between the city centre relief road and the railway boundary, where there was an intention to stimulate ideas for its future role and enhancement.

In 1987 Morbaine Properties, acting on behalf of Safeway (then newly integrated into the Argyll Group), lodged a planning application for a 50,000 gross sq. ft. supermarket for which permission was given in September, 1987. The access road was designed to serve as the first phase of a spine road for the whole sector and improvements were made at the junction with Commercial Road, which became signal-controlled. In addition a new spur road was designed to improve access to Barrs Court station, Peak Engineering and Rockfield D.I.Y. Brand loyalty apart, the Safeway store tended to serve the needs of shoppers from the north and east of Hereford and, like Sainsbury to the west, was not too distant from the city centre and its range of 'comparison' shopping and other services. The store was the first in Hereford to incorporate a former pharmacy, Lewis Smith of Commercial Road, but it took until 1999 before Sainsbury followed suit with The Dispensary from 135 Eign Street, whilst Tescos took T. Lloyd Davies of 7 St. Peter's Street as their 'in store

pharmacy', all offering the advantage of being open during the long supermarket hours.

The Co-op, fourth of the 'Big Five', chose not to continue with their self-service grocery store at 9-11 Widemarsh Street and for several years confined their business to non-food goods in a newly built department store under the name 'Living' until it was closed in 1999. As 'Leos' they moved out from the city centre into a new purpose-built store and car park at Bobblestock which serves a large residential area to the west of the city and beyond. In due course they were joined nearby by a long sought-for branch doctors' practice, but contrary to the trend in the city centre a new dispensing chemist opened for business, not under the supermarket roof, but among local shops in the nearby Grandstand Road. After further refurbishing, a modernised store became the Co-op again in 2000.

Another large Tesco store, petrol filling station and car park was built alongside the A465 Abergavenny Road to serve the growing Belmont community and areas to the west, but it seemed that Hereford was to be denied the fifth of the 'Big Five' supermarkets of the era. However, in 2000, after trying to get a foothold in Hereford for 20 years, ASDA, with Eign Enterprises (developers of The Left Bank Village) announced a £50 million plan for a store, 494 car-parking spaces and the familiar lure of 500 additional jobs, combined with a range of community projects, on 22 acres of land at the former Causeway Farm.

Between them the supermarkets provide full and part-time employment for a significant number of local people. For example, before any potential enlargement, Sainsbury employ over 300 people, 30% of them full-time, at the

Hereford branch. This is, however, at the price of many other jobs formerly provided by independent producers, farmers, market operators, wholesalers and retailers, for the big stores buy most of their food from distant large concerns. Some firms do permit their local managers to seek out suitable local suppliers.

The rise of the supermarkets was to be challenged by new arrivals on the retail scene in the

Maylord Street, South Elevation

Bell Passage and Gomond Street, East Elevation

form of discount stores in austere warehouse-type buildings, offering cut-price food and non-food shopping at rock bottom prices. In 1998 Hereford saw the first of these, Lidl—a continental-based chain—enter the fray on the former Ravenhills

Left: The Atrium as shown in the proposal's drawings and (above) Trinity Square as built

site at the entrance to the city centre off Commercial Road (a site that many had hoped would instead have been added to the adjacent County Hospital site for the purposes of the new District General Hospital). This was part of a 'retail park' requiring further elaborate road-works to join with Commercial Road, extended by a new access and traffic signals to serve the hospital and neighbouring petrol filling station. Sainsbury was also to face competition from a branch of Aldi following a successful planning

appeal against a refusal of permission on the grounds that it encroached too much on the Great Western Way footpath and cycle-way.

Maylord Orchards

With the help of the development brief, the city council proposed entering into partnership with a developer for Sector C. A national advertisement brought 270 requests for more information and in April 1981, 44 developers expressed further interest, of which ten were selected for interview and four finally shortlisted. Each submitted proposals in October 1981 and full details were placed before the public in an exhibition which attracted 975 people, the overall process resulting in the selection of Norwich Union as the nomi-nated developer 'on the undertaking that due weight would be given to public and other comments in refining the final design details'. Further land acquisition followed and work commenced in November 1985. The Maylord Orchards, as the scheme was called, consisted of 48 shop units, some incorporated in the Atrium fronting the new Trinity Square, a basement car park providing 220 spaces and, at second floor level, 21 flats. This level also contained a restau-rant complex, a public meeting room and upstairs entrances to some of the main stores. The largest of these was C&A, then a good 'anchor' store for the scheme. One proposal was that Maylord Street and Gomond Street should follow the medieval street pattern, and in June, 1983 acceptance of the

Bell Passage and Gomond Street, West Elevation

Commercial Street in the late 1970s showing the Focus Cinema (previously the Odeon and afterwards the Classic) and adjoining buildings demolished to be replaced by the Maylord Orchards scheme. Note the former Labour Exchange (as Halfords) in the top picture, and how the link is made alongside Laura Ashley to Trinity Square today

planned alignments was received from the Council for British Archaeology, following earlier endorsement of the 'sensitive approach of the problem of fitting a large commercial development into the fabric of an historic town' by the Royal Fine Art Commission. The first shops opened for trading in October, 1987, many more by that Christmas and the scheme was almost completely let a year later, producing a significant rent for the benefit of city ratepayers.

Apart from its financial and trading benefits, the Maylord Orchards design was generally well received locally, regionally and at national level. Entered for the 1988 Royal Town Planning Institute's regional award it came first as 'a significant contribution to town planning in the West Midlands'. It was duly entered in the RTPI national competition between 36 schemes and won praise for its 'environmental quality, social and economic benefit, originality, visual amenity, professional standard and usefulness as a model to others'. Placed second and 'Very Highly Commended', Maylord Orchards was described by the judges as 'a most successful development adding small shops and a major shopping complex (and housing) with car parking and pedestrian areas, sensitively tailored to the grain of an important historic city'. The project was also cited in the 1988 Europa Nostra awards. Little wonder that the scheme architect was not over bothered by a charge from some local quarters that the scheme was a 'missed opportunity', being rather more struck by accounts concerning visitors to the city who have failed to realise that Maylord Orchards was in fact a new addition to Hereford's shopping outlets! Even some local residents found it difficult to work out where 'the join' occurred in High Town (where the former Odeon/Focus/Classic Cinema/Cherry's Disco had stood), others were impressed by the way that the one-time Ministry of Labour Employment Exchange (and latterly Halfords), with its discreet date stone of 1910, had been restored to become a prize-winning building for Laura Ashley at a strategic entrance into the newly brick-paved Gomond Street.

The development linked the Mansion House Walk path to Sector A/B and Tescos and also dovetailed into the Butter Market Hall in Maylord Street with a subtle transition of architectural styles. Brewers Passage was a revived pedestrian link between Trinity Square and Commercial Street and this provided access to some of the number of smaller units which were provided for local family businesses. It also served a new rear entrance to John Wilson's imposing gardening and florist shop, which had been a prominent feature of Commercial Street since it first opened in 1915.

Framework for renewal—after 25 years

Directly or indirectly the building of Greyfriars Bridge and the inner relief road, which began in 1965, changed the face of the city centre to an unprecedented degree. With the many associated public sector improvements which took place or subsequently got under way they formed a framework for renewal, the Tesco supermarket and Maylord Orchards being the most obvious new appearances, expanding the city centre trading floor space that existed in 1981 by 23%. But there were many other smaller developments too, a notable example being that at Bewell Square (until the 1920s near the squalid 16th-century Bewell Street 'stews') where a local businessman, Mr. Fowler, developed a courtyard of covered shop units on two levels. Elsewhere in the main shopping areas shopkeepers and property owners refurbished, extended or developed their premises and many of the 70 or more listed buildings attracted grant aid under initiatives such as the Hereford Town Scheme. The money came from both central and local government sources: because of the special quality of the nationally designated central Conservation Area of Outstanding Merit, a substantial contribution was paid by the Department of the Environment towards the expense of repaving and upgrading High Town.

In 1991 Hereford was entered, alongside York, Macclesfield, Banbury, Gloucester and 16 other towns and cities, for the prestigious national award of the British Council of Shopping Centres for 'the community which had most contributed to the greatest improvement of their shopping environment' in recent times. Hereford was the winner.

This success was no mean achievement, for by the 1990s the traditional shopping area had started to lose numbers of businesses which had hitherto contributed to its intrinsic market town atmosphere and appeal. Some had been long-established family concerns which made way for chain and fashion stores of the kind found in most other high streets of the United Kingdom. The appeal and reputation of Hereford as a major sub-regional shopping centre was also impaired by a growing proliferation of cheap plastic goods, book-remainder and other bargain basement stores. With a minimum of shopfitting, style and decorative effort, these moved into premises vacated by local traders, such as Jennings (based in Eign Street/Eign Gate since the 1850s), Copes and Lindsey Price. By 2000 there were also 18 charity shops, several in prime positions and all benefitting from at least 80% relief from the normal business rates. Many small shopkeepers regarded this as unfair, particularly where some organisations, one with 840 branches, sold 'bought-in' goods in addition to their range of cast-off clothing and other surplus items. Other businesses were lost to petrol filling stations, garden centres and catalogue stores.

The growth in car ownership has also encouraged an exodus from the city centre of white goods, electrical equipment, motor accessories, furniture, carpets, do-it-yourself and other bulky goods retailers. These have moved to roomy, purpose-built (if not lovable) warehouses on former industrial brownfield parks, mainly at Holmer and Three Elms. They all have spacious free car parks with easy access to main roads and sell most of the merchandise formerly found at the high street shops—and much more. In early 2000 the School of Farriery site at Newtown Road (formerly intended for industrial employment use) and adjacent police traffic department land were set out for P.C. World Computers, Harrap Furnishings, Carpet Right and Pizza Hut, along also with Currys who had outgrown their first new building at Holmer Road. Not surprisingly most motor vehicle main dealers had by then opted for new fringe sites with more room and better road access.

One outcome of these changes was that whereas in 1981, when the city catered for a total county population of approximately 150,000 people, some 80% of its total trading floorspace had been in the central area, this proportion was down to below 60% just ten years later, despite major new city centre developments. The downward trend continued and the resulting drastic reduction in capacity and variety in once flourishing locations clearly put the viability of remaining high street shops in jeopardy. They were already beset with other difficulties, not least in having to make the most of inefficient, outmoded premises.

The brunt of this transformation was borne along the primary shopping axis, between Chadds in Commercial Street to the east and Jessons in Eign Gate to the west. Commercial Street had contained 42 individual family businesses as recently as 1960. They offered everything from clothing and shoes, wools and hosiery, sports goods, grocery, fish, meat, tobacco, confectionary and wines, to radio and TV, newspapers and stationery, watches and clocks, house furnishings, decorating materials, ironmongery and even motor cycles. There were 13 non-retail concerns, consisting of the Odeon cinema, Trinity Almshouses, the Gospel Hall, the Kerry Arms, Coach and Horses and Tabard public houses, four milk bars or cafés and a fried fish shop, a pawnbroker, an optician and a dry cleaner. By the end of the century there were just 26 retail businesses, comprising far fewer trades and offering much less choice (except for Chadds which had expanded to become an important 'magnet' department store for the street). Of the 15 non-retail businesses, six were banks and building societies, with frontages mainly devoted to cashpoint machines and interest rate notices, a betting office and a travel agency whose window displays also did nothing for the image of the street. The draw of well-dressed windows, so important to former generations of shopkeepers, was broken by these drab and lifeless frontages. The many breaks in shop window continuity ran contrary to one of the cardinal rules for successful retail trading in a main shopping street.

Similar changes were occurring in the High Town area. The short length of St. Peter's Street contained four charity shops, a bank, a building society, a travel agency, a post office, a public house, a café and only eight shops. These included a bargain bin store in place of a long-established pharmacy, and one of many mobile 'phone outlets (sited next door to another, in High Town).

There had been 47 widely diverse retail shops in Eign Gate (part of Eign Street in 1960). These were mostly family run, except for Woolworths, and the nine non-retail businesses included two public houses, two cafés and a fish restaurant. The pubs had gone by the end of the century, an amusement centre replacing the Three Crowns. There were five other non-retail outlets and of the remaining 32 shops, three were charity bazaars and about a fifth of the remainder were various bargain basement or cut price clothing chain stores.

In contrast, the new shops in Maylord Orchards had been designed to meet modern trading approaches and techniques by being built of adequate size, to the right proportions and with ample frontages—all to help maximise sales. Tenancies were rigidly controlled in order to secure a variety of trades, with an unbroken sequence of retail shop-front displays to attract shoppers. Various entertainments and events were organised, both in Trinity Square and in the Atrium, and there was a choice of restaurant facilities. The whole was supervised by a Shopping Centre Manager, aiming to make shopping at Maylord Orchards pleasurable and relaxing, and therefore for the shop-keeper a profit-producing, experience.

But as in the high street, the managers of Maylords Orchards need to be sensitive to developments in the retail industry. Rising living standards and increased access to credit arrangements produced dramatic shifts in what people bought. This was well illustrated when a form of 'technomania' set in with a big surge in the sales of electronic goods. As an example, well before they closed for Christmas, 1999, Hereford retailers had run out of huge numbers of personal computers, word processors, digital cameras and 'must have' gadgets.

New suppliers included the supermarkets, which had already moved a long way from their native grocery territory into general merchandise, toiletries and banking. They had absorbed and closed three city centre pharmacies and were in strong competition with Boots, Superdrug and the remaining smaller chemists. The entry of Tescos into clothing, albeit in a relatively small way, put further pressure on neighbouring Woolworths and could have been one of the factors in the eventual closures of C & A and the Co-op's Living store. In the fiercely combative clothing and fashion trade, even high street favourites Marks and Spencer have been 'struggling'. Clothing, footwear shops and new 'discounters' such as Primark fight it out for a greater market share, their price-wars producing windows constantly covered with huge 'Sale' posters. Much 'value-led' fashion ranges and leisure wear (often made of inexpensive low grade far-eastern and other foreign material) cater for a growing tendency to 'dress down' with informal attire for both work and play. This has made life much tougher for the 'mid-range' shops such as Marks and Spencer, Next, and brands of the Arcadia (former Burtons) Group.

Not everyone has the money to enter this new consumerism, however cheap some products become. A 'New Earnings Survey' in 1999 reported that the proportion of employees living in 'poverty' in Herefordshire, a county often synonymous with low pay, was double that anywhere else in the West Midlands Region. Average earnings of men in the county were said to be 18% below the regional norm: 15,000 workers, representing 37% of the workforce, were paid less than £250 a week—compared with regional pay for full-time male workers of £375.60.

E-mail commerce and the internet provide another conundrum for the future.

The typical high street is thus beset with a catalogue of issues, and Hereford is no exception. Fragmented property ownerships, inflexible leases, conservation areas, town planning, listed building and building regulation requirements compound the effects of profound changes in late 20th-century shopping practices. The scorching out of family-run shops and domination by large chains (the Arcadia group comprising 16 brands alone operated six different stores between Eign Gate and Gomond Street) tend to produce a lowering of local involvement in economic or physical revitalisation efforts. With few exceptions, it is only in smaller 'secondary' shopping streets where individual initiatives, and unified ownerships (such as in Church Street and Bridge Street), produce the commitment of earlier shopkeepers in and around the city centre. Another unhelpful drawback is inertia in relevant matters of management and funding, not least among landlords, shop tenants, investors, and public sector agencies.

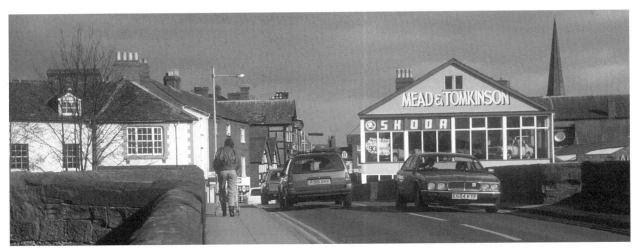

Looking across the old bridge towards the cathedral, when Mead and Tomkinson had their showroom

Also, if the city centre is to hold its own at the heart of the community, it must offer something more than historic associations in order to compete with the convenient, clean and tidy and well maintained new-style shopping emporia, or the temptations of new forms of armchair shopping. One approach has been taken by the Left Bank Village which is promoted as 'the new heart of Hereford', occupying earlier shop premises in Bridge Street between the Crystal Rooms Entertainment Centre (previously Franklin Barnes, corn merchants) and replacing Mead and Tomkinson, the former motor cycle agents (whose riverside showrooms marred many a Wye Bridge picture postcard view!). A wine merchant, delicatessen, bakery, patisserie, Dutch style coffee corner and 'trove' of gift items lie at different levels along with an outdoor Piazza. In summer 2000, Eign Enterprises also opened an adjoining new restaurant, brasserie, banqueting suite and cocktail bar overlooking the Wye.

Another enterprise, inspired and led by the Reverend Andrew Mottram, has introduced a rather exceptional amenity into the late 13th- and 14th-century walls of All Saints church in High Street. A meeting place for music, drama, exhibitions and other events has been created as part of a massive £1.7 million restoration scheme, aided

The Left Bank complex which has replaced Mead and Tomkinson and some adjoining properties

by English Heritage, the Heritage Lottery Fund and other donors which, opened in July, 1997, also includes the Café @ All Saints. Owned by the parochial church council through its trading company, Spire Trading Ltd., café profits are spent on keeping the whole building in good order. Regular services still take place on Sundays, and during the week the Lady chapel is always available for prayer and quiet. Mid-week celebrations of the Holy Communion regularly take place in full view of people having lunch in the nave and new south gallery.

The creation of traffic-free streets since the 1960s has done much to produce a more civilised 'environment', free from the former intimidating traffic and its noise, fumes and chaotic danger. People have been able to hear each other and look around them in the pedestrianised areas, and after early gloomy prophesies about ruinous loss of trade, most shopkeepers have accepted that relaxed shoppers have in fact made for increased

trade and turnover. Shoppers with parking problems cannot, however, be totally at ease. At a 1980s conference of town planners, Lord Sainsbury went as far as to assert that 'the success of a city centre to a very large extent depends on the capacity of its car parks'. This was not news for Hereford and District Chamber of Commerce or any city shopkeeper, but in a rather cramped historic city, serving not only residents but visitors from many surrounding county and Welsh districts as well as tourists, no amount of space would have been enough to serve everyone wishing to park close to the centre during busy times. By the start of the 21st century pressure on available kerbside and off-street spaces has become ever greater as car-ownership continues to expand. Special traffic limitation arrangements will soon become essential if frequent 'gridlock' of the limited road system is to be avoided.

As a gateway and introduction to the city for long distance and country travellers, the council's

All Saints, showing the east end (left), part of the area retained for worship and (right) the café on two floors at the west end

shabby 1930s Union Walk bus station compares badly with Railtrack's recently refurbished Victorian Barrs Court station, whilst the Tesco/Fryzer's Court bus station, not designed to become the principal city-service terminus, is frequently overwhelmed with passengers and buses, according to modern standards of amenity and safety. Similarly, the bus stops at St. Peter's Square, lacking any form of weather protection or adequate seating, are equally not up to the much higher standards needed to attract people out of their comfortable cars.

As for shoppers walking from outer fringe areas, a lack of planned maintenance shows in the condition of many footways, whilst the longer established pedestrianised streets have lost their early freshness and 'sparkle'—in the USA shopping centres are refurbished every 5 to 7 years, compared with 15 to 20 years in the UK. The benefits show in new paving work carried out in Church Street, Palace Yard, King Street and the Wye Bridge and further planned refurbishments will do much more to lift the image of the historic core when funds become available.

Much good can also be undone by ill-planned or badly reinstated road works by highways or services agencies, even more by excessive traffic engineering signs and plastic paintwork lettering, lines and strips. Those imposed upon Hereford's 'Central Conservation Area of Outstanding Merit', as part of the traffic reversal (and then re-reversal!) measures from Widemarsh Street to and from Bridge Street, were extreme examples of this in the late 1990s.

Because of the wide range of areas to be covered in dealing with the needs of the city centre as a whole, and the many different departments and interests involved, the city council decided to follow the concept of the commercial shopping centre manager by appointing a 'City Centre Manager' in the late 1990s. Covering everything affecting the success of the centre, the role is to serve as a co-ordinator with a wide range of managerial functions. This involves a development of the corporate spirit of the centre and its

place in the promotion of the city, both for shopping and tourism. It requires co-ordination of public works (such as car parking, repair and maintenance, cleansing and litter bins, seats, street-lighting, public toilets and street planting and floral decoration), liaison with police, public transport, underground services bodies, planners, Chamber of Commerce, and individual traders. The Manager is also in a good position to organise events and activities, especially in High Town, and establish connections within both the public and private sectors to help sponsor and finance various initiatives. The post has encouraged the formation of a City Centre Forum comprising local shopkeepers, chain store representatives, estate agents, local authority members and other interested individuals, which has embarked upon a number of ideas, most successfully a participation in the Britain in Bloom competition. This move is seen as a prime example of a way in which large and small businesses, private residents and the local authority can join in injecting more colour and life into the city centre in the new century. Specially priced window displays and hanging baskets with a free watering service were made available, with the co-operation of Herefordshire Parks and Countryside Services, to all city centre businesses and private dwellings within one square mile of High Town. Sponsorships were also invited for the planting of shrubs and floral displays on roundabouts, greenswards and other floral sites in the city. On their first attempt Hereford were 1999 regional runners-up and in 2000 repeated their success but also came second in the national finals.

The future of the city centre in the 21st century will depend a great deal on distant commercial considerations and a more local political perception of priorities for the application of funds for the financing of infrastructure and support services. Meanwhile it has been shown that it is still not too late to explore ways of improving the shopping environment, and therefore economic and social health, of Hereford.

Chapter III
Transport

The road system along which the Romans withdrew after 400 years formed one of the major bequests of the departed Empire. Although surfaces must have become heavily potholed, the deep foundations and proficient drainage ensured that they could survive as important thoroughfares.

By the Middle Ages the local road system had become quite extensive, even in a remote territory such as Herefordshire. It was chiefly suited to travel on foot or by horse, but almost every important feature of the countryside had some form of vehicular access. Moreover it is certain that the city could not have developed in the way that it did without adequate provision for the transport of large quantities of various building materials, as well as foodstuffs and other necessities for the increasing population and visitors. All the kings of England until Henry VIII are said to have visited Hereford, and royalty were not known for travelling light or on their own. They would be attended by their household, there would be ecclesiastical and lay members of the establishment along with their retinues. In addition there would be merchants, soldiers and many officials. At the cathedral, the shrines of St. Ethelbert and St. Thomas Cantilupe became leading places of pilgrimage—to the extent that at one time revenues from believers enabled 50 additional masons to be employed on enhancing and extending the fabric, with stone obtained from distant quarries. All this activity required roads.

Unfortunately medieval man was no better at road building than the Saxon, and neither was the Elizabethan and Stuart. In their time countless lanes, tracks and paths gradually vanished, many of them in the processes of enclosure. Mobility became increasingly difficult even in the Summer. In July 1645, during the Civil War, the Earl of Leven complained to Parliament about the state of the roads in Herefordshire, which he described as being the worst that the Scots had encountered since entering England, such that his army could accomplish only 8 miles in a day between Bromyard and Ledbury.

Up to the middle of the 18th century, goods were mostly transported on trains of pack horses. Even so, such was the state of roads in north Herefordshire that 'from Autumn until the end of April all intercourse between neighbouring families was suspended, unless they would consent to ride on pillions', a mode of travel in general use at that time. In the Spring, roads were levelled by means of ploughs, drawn by eight or ten horses—and in this state they remained until the following Autumn. Not everyone welcomed this process; the drovers who walked their animals in vast drifts to the many markets were strongly opposed to the resulting 'roads', which they held to be injurious to the feet of their beasts. The results were in any case inadequate for stage-coach travel, but the costs of a higher standard of road repair and maintenance, bridging and culverting were beyond the meagre resources of an impoverished rural Herefordshire. Drovers had flourished since at least as far back as the Norman Conquest and had always played a vital part in the rural economy of Wales. They were entrusted with the precious animal resources of often impoverished farmers and sometimes, buying and selling quite legitimately, were able also to operate a convenient, safe and reputable banking system in the big cities on behalf of country people. As regular long distance travellers they were always better informed than most others and were greatly relied upon as bearers of news: in 1815 they are said to have brought the first account of the great victory at Waterloo to rural Wales.

Matters changed with the Turnpike Trusts. These were companies made up of enterprising local men who obtained private Acts of Parliament empowering them to take over the making or improvement of sections of road and to erect gates and toll bars and to charge tolls. In 1730 an Act was obtained 'for repairing the roads leading into the city of Hereford' and by 1800 about 2,000 such Acts had been passed in respect of what were later to be classified chiefly as 'A' roads. The improvements eventually made it possible for pack-horses to be replaced by wagons, which were more efficient carriers of goods. Whereas each packhorse could carry about two hundredweights (100kg), the same animal could draw at least five times as much on wheels on a good surface.

Daniel Defoe, in his commentary on turnpike roads, appreciated their benefit to trade, observing that 'as for trade, it will be encouraged by it in every way; for carriage of all kind of heavy goods will be much easier, the waggoners will either perform in less time, or draw heavier loads, or the same load with fewer horses; the pack horses will carry heavier burthens, or travel farther in a day, and so perform their journey in less time; all which will tend to lessen the rate of carriage, and so bring goods cheaper to market'. He also thought that the better surfaces would benefit the produce which travelled on the hoof, which could be driven to market more easily and speedily and with less loss of weight. He had not, however, allowed for coyness on the part of the

Widemarsh Street Toll Gates in 1860

drovers in meeting toll collectors, for turnpike roads, tollgates and bars were generally avoided whenever possible. Typical was the old drove route which entered the county from Wales at the Rhydspence Inn, once the Cattle Inn, an important collecting centre. It continued to Hereford's markets via Monnington, Byford, Bridge Sollars, Green Lane at Breinton and a resting and watering stance at Kings Acre (so named in that connection), avoiding the road now classified as the A 438. The scale of such movements may be gauged from the count of a thousand head of cattle which are said to have been bought and sold on the streets of Hereford at the October Fair before the Winter of 1788.

Greatly improved roads also paved the way for speedier and more comfortable personal transport and, as both roads and coaches improved, ever faster times were accomplished on journeys. In 1774, the coach from Hereford to London took 36 hours to cover the distance; by 1800 this had been reduced by a third. Mounted

'Turnpike House', 20 Barton Road, formerly part of the Royal Oak inn

post 'boys' were also able to provide a far speedier mail service than before, and were somewhat safer from highwaymen.

As the number and efficiency of the coach services built up there was a corresponding demand for more hotels and with this went a need for stabling provision—later to be replaced by garaging and car parks. An example of such a conversion remains in Aubrey Street at the rear of the Green Dragon Hotel, now considered 'ripe' for further commercial development. In Hereford, Charles Howard, 11th Duke of Norfolk and Chief Steward of the city, bought the ancient coaching and posting inn, the Swan and Falcon and in 1790 rebuilt it on a new alignment in Broad Street, for it eventually to become the City Arms Hotel. Among the other principal inns listed in the *Hereford Guide* of 1808 were the Green Dragon, also in Broad Street, the Greyhound in Eign Street, the New Inn in Widemarsh Street, the Redstreak Tree in High Town and the Black Swan in Widemarsh Street.

Every Monday, Wednesday and Friday morning the 'Mail' set out from the City Arms Hotel at 5 o'clock and, travelling through Worcester, arrived at the Bull and Mouth in London on the following morning. It returned to Hereford on Tuesday, Thursday and Saturday evenings. A rival service departed from the Green Dragon at 6 o'clock on the same mornings to travel through Ross and Gloucester also bound for the Bull and Mouth, whilst on Sundays, Tuesdays and Thursdays at half-past four another coach set off in the Ledbury direction—also to arrive in London 24 hours later. From the Greyhound the 'Opposition' coach followed the Ross, Gloucester and Oxford route to terminate at the Bolt-in-Tun in London. Other services ran to Monmouth, Chepstow and Bristol, with connections to Newport, Cardiff, Neath and Swansea, to Ludlow and Shrewsbury through Chester to Holyhead for Ireland and to Brecknock, Carmarthen, Milford and Ireland.

The Post Office was kept in a part of the City Arms Hotel, letters being put into a letterbox in a window on Broad Street. The post went out every morning, coming in every evening. The Stamp Office was to be found at the house of Mr. Watkins, bookseller, in the western part of High Town.

Farmers and tradesmen, formerly restricted in range to very short distances from home, could widen business contacts by arranging a trip on the coach to the big cities and industrial centres at last within easy reach. Much extra business was gained in the provision of horses for the coaches by the hotels and inns, who also let post-chaises, four-wheeled closed carriages and other means of transport for more local journeys.

Better roads helped the development of long-distance freight services. Morris's Wagons set out every Sunday evening at 10 o'clock from the Warehouse in Broad Street, calling at Ross, Gloucester and the Black Bear, Piccadilly—terminating at the Saracens Head, Friday Street on the following Friday morning, before setting off for the return journey during the same after-noon. Messrs. Moles and Dadd and Co. provided competing services for London and elsewhere and they undertook more local return journeys which could be achieved within a day from the Black Swan, such as to Kington, Hay and Brecon.

Carriers operated to and from the villages, among them Mr. Thomas Payne of Mullings Farm, Bosbury, who was the 'last word in moder-nity, for his association with town life was regular'. For 20 years of the 19th century he conveyed people on the Bosbury, Canon Frome, Ashperton, Eggleton and Yarkhill route to Hereford 'to do business with the Gurneys, Edwardses, Philip Morrisses, and the like, to put up regularly at the sign of the Coach and Horses in Commercial Street - or in Union Street for the stables and market room - and to carry out commissions for those who could not themselves make the journey to and from Hereford'. While the May Fair was always a busy and enjoyable occasion it was at the October Fair and in the Autumn when villagers would stock up before the roads became blocked by winter rains and snow.

An element of Mr. Payne's charges would go towards payment of tolls at the turnpike gates in the suburbs of the city—the new city gates. For a single payment the traveller was entitled to pass through all the gates on the same day and also use the roads of the Hereford Trust. Payments on Sundays were double the weekday terms.

A glance at any road map shows Hereford to be at the hub of a radiating road network, one of its chief assets. The improved means of access resulting from the efforts of the Trusts did much to counteract the isolation and stagnation from which Hereford had suffered for so long, but the local road network remained largely in its ruinous state, left to arrangements which had really not worked since they were devised in Tudor legisla-tion 250 years before.

River

Although by 1800 the condition of many main roads had considerably improved, the cost of carriage by wagon was ruinously expensive. Boats and barges held more than wagons, could accommodate far more heavy and bulky goods for every horse used for towing, were also much safer when it came to handling anything fragile, and were easily the cheapest modes of trans-port—when they were available.

The Wye is one asset which Hereford has always had difficulty in exploiting. George Borrow, the 19th-century author of *Wild Wales*,

Wharf in front of the cathedral in 1805, from a drawing by Wm Varley

Craft on the Wye at Hereford at the end of the 1700s by James Wathen

went as far as describing it as 'the most lovely river, probably, which the World can boast of'. Daniel Defoe, equally well travelled, was also favourably impressed in an earlier century, although he noted that at Hereford it 'sometimes incommodes them very much, by the violent freshes that come down from the mountains of Wales'. Described as 'the keenest observer of economic growth of his time', he might have been expected to describe rather more than just the inconvenience of flooded property and fields and disruption to transport caused by these 'freshes'. Whilst the winter flows made navigation nigh on impossible, during the summer, river levels became so low that for the opposite reason use of the river became impracticable. Attempts were made over many years to engineer ways of navigating reliable and regular traffic to tidal Brockweir, near Chepstow, but nothing effectual or lasting ever came about.

Nevertheless, at favourable times barges of from 18 to 30 tons were brought laboriously upstream more than 60 wild and meandering miles from Brockweir to the quays of Hereford, 152 feet above ordnance datum at summer level. They were towed by teams of men—bow haulers—who brought cargoes of coal, building timbers, slate and a great variety of heavy goods for sale in the shops.

The return journey was much easier and faster and great quantities of Herefordshire cider, hops, oak bark for tanning, wool, wheat and timber were conveyed downstream to be shipped off to Bristol, London, Ireland and other distant places.

Sir William Sandys of Ombersley Court and others had obtained wide powers under the Rivers Wye and Lugg Navigation Act of 1662 to provide for 'the making navigable of the River of Wye and Lugg, and the rivers and brooks running into the same in the Counties of Hereford, Gloucester and Monmouth'. Provision was made for 'erecting, building, setting up and making of locks, weirs, turnpikes, penns for water cranes, wharfs, ways, passages, new channels, foot Rayls or other things &c.' and making use of a flash lock system. Funds were raised and much work was done to assist barge traffic up the river, but a system which had worked for Sandys on the Avon did not succeed on the Wye, essentially due to the volume and speed of the water. Subsequently Lord Coningsby and other landowners adopted different principles under an Act of 1695, but without much greater success.

The river would only become freely navigable throughout the year if a system of locks was introduced, and in 1763 a plan was duly submitted by Isaac Taylor for 22 weirs and locks between Bigsweir and Hereford. Estimated to cost £20,000, it would have catered for 40-ton barges, but it was not to be.

There had always been conflict on the river between those who wished to build weirs as a source of power for mills and iron forges and a breeding place for fish, and the boatmen who needed freedom of passage. In 1301, the city of Hereford was the plaintiff in an action to inquire into weirs and dykes between the Wye Bridge and Monmouth, and over the years there was much legislation to regulate the use of the river, especially after the end of the Civil War.

In 1805, a Mr. Jessop submitted recommendations for the improvement of navigation on the Wye. He concentrated in particular on the comparable costs of manpower, at two tons for every bow hauler employed, against horse-power, plus one man or boy for each barge. For his calculations, he allowed for annual carriage of 2,000 tons of goods from Brockweir to Hereford, 10,000 tons of coal from Lydbrook and 2,650 tons of goods from intermediate places. For the return to Brockweir the figures were 11,250 tons of goods from Hay and Hereford and 14,400 tons from intermediate places. He arrived at a likely annual saving to the public of some £4,233 and saw further advantages arising from 'dispatch and regularity; and that of restoring about 500 men, who are no substitute for horses, to more useful employment'. After prolonged discussion, doubtless joined by those selected for 'early retirement', a scheme was settled for the laying of a 10ft. wide towing path. Provision for this and a great many detailed matters were set in the clauses of the Rivers Wye and Lugg Navigation Act, 1809.

The Act came into force at one of the busiest periods seen on the Wye. In a *Guide Book* of 1809 it was recorded that 'the quay walls were thronged with barges', with names such as *Mayflower*, *Eliza*, *Charles*, *Hereford* and *Charles and Henry*. Later on, the *John and Mary* and the *Wellington* were said to have joined the fleet. At tolls not to exceed 6d. per mile for every horse, and no charge for barges still hauled by men, the tow path opened for business in 1811.

It was almost too late, for despite the many clear advantages it gave—particularly in reducing the cost of coal at Hereford, as it prepared to 'modernise' and enter the new dynamic Victorian era, they were not enough. By then, other more reliable, competitive and cost effective transportation ideas had, for some time, been 'in agitation'.

Tramroad

The strings of men hauling coal barges up-river from Lydbrook to the Hereford wharves faced 30 miles of difficult twists and bends and thought was given to finding a shorter and more dependable overland approach. Pack horses could make little impression on the annual 20,000 tons of coal needed in and around the city, and certainly not on the delivery price, and thoughts of a horse-powered tramroad were aired in 1801 at a meeting at Ross-on-Wye. A plan showing a line of only 24 miles followed soon afterwards. The route left the Wye at Lydbrook and ran via Goodrich Castle, Bridstow, Michaelchurch, St. Owen's Cross, Wormelow and Hunderton to a wharf near Hereford's Wye Bridge. However, investors were not impressed and the scheme fell for want of financial support.

This was not to be the end of such an idea. Less than 10 years later a meeting at Abergavenny considered the merits of bringing coal from the Monmouthshire coalfield via Govilon, on the Brecon to Abergavenny canal. In 1811 a further gathering at the Mitre Hotel in Hereford heard a proposal for a 15 mile tramroad from the terminus of the Llanvihangel Railway, under construction that year—but nothing ensued. Meanwhile the Grosmont Railway Company was formed and received Royal Assent for an extension of the track from Llanvihangel Crucorney to Monmouth Cap in 1812. It took another 17 years for the promoters to raise the money and overcome forcible opposition from barge-owners and other vested interests before the Hereford Railway Company could complete the 25 miles link with the canal.

It was not until the year 1829 that the final section reached the Wye Bridge wharf, the first consignment of coal, made up of 15 trams from the Blaenavon pits, 18 from Pontypool plus a tramload of grain, arriving on 21 November. The price of South Wales coal at Hereford came to just over £1 per ton, cheaper than the Forest of Dean coal, but the tramroad could not have achieved financial success once the Gloucester, Ledbury and Hereford canal opened in 1845. In that year it was bought by the Newport, Abergavenny and Hereford Railway and closed in 1851. Part of its route was used by the railway but in Hereford many signs remained visible into the 20th century, the tramroad terminal building finally making way in 1965 for the new 'Motor Age' Greyfriars Bridge.

Canal

Prior to the steam age, canals were the most effective mode of industrial transport available and they flourished for at least 70 years. One of the earliest was the Duke of Bridgewater's canal of 1761 which linked his mines at Worsley to Manchester, so enabling the cost of his coal there to be halved. Five years later more customers were enjoying similar benefits after its extension to the Mersey. Many other canals in Lancashire, the Midlands and Wales were constructed, with coal conveyance comprising one of their principal sources of revenue. Its uses extended from

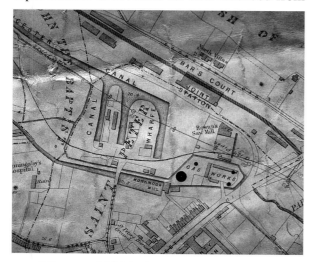

OS map of 1886 showing the canal basin south-west of Barrs Court Joint Station

the heating of homes, brick-making, brewing, iron and and many other industries — to the generation of steam, by 1800 the indispensable form of energy for the new age.

Hereford's coal had to be transported from the Forest of Dean collieries either by barge or packhorse. By 1800 the price on the quays at Hereford averaged a then very expensive 30s. a ton, limiting commercial competitiveness. Attention inevitably turned to the idea of a canal. To 'give encouragement to commercial enterprizes', an Act was passed in 1791 for the cutting of a canal between Hereford and the River Severn at Gloucester. The route would go by Ledbury with a collateral branch to Newent, at an estimated cost of £72,000. By March 1798, after numerous difficulties and with available funds exhausted, the canal had almost reached Ledbury from the Severn, allowing coal there to sell at 13s. 6d. a ton. But another 47 years were to pass before, in May 1845, the canal reached Hereford. It was the last mainline canal to be built in Britain, apart from short stretches in the Birmingham area and the Manchester Ship Canal, and was too late to be of any great commercial value to the city, then considering how to tap into the rail network. Nevertheless, for a short while it provided a reasonably cheap and efficient form of transport, still carrying 47,000 tons of goods in 1858, six years after the Shrewsbury, Hereford and Newport railway had opened. But by then the railway had arrived in Hereford and no such loading would ever be achieved again, except, ironically, in 1860 when it earned its highest revenue ever from carrying material for the construction of the Ledbury and Gloucester Railway.

Even before opening, the Herefordshire and Gloucestershire Canal Navigation Company received and accepted an offer from the West Midland Railway. Although this did not proceed, in 1862 the canal was leased jointly to the Great Western and West Midland Railways. In 1881 it ceased to function, part of the route was turned into railway as first intended and the GWR continued to pay £5,000 a year for the lease to the canal shareholders until railway nationalisation in 1947.

Stephen Ballard's skew bridge at Monkhide

Of all the products of 'Canal Mania', few have vanished quite so fully as the Hereford and Gloucester Canal—but remnants still survive in scattered places. Some, such as the long tunnel under the College Hill Estate, between Painter Brothers and Holmer Trading Estate, are on private land but others—notably Stephen Ballard's masterly skew bridge of 1839 at Monkhide—are well worth a visit thanks to energetic works by the Herefordshire and Gloucestershire Canal Trust.

Railways

In 1825, the Stockton and Darlington line was laid out using horse-drawn trains with the similar purpose of achieving cheaper and quicker means of transporting coal. The engineer was George Stephenson, builder of the Rocket, and the gauge was 4 ft. 8½ ins.—based on the width of track of the local country carts, Stephenson went on to pioneer the true start of public railways in Britain with the Liverpool to Manchester line. This opened in 1830, and in that year a correspondent in *The Hereford Journal* looked forward to the day when Hereford too would have a railway service. Characteristically, the 'Railway Mania' raging elsewhere took quite a while to gain a hold locally and it took another 16 years before Acts were passed in Parliament authorising land acquisition and construction of the Newport, Abergavenny and Hereford Railway and the Shrewsbury and Hereford Railway. The line from Shrewsbury and Ludlow to Hereford built by Robert Stephenson, to the standard gauge adopted by his father, followed closely that of the old coach road. It took six years to build and opened for freight traffic on 30 July, 1852. The first passenger train, consisting of two engines decorated with flags, a splendid saloon coach occupied by the chairman and his party, six first-class carriages, and a luggage van occupied by a 'band of music' arrived in Hereford on Saturday, 28 October, 1853. On 6 December, the first train of the Newport, Abergavenny and Hereford Railway, drawn by three engines, left Newport at 9 a.m. and, after much celebration on the way, at 1 o'clock steamed over the handsome new Bartonsham Bridge across the Wye and came to a halt at Barton. The train from Shrewsbury and London arrived at Barrs Court at 2 o'clock and

Train crossing Bartonsham Bridge in the 19th century

Barrs Court Station in c.1908. Connelly's motor bus sets off for High Town and Whitecross as the home signal is 'pulled off' for the departure of a train from platform 3

from then on, a local holiday having been declared, the whole of the city celebrated. The occasion was also of some national significance for it marked the completion, through Hereford, of the first strategic 'standard gauge' main line from the Bristol Channel to the Mersey and North-West. It had been a long wait: Hereford was the last English cathedral city, and town of comparable size, to be served by the rail system, which by then exceeded 12,000 kilometres of line and carried over 100 million passengers a year. Barrs Court Joint Station opened in June 1855.

A fragment of Barton Station that remained until it was cleared to make way for the Sainsbury development

There had been at least one other ambitious plan for a profitable South-West / North-West link through Hereford. In 1833 Isambard Kingdom Brunel, then aged 27 (having designed the Clifton Suspension Bridge when he was 23), became the chief engineer of the company building the Great Western Railway. He was totally committed to the broad gauge of 7ft. (2.1m) on the grounds that it was safer than Stephenson's narrower gauge and would allow for higher speeds and greater comfort. He was probably right. Brunel had looked from Gloucester and Bristol towards the North-West in his early days with the GWR and had urged a broad gauge route through Hereford and Shrewsbury. The necessary powers were, however, not forthcoming and Stephenson's designs were approved instead. Nevertheless, Brunel continued his interest in planning a broad gauge route from Gloucester through Ross to Hereford and promoted it at a meeting at Hereford's Shirehall in 1850. This time he gained the necessary support but it was to be another five years before the broad gauge Hereford, Ross and Gloucester Railway opened. For a while, Barrs Court Joint station was served by both standard and broad gauge lines. The new line also provided a link to Monmouth from Ross-on-Wye. The Worcester and Hereford Railway arrived at Barrs Court in 1861; by then it was a part of the West Midland Railway, itself shortly to be absorbed by the Great Western Railway. Then, from 1869 to 1874, the Hereford, Hay and Brecon Railway operated from the city's third, albeit very basic, station at Moorfields instead of Barton and connected later with lines leading to Swansea and other parts of South Wales.

Thus it was, during the short time between 1853 and 1874, that Hereford, from being virtually 'off the map' for so long, found itself with three stations at the hub of a network reaching out in no less than five directions, operated by as many private enterprise railway companies.

Inevitably long distance travel, freight transport and postal services were quickly transferred from stage coaches and wagons, many of which ceased to operate almost overnight. Just a few coach services continued to run for a while to places still not conveniently served by rail, and wagon services to the stations, halts and goods yards on the main and branch lines became an essential part of the new freight system.

During this time there was an amount of adjustment and consolidation as running powers and leasing arrangements were negotiated between the companies. In 1863 the number of these at Hereford had reduced to three: the Great Western Railway, London and North Western Railway and Midland Railway. Some sections of track were doubled and in 1866 a cut off loop line was laid between Red Hill and Rotherwas. A further significant measure was the conversion of the broad gauge line via Ross to Grange Court and Gloucester in 1869, during an amazingly short period of five days. This was to have a marked effect on the volume of rail traffic to and through Hereford, especially after conversion to the standard gauge on all Great Western lines and also the 1886 opening of the Severn Tunnel. However, it was not to develop as a trunk line from the North-West to London, as had been hoped when Barrs Court Joint Station was so lavishly designed and opened in 1855. Instead the rather grim looking Barton Station of 1854, serving the through route to South Wales, the Severn tunnel and Bristol, gained ascendancy and seemed likely to be Hereford's only passenger station with Barrs Court becoming a freight depot. This idea did not appeal to the powerful Midland Railway, which had acquired the Hereford and Brecon line as their cherished route from the North to South Wales and Swansea. They were able to prevent it happening, and after much argument all three companies settled at the modernised Barrs Court station. Originally built by Johnson of Birkenhead, it has since been listed as a Grade II building of Special Architectural and Historic Interest. Without this protection, it might well have been reduced to little more than a prefabricated 'bus stop' type of station building towards the end of the 20th century, but instead was conserved and protected substantially in its

Year	Population
1757	5,597
1785	5,638
1801	6,828
1811	7,306
1821	9,076
1831	10,282
1841	10,921
1851	12,128
1861	15,565
1871	18,345
1881	19,821
1891	20,265
1901	21,382
1911	22,568
1921	23,322
1931	24,159
1941	26,650 (estimated)
1951	32,490
1961	40,431
1971	46,503
1981	47,804
1991	50,234
2000	56,500 (greater Hereford)

Population of Hereford over the years

original state at a cost of £280,000—although with not the same imposing internal uses. Moorfields and Barton stations were closed to passenger traffic and Barton engine shed, opened in 1854, was used for stabling, fuelling, watering and maintaining some 40 widely varying loco-motives at a time. It did not close until October 1964.

The centre of Hereford would have acquired quite a different shape in the 20th century had the 40-year battle between the three former railway companies ended with the passenger station being established at Barton and not Barrs Court.

The effect of the railways on Hereford was soon apparent as city and county began to connect with the busy and hungry communities of the North-West and Midlands, the huge coal fields and iron industries of South Wales and the ports. With such a widening of horizons the opportunity arose to participate in a booming national economy. The railway companies themselves were highly labour intensive with Hereford initially having three stationmasters, together with their staffs and operatives in strict grades of operational, commercial, technical and related departments. These employees and their families must have accounted for a good propor-tion of the increase in the city's population, from 12,128 in 1851 to 18,347 just 20 years later—the steepest rise in its history. The business directo-ries for the second half of the century give an important indication of the extent of economic growth, whilst the greater opportunities provided for more people to travel at manageable fares presented scope for new initiatives, including the first beginnings of tourism.

The city's role as the traditional market centre for its agrarian hinterland was greatly enhanced when produce could more easily be conveyed from local stations, although it was also possible for large amounts to be railed direct to anywhere served by the railway system. The effect on the cattle trade was revolutionary, both for the drovers from Wales and for local beef farmers. Although movement by rail in cattle trucks was more expensive than it had been on the hoof, there was more than enough benefit gained in the condition and weight of the animals when they arrived at the markets and when they were sent for slaughter in distant towns and cities. As it turned out, the railways would be involved in the movement of cattle for a considerably shorter time than the nine centuries of the drovers. They did however, through mass transportation of newspapers and journals, take over the wide circulation of news for much longer than the cattle men, whilst the postal service also bene-fitted greatly from a speedier and more reliable form of transport.

The punctuality achievable by trains quickly produced a problem with the existing national time system, which had always observed east to west local variations according to the position of the sun. With the development of direct telegraph communication, standard 'railway time' was adopted throughout the network for the benefit both of rail users and operating crews and staffs. Railway time-tables were produced showing precise arrival times at each station based on Paddington or Greenwich Mean Time—and this standardisation gradually came to replace local time across the country. The citizens of Hereford 'lost' 11 minutes of their lives in the process!

As the value of rail transport for bulk freight became increasingly recognised, private sidings were laid to developing commercial and industrial sites. They included the municipal livestock market where, in 1856, provision had been made for future service by rail. By the end of the 19th century the annual 'throughput' had grown to over 150,000 animals and in 1914 a layout of track, ramps and pens was arranged with the Great Western Railway at Canonmoor on what became known as the Worcester Sidings. Rail service was later extended across Edgar Street, through the market, to fuel the Electricity Generating Station. As time went on other sidings were negotiated with Watkins Flour Mills, Painter Brothers, the Gas Works, H.P. Bulmer, Henry Wiggin and some smaller companies. During the First World War, considerable installations were built to serve military ammunition factories at Rotherwas and Credenhill.

In 1914 the 120 different railway companies in Great Britain were placed under control of a central committee and after the war all were 'rationalised' and placed under a measure of state control in a 'Grouping' of just four. Prior to this, the railway history of Hereford had involved 11 railway companies and one joint committee. From 1923 the three companies then operating at Hereford merged to two and until after the Second World War the carriage livery to be seen at Barrs Court Station was the 'Crimson Lake' of the London, Midland and Scottish Railway and the 'Chocolate and Cream' of the Great Western Railway.

The deterioration of track and rolling stock during the Great War meant that far more than new livery was required to restore an effective rail service, and it took until the end of the 1920s before even the express lines were in adequate shape to catch up with pre-war speeds and effectiveness. Revenues inevitably fell in the face of relentless and mounting competition from road transport. The advantages introduced by the internal combustion engine, pneumatic rubber tyre and tarmacadam-surfaced roads weighed heavily against the fixed infrastructure, land, rolling stock and operating costs of the railways—handicapped as they had also been by state control of fares and freight charges since 1923.

From 1939 the whole system was again subjected to heavy wear and tear in the movement of munitions and other war materials, troops and evacuees. In Herefordshire the war greatly increased the number of people employed in central and local government, in war production and in certain food industries that had been evacuated, and together with R.A.F. units at Shobdon, Madley and Credenhill all made a full call on railway services.

The Royal Ordnance Factory sidings at Rotherwas were again put to use (including involvement in the movement of some munitions to a secret bomb-proof naval armaments store in the disused first Colwall railway tunnel beneath the Malvern Hills) and further tracks were laid to

One of the ex-railway sidings at Rotherwas, showing how they were surrounded by blast walls. The trains even ran on wooden sleepers within the sidings so as to reduce the risk of a spark igniting the stored munitions

serve new government installations at Moreton-on-Lugg and Elm Bridge near Pontrilas. During the early part of the war an ambulance train occupied a siding at Barrs Court.

After the war the railways were again in a poor physical state, but they managed to maintain a hold on passenger and freight traffic during the subsequent years of austerity and rationing, whilst road transport slowly resumed its challenge. The election of a Labour government led to nationalisation from January 1948. Under the British Transport Commission, Hereford was served through one of six new regions, but from 1952 operating profits progressively declined and despite an extensive modernisation plan commencing in 1955 annual losses increased.

The British Railways Board took the place of the Commission in January 1963, and under the Chairmanship of I.C.I.'s Dr. Beeching it embarked on drastic surgery which added to rail closures in Herefordshire which had started in 1941 on the Golden Valley Line. By 1966 the only stations remaining in the county were at Barrs Court, Leominster, Ledbury and Colwall: the Hereford to Hay, Leominster to Kington, Leominster to Bromyard and Hereford to Ross lines were either being taken up or had already gone.

For a while during the 1970s there were fears that the Marches Line to Shrewsbury north of Shelwick Junction would join them and there was wide unease about the high level of subsidy required to retain the line to Ledbury and Malvern, reduced to a single track in 1984. From that time, however, more freight traffic was being gained along these routes—a promising trend when the first stages of re-privatisation were approaching.

In April 1994 Railtrack inherited Britain's 16,000 km of railway infrastructure and two years later was privatised for £2bn and became listed on the FTSE 100 share index (only to be relegated in June 2001). It provides management services for the rail structure, coordinates all train movements and, for a reducing and reviewable charge, it provides access to 25 passenger 'train operating companies' (TOCs) and to companies who run freight trains. The train-operating companies no longer have their own locomotives and carriages but lease them as needed from 'rolling stock companies' (ROSCOs)—who bought 11,000 ageing passenger trains from British Rail. Separate companies and service providers maintain the infrastructure, track, telecommunications and other facilities for Railtrack, and heavy maintenance suppliers provide services to the rolling stock and freight companies.

The iron wheel has turned full circle and once more Hereford is served by several private railway companies: Wales and Border Trains and Wessex Trains, Central Trains, Thames Trains and Great Western Trains, all operating from Railtrack's Barrs Court Station. There was initial optimism as investment was made in trains and services, with some disused routes reopened and more freight was transferred to rail. 50% growth by 2010 was being predicted by the industry. But the 20th century ended badly. The route from Hereford and the West suffered two rail disasters at the approach to Paddington, first at Southall and then, in October 1999, at Ladbroke Grove. After revelations of regular red danger signal violations and other rail safety faults, it was the final straw when in October 2000, a 117 mph passenger train was derailed on a bend on the east coast main line at Hatfield. All the evidence pointed to rail fracture, resulting from poor maintenance and 'gauge corner cracking'—a form of metal fatigue—a problem then found to be widespread. Over 400 miles of track across the network were replaced, creating severe blanket speed restrictions and causing long delays, cancellations and chaos. Hereford shared fully in the consequences, with *The Hereford Times* carrying accounts of passengers travelling from Paddington being regularly 'thrown off the train at Great Malvern without advance warning', and transferred to a slow bus for the rest of their journey. The operational failures were unprecedented, even during state control, and although the short term disruption has been resolved, there is a huge question mark over the time it will take for the train companies to regain passenger confidence and growth.

Motor Mania

The 19th century saw the ending of an age-long dependence on the horse or 'shanks's pony' for overland travel and transport. By the end of her reign, Queen Victoria had journeyed by steam train and witnessed a first faltering appearance of the petrol-fuelled automobile. But whereas in 1801 Great Britain had led the way with Trevithick's first steam carriage, it lagged behind in the introduction of the motor car. This was largely due to the bad state of most roads and the not unconnected Light Locomotives on Highways Act of 1865 which limited machine-powered vehicles to 4mph and required three drivers on board and a man walking in front with a red flag. The first motor vehicle to run on the roads of Britain was a Benz three-wheeler imported from the Continent in 1888 and there were still very few when the Act was repealed in 1896.

By 1900, Hereford's first cars were being assembled by the Smooth-Geared Auto-Car Syndicate of Commercial Road who as Connelly and Sons were among the makers of the 198 different models available in Britain by 1913. The new vehicles were all carriage-built by hand, in some cases at the premises of craftsmen of the horse-drawn era. One example was at 20 Bridge Street, now part of the Left Bank Village, where Richard Sully—'Carriage and Motor Body Builder; Rubber tyres fitted in a few hours'— succeeded John Watkins, who in 1876 had been listed in a trades directory as one of three builders of horse-drawn coaches and carriages. The vehicles were sold to a limited clientele as shown in the local advertisement of someone who 'begs to return his sincere thanks to the Nobility, Clergy, and Gentry who have honoured him with their support, and hopes to merit a continuance of the same.'

To begin with, the motor car was affordable only by the well-off and used mainly as a novelty for pleasure, excitement—and as a symbol of prestige. Before thus indulging themselves, the pioneers needed to know not only how to operate the unfamiliar levers, pedals and other mysterious controls to steer and manoeuvre on dusty unmade roads, but also what to do in the event of a break-

EIGN STREET, HEREFORD.

JAMES STOWE,
COACH & HARNESS
MANUFACTURER,
BUILDER OF CARRIAGES

On the most Approved Principle, at a Moderate Price.

All Carriages built at this Establishment are warranted, the whole being Manufactured on the Premises, and under the superintendence of the Proprietor, who has had many years experience in the trade, both in and out of London. He begs to return his sincere thanks to the Nobility, Clergy, and Gentry who have honoured him with their support, and hopes to merit a continuance of the same.

N.B.—OLD CARRIAGES TAKEN IN EXCHANGE.

Advert for coach manufacturing in Hereford

down. Very few would have had any relevant skills or aptitude and it was common for the dealer to find a chauffeur when supplying a first car. Even so, in the early years of the Motor Car Age there were almost as many suppliers in Hereford as there are now.

Due partly to competitions and trials promoted by the new motoring organisations reliability of cars improved fairly quickly. To celebrate the repeal of the Red Flag Act, and at a greater top speed of 14 mph, the first London to Brighton trial took place in 1896, and by 1904 the 6th National Light Car Trials were being held in and around Hereford. These were to test the endurance of vehicles costing less than £200 and each day their drivers motored over six different routes, covering two non-stop laps of 50 miles. In the same year licencing and number plates were introduced and Hereford formed its own Automobile Club which organised an annual hill-climb at Fromes Hill, attracting 112 entries in 1907.

Although some vehicles were used for day-to-day travel, they were not to displace local horse transport until the 1920s and there was still plenty of work for blacksmiths, farriers and wheelwrights for some time afterwards. In 1914 there were over 130,000 licenced private cars in Britain, but despite such a rapid growth no-one could then have predicted that by the end of the century the total would have increased some two-hundred fold. The war brought motor car production to an end and resources were directed to military purposes. Although horses and mules were still being used in large numbers, mechanisation was gradually taking over many functions and introducing and developing others, notably in the air. As in motoring, use of the internal combustion engine in aviation was very much in its infancy—the people of Herefordshire did not see an aircraft until 1912 when in April a Bleriot monoplane made a forced landing near Weobley and another landed at Hereford racecourse in July. Yet, at the Armistice six years later the Royal Air Force, in succession to the Royal Flying Corps, operated 22,000 aircraft with a complement of 291,000 officers and men. Another new instrument of war was introduced in 1916—the tank, which evolved from the Hornsby caterpillar-track petrol driven agricultural tractor, and by 1918 there were many thousands of army, navy and air force men trained to drive, service or repair all manner of vehicle and mechanical equipment. This was of great benefit to the motor industry as it resumed production, stimulated as it was also by the lessons learned during the war.

By 1922 there were almost a hundred different makes of car, most individually built and costly. It was only with the introduction of assembly-line methods that prices fell. This method of production had been brought to Britain in 1911 by Henry Ford. By the mid-20s Ford's UK plants were producing cars which were far more within

people's means, notably the pioneering model 'T'. William Morris and Herbert Austin were the first English manufacturers to adopt these mass-production techniques and during the inter-war years they became responsible for the output of 60% of all British cars. With some 30 other car manufacturers, they were the foundation of a major industry that included a wide range of accessories and other trades, distributors and service agents.

In Hereford increasing numbers of people could afford to buy and run a car despite the fact that many of the working population earned less than £5 a week. Just before the war, the cheapest new saloon, a Ford 8, cost £117 whilst a medium range car might cost more than the average annual income of most families, and about half that of a semi-detached house.

Those who could afford to own a car were well catered for at numerous agents, dealers and repairers, some of them early pioneers notably James Fryers. After coming to Hereford in 1908 they undertook a luxurious glass roofed development of the former posting yard of the Green Dragon Garage at Aubrey Street in March 1915. Even in those early days they had already dealt with names such as Rolls-Royce, Daimler, Wolseley, Napier, Sunbeam, Minerva, Rover, Humber, Sheffield-Simplex, Buick, Saxon and Ford. They and competitors, including R.P. Ravenhill of Commercial Road, Hereford Motor Company of Eign Street (who suffered a devastating fire in 1942), Imperial Motors of Commercial Road, Marriotts of St. Owen Street, West End Garage of Eign Street, Wye Valley Motors of St. Martin's Street and White Cross Garage, dealt in or serviced the wide range of makes and models of British cars then available.

Congestion

The road pattern at the medieval core of Hereford was shaped well before the Norman Conquest and has not been altered essentially for a thousand years. In places the trunk and main roads within the city were as narrow as 16ft. and the only bridge over the River Wye provided a carriageway width of 17ft. 10ins. and footways of

4ft. 7ins. and 1ft. 5ins. between parapets that were just 23ft. 8ins. apart. The nearest road bridges were six miles upstream and five miles downstream and both had poor approaches and were subject to weight restrictions.

The daily number of vehicles using the Wye Bridge in 1938 averaged almost 5,500 and although Hereford had long been accustomed to street congestion from horse drawn carriages, carts and animals at busy times, this new ingredient gradually introduced a new form of 'traffic jam'.

The Ministry of Transport, which had become responsible for trunk roads in 1936, developed plans for a new route from South Wales to North Wales and the North-West of England through Hereford, entering into discussion with the city and county authorities about ways of saving the medieval city's central streets from overloading. Studies showed that because of its focal attraction as a county market town some 80% of all drivers had reason to call and stop; at certain times of the week barely 15% of vehicles could

be classified as 'by-passable'. And so in 1939, a route was agreed for a new bridge close to the city centre not many yards upstream from the old Wye Bridge. It was to be aligned with a new north-south dual carriageway along Victoria Street running parallel with the western medieval wall-line.

The Second World War put an end to any further action and the narrow ancient bridge, rebuilt in stone it is said in 1490, carried an increasing volume and weight of traffic, including much of a military nature. After the end of the war the usage intensified. Eign Street and Widemarsh Street were too narrow for two-way traffic and were often at a standstill, whilst Commercial Street, St. Peter's Street and Union Street were restricted to a clockwise one-way circulation and were also frequently blocked due to severe overloading. Other streets, especially those following the routes of the old walls were narrow and congested and had difficult blind turnings into the main roads.

A relatively calm High Town in the 1950s, contrasting with traffic build up in later years (opposite)

Congestion!
Top right: 'Dean's Corner' and Eign Street
from the A49 Victoria Street in 1965

Above and below: High Town in 1965.
(Just visible, both above and below, at top
left, is the edge of the polythene-wrapped
3 High Street at its temporary home

Right: High Street

In 1946, the theme of the pre-war trunk road scheme was taken up by George Cadbury, a locally connected member of the War Transport Council and of the West Midland Group on Post-War Reconstruction and Planning. In his booklet *Hereford Walls* he suggested:

Opening up the old walls and preserving the centre of the city from through transport, with all its noise and vibration, will enable a truly 'precinct' city to be formed for shopping, business and residence. Hereford would then lead the way in restoring the idea of a walled city - walled against outside noise and disturbance - and therefore become a modern residential and business centre ...

There was to be an incubation period of 20 years before, in 1965, such ideas started to come to fruition. All the preparatory work anticipated much of the Buchanan Report, *Traffic in Towns* published in 1963, which put the problems of Britain's historic towns firmly in perspective:

It is not a question of retaining a few old buildings but of conserving, in the face of the onslaught of motor traffic, a major part of the heritage of the English-speaking world, of which this country is the guardian.

In the meantime the traffic onslaught at the old Wye Bridge intensified and by 1954, following the ending of post-war austerity and the lifting of car-sale restrictions, the average daily traffic flow had risen to almost 9,500 vehicles—amounting to a 75% increase over immediate pre-war totals. Not only was road transport gaining increasing amounts of freight from the railways, but Hereford's population was continuing to grow, encouraged by the arrival of new industrial companies, particularly Henry Wiggin and Company Ltd, who were eventually to employ up to 3,500 people at Holmer, on the north side of the river. Between 1951 and 1961 the city's population rose from 32,490 to 40,431 and by 1971 it amounted to 46,503. In 1965 more than 24,000 vehicles per day were crossing the Wye Bridge,

What Hereford might have looked like. The proposed sunken route for the A49 set out in the pamphlet Hereford Walls

and it might have been even more had it not been for the many commercial operators and motorists who gave Hereford a wide berth because of its reputation as a place to be avoided. All this worked to the great detriment of the entire trade and economy of the city, as well as to the long-suffering motorists who could not avoid the place. The heart of the city was being devastated.

Herefordshire County Council had a duty to produce proposals to deal with the situation and after three years of research, debate and public consultation a statutory Town Map for Hereford came into effect on 11 October 1963. One of its four main listed 'Objects' was: 'To assist in the relief of traffic congestion' through a process of segregation. Through traffic would, for the most part, use only the trunk and inner relief roads, local traffic would have limited entry to the central area, there would be service roads for the purpose of loading and unloading, and car parks for the purposes of long and short period parking. Areas would be specifically reserved for pedestrian use. A further 'Statement of Principles' prepared by the city and county councils asserted that: 'the demands of the pedestrian and motor vehicles in the central area cannot be reconciled; they must be separated by a system allowing for the speedy, safe circulation of both in segregated channels'.

The ideas of the Ministry of Transport in 1939 and George Cadbury of 1946 were reviewed in the context of the Buchanan report of 1963, but not everyone in Hereford was convinced that a new bridge and road situated so close to the existing bridge and the city centre was the correct solution. For some time there was pressure for the alternative of a new bridge and by-pass some distance upstream, to the west of the city boundary (with no mention of any alternative eastern route — the Minister's preferred option many years later!). The Ministry of Transport was still the responsible highway authority and remained convinced by the arguments for the pre-war scheme and finally, amidst great surprise, the Minister visited Hereford in person. In essence, Ernest Marples brought the message that there were other competitors for funds available for

The Minister of Transport, Ernest Marples MP (on the left) visiting Hereford in 1964 prior to issuing his 'ultimatum'. He is accompanied by Mayor Gordon Elcox, David Gibson-Watt MP and city surveyor F. Margerison

road building — including Worcester — and if Hereford did not accept his preferred scheme there would be no alternative and the city would lose its place in the roads programme for an indefinite period. With no chance of a by-pass and faced with this ultimatum there could only be one response.

Experience of all that has occurred since 1964 confirms that the correct decision was made in the circumstances applying and forecasts at that time: it is very difficult to visualise what an appalling shape the city would have been in at the end of the 20th century had Marples' ultimatum been rejected.

Inner relief road
Until the start of the Railway Age most historic towns and cities had evolved gradually and on a piecemeal basis. Generations of builders and tradespeople made their individual contributions

to the townscape, as a rule paying due regard to the nature and scale of what existed and to the levels of business which could be justified. This pattern of sporadic and modest development changed drastically when substantial areas of urban land were appropriated to railway tracks, cuttings, embankments, sidings, engine sheds and stations, and subsequent industrialisation produced further wholesale changes in the pace and scale of town development.

Hereford presented no exception to this, although from 1774 it was already starting to acquire something of a new look in places within its historic core through the efforts of Town Commissioners. Despite their scope, none of these changes would compare in scale with those which were about to occur in and around the city centre from 1964.

Stage 1: Greyfriars Bridge and approach roads
The southerly starting point of the inner relief road is at the Belmont roundabout, where the A49 and A465 meet. The route struck northward on a viaduct approach to the Greyfriars Bridge, named after the 13th-century Franciscan priory which

once stood nearby, close to the north bank of the Wye. Another viaduct led to the busy junction of the narrow northbound A49 route. This ran along Victoria Street towards Leominster, joining other roads leading to Hay, Ledbury and Bromyard and Worcester. Most of the property required for this phase was in the form of yards and rear gardens with the exception of a terrace of houses in St. Martin's Street, Nos 17-23 St. Nicholas Street and the Barton Tavern, the first of five inns and public houses which would be sacrificed to the new road. Another casualty was the terminal building of the short-lived Abergavenny to Hereford tramroad which, although in a poor state, had survived redundancy for over a hundred years. It stood close to the former boat-yard of the Jordan family who had been involved in boatbuilding and hiring for very much longer and had enjoyed a flourishing trade until the days of the motor car. By the time the boatyard made way for the new bridge, very little such boating remained but relics of the river access may still be seen beneath the bridge, close to stone steps which once allowed barges to operate at all levels at the adjacent coal wharf.

St. Martin's Street looking north before the new bridge was built, with the Greyhound Dog on the left

The A49 snaking through Hereford over the old bridge in 1960. Notice the Greyhound Dog, lower left

The temporary 'navvy gantry' used in the construction of the new bridge

Work started in late 1964 at a contract price of £608,000, and it was decided to build the approach viaducts first—in order to use their large surface area for storage of materials with a clear and reliable access above any potential flood levels. As it turned out, the near-record floods of December 1965 provided ample justification for this sequence and work proceeded without any interruption. Rapid flows and heavy debris floating at levels reaching over 18ft. above normal summer level nevertheless caused some worries about the temporary support piles driven into the river bed, but there was no damage. A notable feature of the technique for building the bridge was the use of a temporary 'navvy gantry' extending from the approach viaducts and placed about 4ft. higher than the road surface of the bridge. Steel beams carried a timber deck approximately 15ft. wide and there was a cantilevered footway on one side and supports for a narrow-gauge supply railway on the other. Construction of the main bridge was carried out from this structure.

With a central span of 290ft. and with two side spans of 85ft., the clear height at the centre of the main structure was raised 32ft. above summer water level and 12ft. above the maximum recorded flood level, as measured in 1960. The only serious setback throughout the whole construction was due to vandals who, with black bitumen, badly defaced the special white concrete surface of the bridge spandrels. This took some time and expense to eradicate, but the bridge was handed over for traffic use just before Christmas, 1966.

Stage 2: North-South and East-West Relief Roads
Immediately beyond the northern limit of the new approach road lay Victoria Street, a two-way street barely 16ft. wide in places, carrying all northbound trunk road traffic towards Herefordshire's only set of traffic signals. When Taylor produced his detailed map of Hereford in 1757, he knew Victoria Street as 'Town Ditch' when it formed part of a pathway which ran outside the City Wall line and former defensive moat past Fryers, Eigne, Widemarsh, Bye-Street and St. Owen's gates towards the Castle Pond and the river. On a 'North-East Prospect of the City of

The Greyfriars Bridge well under way in 1966

Greyfriars junction
Above looking past Greyfrairs House towards the river before the construction of the new bridge.
Below: (left) The semi-circular bastion between Greyfriars House and the river before the inner relief road was built, and (right) after

Hereford' of 1732 by S. and N. Buck (see p.8), much of it is shown as being pleasantly tree-lined, and a view of the west (below) shows the wall before buildings cluttered up its face; what neither can show is the 'atmosphere' pervading the neighbouring ditch, fed by water from the Eign Brook and pungently serving as an open sewer.

As Hereford increased in size in the 19th century, areas between the City Wall and the ditch were gradually developed and used by a variety of businesses. The east side of Victoria Street was divided into more than 20 properties, varying over the years from gardens and yards to buildings for trades which included blacksmiths, cabinet-makers, painters and decorators, coach builders and stone masons. One of the builders named in a list dating from 1851 was William Beavan—and Beavan and Hodges Ltd. operated from their site at No. 9 until the arrival of the demolition crews in 1965.

Newmarket Street was named following the building in 1856 of the livestock market on an area of the Portfields where businesses were naturally associated with farming. In the early days these included a manure merchant and agent and a skin and hide centre. In addition there were two public houses—The Wheatsheaf and The Globe—as well as a lodging house. In the early 1960s there were engineers and ironmongers, tractor implement dealers, corn merchants, auctioneers and most agricultural trades.

Blueschool Street, like Victoria Street was also known as 'Town Ditch' until the 19th century. The full name should have been Blue Coat School Street and for a time it was known as Blue School Lane. Over the years it had two public houses—The Vine and The Railway Bell—as well as accommodating a great variety of tradespeople, including a straw bonnet maker, several tailors, a milliner, a maltster and a farrier. The street also attracted numbers of motor engineers and body builders, agricultural suppliers and, of course, the school.

Bath Street was originally Sally Walk, named no doubt after the willows growing alongside the ditch, as depicted on the Bucks' engraving. It was given its new name when baths were provided by the Industrial Aid Society in 1851 (the first had been in the basement of the old Castle Green Museum). Directories again list diverse businesses and trades, including a wheelwright, butcher, iron and brass founder and, latterly, a foundry, motor engineers and warehouses.

Construction of the new east-west relief road was hugely complicated because of the extensive demolition and site-clearance works required and a need to maintain access and keep the city and its vehicles and pedestrians moving. Property purchases, compensation and works of adjustment (or 'accommodation works') involved a lengthy process in spite of being covered by compulsory purchase orders. The work was divided into four phases commencing at the

West prospect of the city showing Friars' Gate and the wall running to the river

Properties at the St. Nicholas Street junction, including the Barton Tavern on the right, which were demolished to make way for the line of the new bridge approach road

A car park against the city walls in Victoria Street also cleared for the new road

*Three views of the A49/A438 junction
before demolition started in 1968.
Looking from:
Top: Edgar Street
Middle: Victoria Street
Lower: Eign Street (east)*

eastern end of Bath Street in March, 1964. The smallest in scope, this contract was complicated by a need to route a part of the road through the closed burial ground of St. Owen's Church, one of Hereford's medieval churches destroyed during the Civil War. This involved the uncovering, reburial and reconsecration of the ancient remains, during which pipework was found which maintained a flow of water to the Castle Pool after the city ditch had been filled in a hundred or so years before. This was replaced with a new surface water sewer and reconnected to the existing system.

Preparatory demolition of a considerable number of buildings commenced in Blueschool Street in the Spring of 1966 when several sections of the City Wall were exposed to view for the first time in many years. Of particular interest was a portion close to the Widemarsh Gate that now forms the north elevation of the Farmers' Club. Since restored, the wall has a small doorway with an inscription, T 1626 C, still showing above it. This is said to have been carved for Thomas Church, a dyer, who in 1582 asked the then powers that be for permission to make a door through to the ditch outside so that he 'may the better washe his coloured clothes'. It would take another three centuries before river pollution laws would put a stop to this sort of arrangement. Other demolished buildings included the farriery of Wm. Watts and Sons which had been in business right up to that time. Archaeological investigation there exposed remains of one of 17 semi-circular bastions known to have been incorporated in the City Wall circuit. Parts of two others were also exposed for a while, one of which was shown to have been rebuilt in rectangular form during the course of its history. Close to the former Jewish quarter of the city, in the 17th and 18th centuries it was known as the Jews' Chimney. The position of the Bye Street Gate was also confirmed during sewer excavation works and, with adjoining sections of wall, it now is buried beneath Commercial Square. The whole appearance of that area was transformed and opened out by the wholesale demolition of buildings which fronted Commercial Street and Blueschool Street. By the end of the century, few Herefordians could remember the Black and White Café, David Greig, the grocers, Eddy Lewis the fruiterer or even Trinity Almshouses. Known also as Trinity Hospital, the charity was founded by Thomas Kerry in 1607 and augmented by a legacy left by Thomas Baker in 1788. The first tenements were built in 1620, at the same time as the Old House in St. Peter's Street, but these were taken down in 1824 to be replaced with new buildings housing poor widows and unmarried men, subsequently under the care of the Municipal Charities of the city. After demolition the site was used as a public car park and a relic still survives in the form of the decorative wrought iron gates and railings, saved from scrap dealers and later re-erected at St. Giles' Chapel in St. Owen Street.

One of the few sections of the medieval street system, part of a communication lane running inside the base of the City Wall, was sacrificed for the sake of Cecil Corey's newly built Franklin Barnes building at the north-east corner of Blueschool Street, and of 20th-century traffic mobility. A casualty on the north side of Blueschool Street was the Vine, which by then had been the only public house in the street for more than half a century after closure of the Railway Bell. For the nostalgic imbiber, traces of this shorter-lived pub may still be found by careful inspection of features on the restored City Wall.

Forecasts of traffic volumes argued for a dual carriageway. Special care over the design was needed in view of the uncertain capacity of the supporting ground in the former ditch area. It was hoped some interesting finds would be made in this area, but the deep sewer trenches failed to rise to the occasion. Rumour has it that during the early part of the Second World War a vaulted passage was discovered by chance near Black Friars Monastery not far to the north, when some ground collapsed. This brought to mind a previous collapse involving much back-

Top: Blueschool Street looking west and (middle) looking east, before construction of the relief road. Once known as 'Town Ditch' it served the Blue Coat School for more than 130 years. The school building is now used as a night club
Bottom: Bath Street after widening. The John Venn building is beyond the car park

filling beneath a cellar floor at an address in Coningsby Street (since demolished)—on a direct line between the monastery and the City Wall. It was thought then that a tunnel might lead to the inner side of the city defences, to be used in the event of an attack, and a volunteer crawled from the monastery site in some danger for about 130 yards before coming up against a complete blockage. After nearly an hour he emerged frustrated, covered with slime and dirt. Unfortunately the excavations of 1966 did nothing further to solve the mystery of yet another secret tunnel thought to be beneath Hereford.

In late 1967 a third contract again brought demolition crews to Commercial Square, (unbecomingly renamed with several other historic streets by city father/businessmen in 1855 in a flurry of modernising zeal), and further sections of old wall were revealed. Among buildings to go at that time were the iron and brass foundry and general engineering and repair shops of Harding Brothers Ltd., one of the oldest such businesses in the city. This had been started in 1850 by Mr. R.M. Harding with workshops and outlets in Commercial Street, Union Street, Gwynne Street, Bridge Street and Berrington Street, and a depot at the cattle market. Further to the east of Bath Street lay De Lacy Street and the end of this was severed as far as the wall line, converting it to a cul-de-sac. For many years it had served as the way to the offices and soup kitchen of the Society for Aiding the Industrious, created in 1841 by the Rev. John Venn. However, the Society's first soup kitchen has survived in Hardings' Passage between Commercial Street and Union Street. This building had been derelict for many years but it has now been preserved to form a shop. A prominent surviving building close to the relief road asso-

Top: Looking along Newmarket Street towards the former NFU offices. The Victoria Hotel was to the left and the Wellington Hotel (now JDs) to the right
Middle: The side wall of the Farmers' Club after the NFU building visible in the top photograph had been demolished. (Note the small doorway, dated 1626, once giving access to the city ditch)
Bottom: Looking over the wall half way along Blueschool Street, near bastion 10

ciated with Venn and the Society is the flour mill built in 1848. Waste steam from this was used to heat the Society's public baths in Kyrle Street (now the Masonic Hall). The mill building subsequently housed *The Hereford Times* after its departure from Maylord Street and continues to provide for a variety of enterprises.

Thought was given by the experts about the possibility of providing a link between traffic signals installed throughout the relief roads, enabling mechanisms to be synchronised for better traffic mobility. The required technology was not then available, but much later a computer-operated system was installed throughout the route and this achieved a great deal in increasing the capacity of junctions— and therefore the circuit as a whole. Known as the SCOOT (Split Cycletime and Offset Optimisation Technique) system, operated remotely from Worcester, it not only had the ability to register vehicle volumes building up at approaches to nine signal-controlled junctions and three pedestrian crossings, but was also able to produce a signal operating sequence which helped to reduce the number of interruptions to flow. However, as traffic volumes relentlessly continued to grow, the effectiveness of this system unfortunately dwindled, especially at busy peak hours.

If for many in Hereford the extent of roadworks completed by April 1968 at Blueschool Street, Bath Street and Commercial Square seemed prodigious, the activities which were about to start between the new Greyfriars Bridge and the northern end of Edgar Street were to become many times more sweeping and spectacular. They would totally transform a vast corridor of land to the west of the city centre, cattle market, football ground and beyond and it was therefore fortunate that, in such a historic city, no buildings of any great architectural or historic merit would be lost, although there were regrets at the loss of the Victoria Vaults in Edgar Street and the Victoria Hotel in Widemarsh Street. Nevertheless, the acres of

Top: The roundabout at the junction of Commercial Road and Blueschool/Bath Street. The Kerry Arms is off to the right
Middle: The Kerry Arms is to the left, the view towards the end of Maylord Street
Bottom: Seen from De Lacy Street, two buildings by the Society for Aiding the Industrious—the corn mill ahead, and the offices and soup kitchen on the left

Maylord Street and Blueschool Street before the inner relief road and the Maylord Orchards scheme

70

unsightly asphalt and concrete to be laid in replacement for the mild tones of bricks and mortar would constitute what someone dramatically suggested was 'the completion of [Hereford's] first new line of fortifications since the Middle Ages'.

Some of the buildings in Victoria Street had been built into the City Wall, as had been found earlier in the programme, and demolition became difficult in view of the condition of the masonry and jointing. Collapses inevitably occurred in some instances and in one of these, at the southern end near Friars Gate, several 10lb. iron cannonballs appeared with the gravel slippage from behind the Wall. These turned out to have been fired during the Civil War siege of Hereford. A diary describing the events was written by the Governor of Hereford, Barnabus Scudamore (later knighted by King Charles) to Lord Digby. The entry for 16 August 1645 reads:

They discover *(aim)* the face of their battery against Friern Gate, with five several gun ports; from hence they played four cannon jointly at our walls, and made a breach which was instantly made up, they doe the like on the other sude, (south by Dr Strange's house) with like success.

One of the cannonballs was treated against further corrosion by a conservator at the City Museum and built back into the wall during later restoration works. The Hereford City Wall is a scheduled Ancient Monument and was under the protection of the then Ministry of Works who approved a grant-aided scheme for its conservation and repair. Stonemasons were sent away for special training which included lessons with experts working at Ludlow Castle. Where possible they paid particular attention to the need to distinguish between 'old' wall and any new rebuilding work so as not to mislead anyone in the future. Meticulous care was taken with the jointing and pointing work to find the right sources of sand and lime and in gauging their proportions for preparing the mortar. At one juncture there was a serious shortage of suitable sandstone but this was overcome through an adver-

tisement in *The Hereford Times* asking for a return of any masonry which might have been bought or otherwise redeployed from the City Wall—a common practice from the 16th century onwards. Whatever the provenance, masonry stone was offered from many sources, promptly examined, collected and, who knows, returned whence it came!

An important defensive feature was revealed at the rear of the old Victoria Mills at No.11— then the premises of Holloway and Webb Ltd., tent and marquee contractors. All that was left standing above ground level was one of only two remaining half moon bastions (the other is at Grey Friars House next to the Greyfriars Bridge), which now forms the northern end of a section of restored Wall alongside Victoria Street. Like all the other exposed remnants of ancient walling, it bears obvious signs of having been repaired and refaced many times. Originally the Wall is thought to have stood between 4.9 and 5.5m high with 10.7m high bastions, and the city's medieval defensive circuit north of the Wye can now at least be recognised for virtually its entire length of 1,645m.

The Normans had followed the same western alignment as the Saxons as far as present day West Street (formerly *Byhindwalle*), and after demolition and site clearance of Beavan and Hodges' premises at No. 9, an archaeological excavation was organised to examine the defensive sequence under the direction of Professor Philip Rahtz (then of Birmingham University). An area excavation identified ten historic periods with a probable date range starting from the mid-7th to 8th century until disturbances of the site after the 13th century. At the lowest excavated level substantial remains of two grain drying ovens were revealed, built partly of re-used Roman masonry including two altars, then the oldest historic features unearthed in Hereford. It was considered that the ovens may have been used to dry grain harvested with an excess of moisture or possibly to parch it to improve the flavour before milling—but nobody has established the origin of the Roman components,

The remains of grain drying kilns discovered during excavations prior to the construction of the north-south relief road

except to suggest that they would hardly have been carried all the way from Kenchester (*Magnis*), the nearest Roman town, some 5 miles away. The Wall had been preceded between the mid to late 9th century and the mid-11th century by either gravel fortifications or turf and clay ramparts superimposed with a stone wall and road. The excavation site now lies beneath a grass verge and a public car park which has been constructed behind a bank symbolising the ancient rampart, whilst also serving partly to screen parked vehicles.

The bastion that originally sealed the end of West Street from Victoria Street was removed in 1898. Eign Gate was at the end of Eign Gate Street and from here the defences took a different construction with an internal communication road built on top of a gravel bank. An example of this appeared at the junction with Eign Street after demolition at Messrs T. and A. King and Co., monumental stone masons, then of Nos. 1 and 3 Victoria Street. Gunner's Lane survives directly behind the wall, but the western end of Wall Street was obliterated by the relief road works together with the north-western remains of the defences and one of the bastions. All features

were either lost or buried beneath the road surfaces forming the large traffic roundabout and junction, but not before a long narrow strip of ground behind the medieval wall was examined in an excavation directed by Margaret Gray. Her research was divided into four main periods commencing before the middle of the 11th century and including a defensive stage dating probably between the late 12th and early 13th centuries. The excavated area had evidently contained parts of several properties, furnaces and hearths and was the site of a variety of industries operating eight centuries ago, as well as possibly the slaughter of animals.

Archaeological work, commenced by Stan Stanford in Bath Street in 1965 and continued by Frank Noble, Ron Shoesmith and others as the relief road programme progressed, was co-ordinated between 1965 and 1969 by the Hereford Excavation Committee. Importantly, it helped to secure vital funding, with help from the Ministry of Public Building and Works, at a time when Hereford was at the forefront of research on Anglo-Saxon and later defences. The time everyone spent, and the discoveries, experience and surprises of the period added greatly to previous knowledge of Hereford's past. In the city, their influence and example awakened the need to safeguard its unique historic heritage and paved the way for action by vigilant guardians

The western end of Wall Street, demolished to make way for the new road

72

such as the City of Hereford Archaeology Committee, the Conservation Area Advisory Committee, the Hereford Civic Trust and all those who care about conservation of the city's historic fabric.

While the archaeologists meticulously applied trowels, brushes and immense precision to their tasks, other forces nearby worked just as hard at stripping away more recent creations, though with a spectacular show of brute force, apparent insouciance and frequent heavy dust clouds.

The southern ends of Edgar Street and Wall Street were flattened, together with Dean's Stores and neighbouring shops in Eign Street, locally known up to then as 'Dean's Corner'. On the western side of the route, the Victoria Vaults public house, South Shropshire Farmers, Jesson's Army and Navy Stores (in both Eign Street and Edgar Street), Bengry Motors and many intervening buildings were all pulled down to expose County Motors of Nos. 56 - 59 Eign Street much more to view. These premises were later to have new owners, whence to inspire 'Steels' Corner' as the new name for the locality. Eventually just one solitary property defied the demolishers— No. 20 Edgar Street standing in splendid isolation until the chemist, Mr. W. Davies, reached agreement about terms and moved to new premises in Eign Street.

Beyond Newmarket Street, the intention was to improve the existing carriageway of Edgar Street for northbound traffic and provide a southbound lane on the eastern side over the market car park, preserving an intervening line of mature trees. This and other calls on land were to lead to a considerable redevelopment and modernisation of the entire livestock market, its facilities for cars and lorries and provision for displaced agricultural and related businesses.

The dual carriageway section was designed to narrow to a single width of 33ft beyond Blackfriars Street, alongside the frontage of Hereford United Football Ground. This involved demolition of the club's covered east-facing terrace and stand as well as other portions of the ground, leading to lengthy negotiations over compensation terms between the club, the city council as landlords and Ministry of Transport. In due course the appearance and facilities at the ground were utterly transformed, the club going on to achieve undreamed of results in the F.A. Cup in 1971-72 and 1972-3, followed by its election to the Football League and subsequent promotion to Division II, all achieved within four years! It is hard to visualise how much of this success would have occurred without the impetus forced on the club by the imposition of the ring road scheme; as it was, for almost a decade United's performance was responsible for keeping Hereford constantly in the national sporting press—and educating the rest of Britain as to its existence and whereabouts.

As the improvement works approached Newtown Road, a new widened bridge was constructed across the Tan Brook, whilst beyond, houses on the east side lost most of their small front gardens. Some property was rendered unsuitable for further occupation, so this and adjacent land at the end of Edgar Street was subsequently used for a new council development named Addison Court after Colin Addison, captain of Hereford United during the club's heady days.

The most difficult part of the new road design was in dealing with the traffic movements at the offset junctions at Newmarket Street and Eign Street (west). These were complicated by heavy pedestrian flows between the city centre, market

Edgar Street and the football ground before the road construction programme

and residential areas to the west. Awesome obstructions were created by a concentration of existing and proposed new sewers, pipes, cables and other underground features. Several different solutions were considered, including a flyover, before the present layout was agreed. Ideally the subways should have had steps and ramps at both ends but the small amount of space available on the west side of Victoria Street allowed for only a compact curved ramp, sloping close to the desirable maximum for pedestrian use. The subway tunnel cut across the line and level of the medieval city ditch, seen during drainlaying and foundation excavations, and an opportunity was taken to represent its cross-section on the side walls with distinctive locally made slip-tiling. Whilst underground passages can create a sense of fear at night, even had bridges been physically and visually practicable, they would have necessitated a greater climb to achieve the necessary road clearance.

The project overlapped in early 1969 with the start of the culminating phase of the new road circuit in Newmarket Street. Again there was a great deal of demolition, exposing the old wall line where F.H. Burgess, West Midland Farmers, R.P. Ravenhill, Brook Brothers, Monkley Brothers, F.H. Sunderland, Passey Nott and other agriculturally-linked businesses had stood. Also to disappear were the Wheatsheaf public house, and the Victoria Hotel at Widemarsh Street junction. The market lost its old fruit, poultry and egg building and other related businesses on the north side of the road. A pedestrian bridge or subway was considered for near to the Market Tavern, but underground complications and lack of space for ramps meant that a subway was eventually built further to the west, on a route between the popular market-stalls and livestock area on the north side and a planned shopping development site to the south. To begin with the subway was regarded as a white elephant, but it came into its own with the opening of Tescos and the adjacent bus station.

In the late Autumn of 1969, the trunk road and Newmarket Street schemes were both completed

The repaired and completed Wall line and bank symbolising the Saxon rampart in Victoria Street

and finally landscaped, including a raised footpath alongside the Victoria Street wall, sloping grass banks planted with bulbs and some token willows to echo the Sally Walk of former years. A 200 year-old cider mill and press were donated by Mr. J. Bristow of Hyde Farm, Woolhope as a symbol of Herefordshire's long association with cider-making and these were installed close to the roundabout beneath the trees at the southern end of Edgar Street.

So ended a vigorous five year programme costing some £2m in terms of construction, land and compensation. The face of a large part of the city had been transformed almost out of recognition by widespread clearance of buildings, including some 112,000 square feet of shopping and showroom space—greater than the combined sales areas of three local 1990s supermarkets. Main contractors for the Greyfriars Bridge were part of a national civil engineering concern, but all site clearance, excavation, drainage, roadworks and brickwork were undertaken by a Hereford firm. Hereford Resurfacing Company went on to tender successfully for the remainder of the relief road works and often employed more than a hundred local craftsmen and other workers. Much of the necessary materials and equipment came through local merchants and suppliers.

The Official Opening occurred on 11 December, 1969. At a national level, *The Times* noted: 'the old city had been celebrating the completion of its first new line of fortifications since the Middle Ages', adding that early results had: 'already been spectacular, nearly halving the volume of vehicles, previously 20,000 a day, which charged down busy Broad Street and past the cathedral'. At a time when traffic moving across the Wye was approaching 30,000 vehicles a day, the M.P. was quoted as saying: 'Hereford people coming to and from work, countrymen coming to the market, and holidaymakers, will never now be able to say "we got stuck in the traffic at Hereford"'. Few of those listening could have predicted that just over 20 years afterwards, the Department of Transport would be fore-casting average daily traffic across the river of 57,000 vehicles by 1995 and 78,000 (almost 10% of them heavy good vehicles) by 2010.

That was all too far in the future, and it was sufficient on the day just to stand and cheer the spectacle of a celebratory parade of 30 vintage and veteran cars, ranging from an 1897 Daimler to a 1965 Rover/B.R.M. turbine car. Led in procession by the city's M.P., the Mayor of Hereford and their ladies in a 1920 Silver Ghost Rolls-Royce open tourer, they drove alongside the re-exposed sections of ancient wall as if they were 'beating the bounds' of the medieval historic core of the city.

Pedestrianisation

The celebrations marked the conclusion of funda-mental 'by-pass surgery' and attention was next turned to the repair of years of damage to the heart of the city caused by the motor vehicle. Congestion, danger, anxiety, noise, fumes and visual intrusion had taken a great toll of condi-tions in the main shopping streets, and Eign Street (within the Gate) had suffered as badly as any. Previously there had been thoughts of widening the street—hence the set-back front of Woolworths—and in the late 19th century there had been a desire to demolish all the buildings on the north side, thus joining Bewell Street and Eign Street to make a wide thoroughfare coming from Wales. From relative quietude Eign Street's share of through traffic had gradually increased to a devastating average of 7,500 vehicles a day, all of them giving way to even greater volumes at the junction with High Street and Broad Street. Footways narrowed in places to less than 2ft. and pedestrians, not least those with children, were exposed to considerable risk. Instant relief from this tyranny came with closure of the street due to the adjacent relief road operations. Fortunately, servicing of most shops and other businesses was possible from Bewell Street and West Street, immediately to their rear.

In late 1969 this gave everyone an enforced opportunity to try out the then revolutionary process of 'pedestrianisation' (for a while also called by the even worse 'demotorisation'!) and early results were not as ruinous as shopkeepers had feared. Despite the fact that some individuals felt that congestion might even be good for busi-ness as it allowed becalmed motorists to 'window-shop', a group of Eign Street traders agreed to join the city council in considering a longer lasting scheme. This led to an experi-mental Order the following June, under which all motor vehicles, except emergency services, were excluded from the street each weekday between 10 a.m. and 5.30 p.m. Any traders' worries soon proved to have been unfounded, one of them even able to report an increase in turnover—but his was a shoe shop in a pedestrian street! Others who had previously suffered from constant petrol and diesel fumes were glad at last to be able to leave shop doors open, maybe encouraging addi-tional 'impulse' customers. It did not take very long for confidence to be such as to make the arrangements permanent, and by the opening week of the Three Choirs Festival in August, 1970 new pedestrian paving had replaced the former carriageway, kerbs and narrow footways. Carefully limited numbers of seats, trees, litter bins and other street 'furniture' were introduced to reduce any 'canyon' effect arising from its narrow 200m length. High level wall mounted lanterns were installed to enhance night-time

Herefordshire's only set of traffic signals, reinforced by PC Derrick Jones, at Dean's Corner, Eign Street, before the relief road and pedestrianisation

appearance and advice was offered to shop owners about ways in which they could add to the attractiveness of their part of the city by tidying of brackets and signs, shopfronts, cables, stockroom windows and also through programmed and co-ordinated facade redecoration schemes By the end of October the council had gained support from the Eign Street Traders Association in imposing a 24 hour ban on all motor traffic. Thus Eign Gate, as it then became, was nationally amongst the pioneers of pedestrianisation.

There was sufficient encouragement from this conversion to continue with the same approach at Church Street, lying on part of the long established route between the cathedral and the 11th-century market area of High Town. Formerly called Broad Cabbage-lane, the street had also been known as Capuchin Lane, although without any justification for Capuchin friars were never resident in Hereford. The true title came from its

history, lasting into the 19th century, as the principal market place for vegetables. As a cul-de-sac it did not suffer from through traffic so a different approach was adopted which would limit entry by vehicles to the few legitimately requiring access. A walking surface of blue paving bricks was laid, replaced towards the end of the 1990s with a new surface, when further refinements were added. As in the rest of the city centre, the effect was quickly fouled by a widespread ingrained spattering of (non-biodegradable) chewing gum.

High Town was able to accommodate a gradual transition from horse-drawn to motor car and lorry transport. A horse-drawn cab rank, equipped with a hut for the cabbies, had been installed between the opposing traffic lanes in the centre and continued in use when motor taxis took over after the First World War. In days of deference, it was not unknown for some shop-

*Eign Street after the relief road
and pedestrianisation*

Gate and Church Street relatively smoothly. High Town was to be a different matter, generating two local inquiries. The first, in February, 1972, led to an experimental prohibition of through traffic by May. Bus operators pressed for a special lane through the middle of the area and the taxi proprietors, all having occupied a prime central rank for so long, not surprisingly felt hard done by at being dispossessed. The Freight Transport Association, National Dairymen, Butter Market Hall Tenants, Chamber of Commerce, banks, frontagers and others made representations.

During the ensuing 12 months everything was regularly monitored with a view to making a permanent arrangement, subject to a second local inquiry in May, 1973. The bus operators did not lodge an official objection and that of the Chamber of Commerce was muted in that 'they supported the Council in their attempt to enhance the environment in High Town', but wished to see better service facilities, traffic management improvements on the inner relief road and a

keepers in High Town to greet favoured customers at the kerbside before conducting them from their parked landaulettes. As a hub for shoppers—'where the pulse of commerce beats fastest', wrote A.G. Bradley in 1905—it contained many prime stores, bearing long established local names such as Greenlands, Wakefield Knight, Frank Stewart and Augustus Edwards on the south side and Gurneys, Fearis and Lewis Smith on the north. Business was such that it eventually became necessary to install a zebra crossing. An 'uncontrolled' crossing, it gave priority to pedestrians over all but emergency vehicles and consequently there was almost always someone walking across. Traffic was continually held up in long queues and it was often necessary for police to intervene, frequently amidst displays of impatience.

It had been possible to achieve the pedestrianisation aims of the 1963 Hereford Plan in Eign

*Cabbage Lane, later Church Street,
by David Cox (1783-1859)*

Church Street in Victorian days, and with yellow lines before pedestrianisation

convenient multi-storey car park. The permanent scheme was duly approved with a few amendments. An area to the west was made available for service vehicles and to the east pedestrians were given almost exclusive freedom for the greater part of the shopping day by restriction of servicing to between 6 p.m and 10.30 a.m. A public participation exercise to attract design proposals was mounted in the form of a competition, and numbers of ideas were incorporated in the completed 'streetscaping' work. The area of the 16th-century market-house and guild-hall with positions of its 27 pillars were defined in exposed aggregate granite paving while other surfaces of different textures and colours were laid to distinguish between pedestrian and vehicle areas. Advice was received on suitable street trees and several were donated by local organisations.

Feelings were mixed about any extension of pedestrianisation to Commercial Street and there was also a loss of momentum following the creation of new local authorities. Another 14 years would elapse before any further changes took place in this, the final section of the principal city centre shopping axis, but in the meantime a separate study was carried out to determine ways of making the most of opportunities presented by completion of the new inner relief road.

Further benefits for shoppers

An area of some 10 acres immediately within the old wall line had gradually become run down and unsightly and this approach paved the way for it to be brought back into beneficial use. After false starts, the site of the former brewery and canning factory bounded by Newmarket Street, Widemarsh Street and Bewell Street was developed as a supermarket of approximately 30,500 sq. ft. by Tescos.

Bye Street (Commercial Street), St. Peter's Street and the Old House before the Motor Age

Bewell Street, formerly *Bewalstrete* and *Vrenschemannestrete* was improved with a new surface of paving bricks to which Eign Gate traders were encouraged to provide additional shopfronts and entrance doors. The repaving was continued beyond the boundary of the new development as far as Widemarsh Street, with some surprising and unsolicited financial help from a local businessman.

The city council had been purchasing land for commercial development between Blueschool Street and the rear of properties fronting the north side of Commercial Street and High Town which led to the Maylord Orchards scheme (see chapter II). This was built along the known line of the medieval street system, comprising the western end of Maylord Street, formerly *Senthomastrete*

and Saint Thomas Street, and Gomond Street. Surfaced for pedestrians with paving bricks, the route linked with Widemarsh Street and Commercial Street. At their junction, Brewers Passage was reinstated as a footpath leading to the Commercial Street shops from Trinity Square (so named to commemorate the old almshouses which had been demolished nearby). It was with much regret and some considerable resistance that a second length of the eastern portion of Maylord Street curving back within the Wall line to Commercial Street, formerly Jewry Lane, had to be sacrificed in the cause of commercial progress and mobility.

The first shops at Maylord Orchards opened in October 1987. The busy pedestrian routes from the new stores and car park linked with established city centre shops, the rear entrance of the very popular Butter Market and a new footpath leading from Widemarsh Street along Mansion House Walk to the new Tesco supermarket with its own car park. Well before then the attitude towards pedestrianisation in Commercial Street had changed. Shopkeepers 'looking enviously at competitors in High Town and Eign Gate' began to feel that they were missing out and becoming relegated to a secondary trading position. This was compounded by ever-hopeful motorists orbiting the street to hunt out rare and unlikely kerbside parking space. When a fire destroyed Goldings ironmongers at Nos.19 and 20, essential road closures effectively pedestrianised the street for long enough to show that trading figures could actually improve with a much safer and calmer environment. It was quite a change for pressure for pedestrianisation to come from shop-keepers, and discussions about alternative measures commenced in early 1986. There were considerable traffic circulation ramifications, for although the lights at Commercial Square would be relieved of a substantial phase of traffic emerging from Commercial Street, many redi-rected vehicles, including buses, would need to be accommodated elsewhere. Union Street was not adequate for two-way traffic or as an alterna-tive route to the signal controlled junction with the relief road.

The pressure also created an opportunity to 'improve' St. Peter's Square. A proposal for a 30ft. fountain in 1865 had come to nothing and apart from providing part of the venue for the May Fair, the square had no special use until 1922 when a 30ft. high memorial designed in the form of an Eleanor Cross, was erected and dedi-cated to some 2,000 Herefordshire men and women who gave their lives in the 1914-1918 War. Later inscriptions commemorate those from the county who fell in the Second World War, the Burma Campaign, in Korea, during the Falklands Conflict, the Gulf War and also soldiers of the Special Air Services Regiment and the Herefordshire Light Infantry who have died on active service.

Eventually a pedestrianisation scheme was agreed for Commercial Street, to include enhancements of St. Peter's Square where there would be better facilities for buses. One-way traffic in St. Owen Street, a revised layout at the Cantilupe Street junction with St. Ethelbert Street and one-way traffic in part of Mill Street facili-tated access to the areas around Castle Street and the General Hospital. The project was completed in 1989 by the repair and rededication of the war memorial in a new setting.

Four months later, the proprietor of Hereford's leading family-owned department store confirmed the benefits of pedestrianisation. Chadds' staff benefitted from 'less fumes, less noise, less dirt and less danger and more customers mean greater financial rewards, due to a profit sharing scheme'. It also produced the same physical advantages for the shopping public. He concluded 'It won't take long to sum up the real disadvantages of pedestrianisation. I believe there are none!' His store was now much more visible from up the street than it had been before and 'this made obvious the fact that it looked tired and old fashioned', persuading him to bring forward a major rebuilding programme. The resulting improvement further enhanced trade not just for him but for everyone in the street due to the key location of this popular store. In retrospect, it is possible to see how the scheme considerably changed the look of the street, even appearing to reveal its pleasing curve and distant view of Churchill Gardens on Aylestone Hill.

So ended a sweeping programme of change which had started over a quarter of a century before with the cutting of the first sod for the start of work on Greyfriars Bridge. Never in its long history had Hereford experienced anything so radical for a city and county of such traditionally conservative tendencies! Less widely known, was that during the 'pedestrianisation' process regular contact was maintained with the Royal National College for the Blind and Partially Sighted at College Road, and allowance was made for the ways that students learn the techniques of the sighted world. Longitudinal path-drainage features acted as 'tramlines' to help guide them along the streets. In addition, the city council learned from the Hereford Access Committee of the special problems arising from the many forms of disability. As a way of encouraging people's independence a shopmobility scheme was established to provide assistance for those who would benefit from free use of a wheelchair whilst in town. Support came from Norwich Union (as the owners of Maylord Orchards), Chamber of Commerce and others, and sponsorships were invited from outside bodies to meet equipment costs. As a result Hereford Shopmobility Centre was installed in Maylord Orchards car park, equipped with a lift and, after tuition, hiring out powered scooters and both powered and manual wheel-chairs without charge each weekday during main business hours. Making use of extensive pedestrian paving, dropped kerbs and other aids to mobility it was possible for users of the service to range throughout most of the city centre, and even beyond to amenities such as King George V Playing Fields and the Leisure

Pool across the Wye. An increasing number of the city's commercial outlets came to recognise the needs of people with disabilities, introducing features over and above those required by Building Regulations, such as induction loops for hearing aid users.

Parking

Throughout many centuries of dependence on the horse for transport, anyone wishing to stop in the centre of Hereford could pull up at the side of the road, perhaps tie one's horse to a hitching-post in Broad Street, or arrange for stabling and provisioning at a local inn or mews. For the first 50 years of the Motor Age there was still enough room at kerbsides for drivers to park without causing any serious problem, but, as numbers of motor vehicles increased, this changed. Gradually the problems of parking overflowed into residential areas, bringing protests and calls for protection and introduction of Residents' Passes. Commuters travelling to work normally arrived first thing in the morning and each one

Broad Street showing hitching posts for horses, painted by James Wathen in July 1799

81

often took up a central space throughout the day which could otherwise accommodate up to 10 short term users. There was not enough room in such a small and densely built-up city to provide adequately for everyone in this way and it was thought necessary to introduce a system to replace the rule of 'first come, first served' with one which took account of location and walking distances for shoppers and tourists who brought additional custom and economic benefit.

Kerbside parking in the centre was therefore restricted to short stays and provision made for longer parking in surrounding streets wherever traffic conditions allowed and undue disturbance and inconvenience was not caused to residents. Inveterate freewheeling parkers failed to register delight at such a loss of their traditional rights, marking as this did an end of what was excitedly compared with 'the introduction of street lighting, main drainage and abolition of the coal fire' as an important event in the life of urban man.

By the early 1960s a small number of off-street car parks had been provided, either by the city council or private owners. The council was hampered in what it could provide, for whereas the cost of providing and maintaining roads was mostly financed by the Ministry of Transport or the county council, the cost of all public off-street parking had to be borne directly by city ratepayers. Sites were mostly unpaved, some being intended only for temporary use pending future building redevelopment. Thus in the central area there were just over 100 potholed spaces off Maylord Street and a further 80 at Bath Street. There were approximately 500 spaces further out, 170 of them being in private owner-ship. One, in Eign Street behind the Horse and Groom public house, occupied space once used for the stabling of horses left by much earlier visi-tors. There were also 380 spaces associated with the market off Newmarket Street, another 300 sharing some very rough ground with used farm-implement displays at Merton Meadow, just north of the livestock market, and a similar number on part of the former railway sidings to the west of Edgar Street. Because of walking distances from the city centre, all tended to be underused except on main market days.

Land requirements for the relief road closed well over 200 off-street and kerbside spaces in Newmarket Street and Blueschool Street and this led to a search for affordable replacements. Requirements of the newly modernised livestock market were met in 1968 by a £103,000 scheme at the partially used Merton Meadow. Once known as Merton Marsh, the 7.5 acre site was not exactly an engineer's dream, lying as it did on 5ft. of soft brown clay, large pockets of highly compressible peat and with a water table rarely more than 5ft. from the surface. Split by the man-made Widemarsh, or Tan, Brook running at a higher level, it was classified as a 'flood storage area' by the river authority and was actually under several feet of water at one stage of the works. The entire area was drained to a pump house, filled with large amounts of suitable foun-dation material from other projects and given deep base courses and specially devised running and parking surfaces to cater for the watery conditions. Its two parts were equipped with high level lighting and parking meters and joined by a new reinforced concrete bridge. The former unproductive and unsightly marsh was laid out to hold 1,000 cars, or 750 cars and 110 lorries (served by a new lorry-wash installation) with scope for providing additional capacity when necessary.

As the years progressed, other factors compounded shortages in the rest of Hereford. Mindful of the need to assist in the provision of adequate hospital facilities for the city, the council agreed to sell off the 200 space Stonebow Road car park, together with a number of nearby houses, to enable the Area Health Authority to develop an Acute Psychiatric Unit linked to the adjacent County Hospital. Other car parks were built or improved off Blackfriars Street, Wye Street, St. Martin's Street and at the Commercial Road Bus Station on the site of the former County Gaol. Additional temporary car parks were estab-lished on land proposed for comprehensive development at Maylord Street and Bewell Street

All that was left of the Garrick Theatre and the Royal George public house before they were replaced by Garrick House and the multi-storey car park

The Wellington and Victoria Hotels at the junction of Widemarsh Street and the relief road before the construction of Garrick House

and permanent provision followed with the completion of the Tesco and Maylord Orchards schemes.

By the early 1980s however, it was clear that more needed to be done, especially as further losses were about to occur at Edgar Street to make way for the Canonmoor housing project. The view was taken that the only way of providing adequate car parking facilities in the city would be by the urgent construction of a multi-storey car park, by 1986 at the latest. Apart from cost, the biggest factor was one of location and this involved many considerations. Any site had to be large enough to provide for an economic and practical layout of bays, aisles and access ways; the height should not threaten the 45ft. roof-line limit set for new developments within the central conservation area; walking distances for laden or weary shoppers needed to be within a reasonable range; and the land had to be quickly available. Many sites were considered against the criteria, but most were discarded, generally because they were too small. The Gaol Street surface car-park site was promising in most respects but was finally ruled out because of uncertainties arising from its ownership by the county council and designation as part of possible future local government headquarters. The two remaining options were either for decks above the sheep pens at the livestock market or a new building on the site of the redundant All Saints School and adjacent land.

Car parks had already been built successfully above animal pens in other market towns and these were visited and studied. It quickly became clear that this proposal was fraught with almost insoluble problems of access and ventilation and so further attention was given to the alternative site. This land had its own problems, notably from multiple ownership and still active uses. The land in Newmarket Street had until recently contained the weighbridge and buildings sited between the Market Tavern public house and the Victoria Hotel in Widemarsh Street, leading thence to the former Herefordshire County Library (once the Garrick Theatre), a long closed Royal George public house, City Housing Department offices in a former Drill Hall, an electricity sub-station with its large underground cables, All Saints Primary School and some smaller less problematical properties! The only hopeful point was that the school was already due to close. In the event, the problems were overcome and six tenders sought for the car park's construction. The new buildings provided for 450 car park spaces, 390 sq. m. of replacement office floor space for the City Housing Department and a further 1,790 sq. m. which enabled the City Surveyor's Department to be transferred from scattered quarters at the Town Hall.

The car park was operating by 1986 and ideas were forming for a second one at Commercial Road bus station, but eventually nothing came of this. By 1994 the stock of public car parking within the ring road totalled 575 spaces in off-street car parks and 280 at kerbsides, of a total of 3,100 in and close to the centre. In addition there was a considerable stock of about 4,700 commuter parking spaces on private land, of which some 1,600 were situated within the relief road. Daily use of these add considerably to peak period traffic congestion.

In November, 1996 the city council, as the district planning authority, adopted its final Hereford Local Plan before local government reorganisation transferred all its functions to Herefordshire Council on 1 April, 1998. In its transportation policies for the period up to 2001 it sought 'to maintain and improve the supply of publicly available short-stay car parking' by considering the provision of new short-stay spaces.

Not long before its demise, the council put this into practice on land straddling the city wall line at Bath Street with the opening of its last new short-stay surface car park.

Public Transport

Among the first forms of public transport were the carriers who operated between towns and villages. Whilst their primary function was to transport goods it was also possible for benches to be provided for a few people to sit on. In 1876, carriers were departing Hereford on Wednesdays and Saturdays for almost 50 destinations around the county, starting at inns such as the Spread Eagle, Coach and Horses, Hop Pole, Nelson, Royal George and Black Lion. Many of the smaller towns and villages had their own carriers who did the journey in reverse. The importance of a market town could always be judged by the numbers of carriers. The arrival of the railways led to withdrawal of most of the longer range stage-coaches, but local carrier services continued to operate successfully well into the 20th century, some 240 of them being listed as regularly putting up at Hereford inns in 1914. In due course the country bus started to replace them.

Whereas introduction of the internal combustion engine quickly led to the rapid development and improvement of the private car, progress with the motor bus took rather longer. In 1907 the Birmingham and Midland Motor Omnibus Company (better known as Midland Red) having tried some out, decided to return to horse-drawn buses for a period of 5 years. One of their rejected buses, a Milnes Daimler, was bought by Connelly and Sons of Commercial Road, Hereford, who were enterprising coachbuilders and hirers during the horse age and soon became involved with the new petrol driven machines. In 1908, in replacement of a competitor's horse drawn service, they experimented with the launch of Hereford's first all-day motor bus on a route between Barrs Court Station and Whitecross. It ran until 1912, when a mishap near Bagallay Street during refuelling led to a blaze and its total destruction, and also to the end of any motor bus service in city or county for several years.

In 1920, Midland Red took the decision to establish a service in Herefordshire in a fairly big way with up to 10 buses. Initially they were based in the yard of the Black Lion in Bridge Street and had to remove all their Tilling Stevens buses on market days to make room for the many carriers' carts and horses from surrounding villages. But the new bus services were seen as exciting and, once the company had worked out their most effective routes, passenger journeys and income grew quickly. Rival operators such as Messrs Fryers (and their successors Hereford Transport), Yeomans of Canon Pyon, Bengrys of Kingsland and Birds of Wigmore quickly joined in to serve most of the county. The majority of services on market days terminated somewhere in Hereford and soon the buses were causing their own congestion, particularly in High Town. There were no shelters or any other amenities for

CARRIERS:

ABERGAVENNY.—Coward Robert, Half Moon, Broad st, daily (Sun. excepted,) 2 30 p.m.

BIRLEY GATE AND MUCH COW.—Derry Charles, Bye st, Wed. and Sat., 7 p.m.

CLIFFORD.—Mills William, Red Lion, Victoria st, Wed. and Sat., 5 p.m.

EGGLETON.—Hartland Thomas, Crown and Sceptre, Bye st, Wed. and Sat., 4 p.m.

EWAS HAROLD.—Lewis Wm., Saracen's Head, Wye Bridge, Wed. and Sat., 5 30 p.m.

FOWNHOPE.—Halford Thomas, Booth Hall Inn, High Town, Wed. and Sat., 4 p.m.

HAY, BRECON, BUILTH, AND ALL PARTS OF NORTH WALES.——Merridith James, Commercial rd, Mon., Wed., and Fri., 6 p.m.

HOARWITHY.——Bond Samuel, Nag's Head, Broad st, Wed. and Sat., 5 p.m.

LAWARNE AND MUCH DEWCHURCH.—— Phillips George Spencer [van,] Royal Oak, Bridge st, Wed. and Sat., 4 30 p.m.

LEDBURY.—Preston George, Sun, High st, Wed. and Sat., 11 30 a.m.

LEOMINSTER.—Whitefoot Thomas, [van,] King's Head, Broad st, Wed. and Sat., 4 30 p.m.

LLANWARNE—Roberts John, White Hart, Broad st, Wed and Sat., 4 30 p.m.

MOCCAS.—Jenkins James, Globe, Broad st, Wed. and Sat., 4 30 p.m.

MONMOUTH.—Nash Isaac, Bewell st, Wed., 12 a.m.

MONMOUTH CAP.—Morgan Daniel, Saracen's Head, Wye Bridge, Wed. and Sat., 5 30 p.m.

OCLE.—Williams Thomas, Coach and Horses, Bye st., Wed. and Sat., 4 p.m.

PEMBRIDGE.—Williams Wm., Horse and Groom, Above Eign, Sat., 4 p.m.

PETERCHURCH.—Garratt James, [van,] King's Head, Broad st, Wed. and Sat., 4 30 p.m.

PETERCHURCH.—Phillips George, [van,] Duke's Head, Norfolk ter, Wed. and Sat., 4 p.m.

PETERCHURCH.——Powell John, White Hart, Broad st, Wed. and Sat., 4 30 p.m.

PRESTON-ON-WYE.——Morris Thomas, Half Moon, Broad st, Sat., 4 p.m.

ROSS.——Southan Wm., Half Moon, Broad st, Wed. and Sat., 5 p.m.

STAUNTON-ON-WYE.—Gritty William, Horse and Groom, Above Eign, Wed. and Sat., 4 p.m.

TEWKESBURY.—Preston George, Sun, High Town, Wed. and Sat., 11 30 a.m.

UPPERTON AND NORTON.—— Caldwell Thomas, Red Lion, Victoria st, Wed. and Sat., 5 p.m.

WELLINGTON.—Rowberry Wm., Maidenhead Inn, Eign st, Wed. and Sat., 5 30 p.m.

WEOBLEY.—Davies Uvedale, Red Lion, Victoria st, Wed and Sat., 5 p.m.

WHITNEY.—Crumpton John, Sun, High Town, Wed. and Sat. 3 30 p.m.

WHITNEY.—Lilwell John, Maidenhead Inn, Eign st, Wed. and Sat., 5 p.m.

WHITNEY.—Smith Richard, Red Lion, Victoria st, Wed. and Sat., 4 30 p.m.

WOOLHOPE.—Wood Wm., Sun, High Town, Sat., 3 30 p.m.

YARKHILL.——Jones John, Coach and Horses, Bye st, Wed. and Sat., 4 p.m.

YAZAR.—Lawrence Ann, Maidenhead Inn, Eign st, Wed. and Sat., 5 30 p.m.

A list of carriers operating out of Hereford in 1851

passengers though different solutions were suggested, including conversion of the Old House to what would have been a unique Jacobean bus shelter and toilets. Other counsels and schemes prevailed, however, and towards the end of the decade St. Peter's Square was adapted to receive buses. A permanent specially designed glass and wrought iron bus shelter was installed in 1929 at Midland Red expense (just for its own passengers) against the front of St Peter's church. No-one will ever know what the Reverend John Venn would have felt about such an appendage in his time, but the vicar of the day soon became disenchanted with both it and the unsettling new ambi-

ence of his late 13th- and early 14th-century church, and he initiated pressures for a proper bus station. In spite of his displeasure, the small terminus continued in use and the splendid shelter, sited on the wrong side of later bus entrance doors and of the square, was completely renovated in the 1980s. After suffering vandalism and abuse as a covered sitting area it remained as a rather grand bicycle-rack shelter at the end of the century, in tantalising view of unprotected passenger queues on the opposite side of the square, for which slender shelters finally came in early 2001, much to the disgust of some conservationists.

As it happened, the city council had decided to acquire the disused county gaol in the late 1920s and, after everyone was given the opportunity of taking a last (6d.) look round, all the buildings except for the Governor's House were demolished. The considerable expanse was laid out as a bus station with added provision for a cinema, café and shops along the Commercial Road frontage. A small bus garage was added alongside Union Walk, a bus parking area marked out and five platforms and shelters built for rental by bus companies, who also paid the council a departure fee for every bus. The former Governor's House was converted into a waiting room and offices for the two major bus companies, and with public conveniences installed at the rear, all uniquely settled in what was partly a John Nash designed building.

After much heavy use the bus station was ready for major repairs by the late 1980s. The passenger shelters had become unsafe and they were replaced, passenger waiting areas were resurfaced, new lighting installed and a part of the area converted to a medium-stay car park. The Governor's House, by now a Grade II listed building, required considerable structural attention in the course of which the public conveniences were removed and replaced in a new block nearby.

Recognising the value of the trade it brought in, the city council had been to some lengths and expense to provide for the humble bus. In the eyes of the public it failed to achieve the recognition and glamour of a branch steam train, yet at a time when few people owned any form of transport the country buses brought countless benefits to rural areas.

Indeed, the 1930s were described as the Golden Age of public transport, but after the Second World War the role of buses was undermined by fundamental changes in the social structure of the countryside. New technology and greater mechanization of farming caused more agricultural workers and country craftsmen to follow those who had long since left for the towns and other employment. Their places in the villages were gradually taken over by an altogether different population made up largely of residents with no rural background, some newly retired from other parts of the kingdom and others with town jobs but a preference for country life. Most could afford to run their own vehicles or needed them for work, and by the late 1960s the long isolation of most rural communities had become a thing of the past. Soon Herefordshire was not far behind neighbouring Radnorshire in its distinction of having the greatest number of cars per head of population in all Britain.

It was no coincidence that this was also at the time of Dr. Beeching's closures of uneconomic county branch lines and stations and because of their own diminishing patronage, many city and county bus routes were at similar risk. Some loss-making Midland Red routes could be sustained with revenues from profitable running in other parts of their operating area, by the process of cross-subsidisation, but this course was not open to their smaller competitors. It was as well therefore that in 1968 government measures were

The bus station offices in 1992, formerly the Governor's House of the gaol

introduced which enabled subsidies towards the support of struggling services to be considered by local authorities. Then in 1972, fundamental provisions, forming part of local government reorganisation, imposed the duty on the new Hereford and Worcester County Council of co-ordinating all public transport operations throughout the forcibly merged counties. The council devised a scheme to ensure at least a weekly bus service between all rural communities and their local urban centre, whilst within towns particular emphasis was placed on adequate transport for work and school journeys and also for the needs of the elderly or disabled. Some subsidies were paid to bus operators 'for socially necessary services' which they could not provide on a strictly commercial basis. But many services remained under threat.

In 1980 the government invited county councils to volunteer for 'Trial Area' status in a new approach to bus services. The Ministry of

Transport was not overwhelmed with applications, indeed there were just three, one being from Hereford and Worcester in respect of the former county of Herefordshire. Each was accepted, but whereas very little was heard from mid-Norfolk and mid-Devon, subsequent experience at Hereford produced even more national exposure than that of United's progress in the F.A. Cup and Football League ten years earlier.

The 'Trial' (in more ways than one) allowed new entrants to start a bus service anywhere they chose without the need for the route licence normally required, provided that they could qualify for an operator's licence. This had long covered matters such as mechanical condition, size and seating arrangements, financial state and general competence. The idea was to open the way to new operators and so introduce the benefits of competition. The news-worthy outcome was that from 1981 new operators often clogged city streets with numbers of second and third hand buses, as lucrative routes were invaded, Midland Red/Yeomans and Stretton Coaches vying with free seats and chasing each other along residential streets. Conversely some previously serviced though little used evening and Sunday routes were abandoned. Hereford's 'Bus Wars' lasted for several years as some combatants retreated injured or were removed from the streets by vehicle inspectors. Eventually 'deregulation' was introduced nationally with not altogether different consequences. Direct blanket subsidies were phased out and some equilibrium was reached, but it is difficult to judge how much was actually learned from the damaging years of farce and chaos at Hereford.

The future of public transport is closely bound up with efforts to reduce worsening congestion and pollution through 'integrated transport policies', and one of many brave approaches is to try and co-ordinate policies affecting all means of travel with the aim of making journeys by public transport as attractive as using the car. Great ingenuity will be needed if drivers are to be persuaded to forsake the comfort and other many appealing qualities, for in 1997 the Lex Report revealed that, nationally, only 7% of motorists would use public transport, even if congestion doubled their journey times—no matter how much it cost in time or money (a 1990 study in Hereford indicated 9%). On the brighter side, government figures for 1997-98 showed that public transport journeys rose by 1.5%, with rail journeys increasing as much as 6% during the year, though this was reversed following the Paddington and Hatfield disasters.

At the end of the 20th century Herefordshire, like everywhere else, presents its unique mobility problems, not least within the city centre. Whilst concessionary fares, 'one off' special government rural bus funds, Park and Ride experiments and Bus Only lanes have their place as palliatives, they form an infinitesimal part of what might well become the hardest measures that central and local government will have to face and present before volatile motorist electorates during the early 21st century.

Cycling and Walking

A new railway bridge was built on the Abergavenny to Hereford line in the later 1960s but it was hardly ever burdened, except by trains removing rails and ballast made redundant by Beeching reorganisation. However all was not lost, for the city later bought the bridge and 2.2 km. of track on what had been the culminating section of the 1853 Newport, Abergavenny and Hereford Railway. The amount paid was just £1, and the route was duly laid out as Great Western Way in 1983, a landscaped 5m-wide traffic-free tarmac footpath and cycleway between Beaufort Avenue, Newton Farm, over the Belmont Road Bridge and the refurbished Hunderton Wye Bridge (both repainted in former G.W.R. colours) as far as Barton Road and Broomy Hill. Further stages of private and council development carried it on in different forms past Sainsbury's supermarket, beneath Whitecross Road, through Canonmoor (close to the Courtyard Centre for the Arts and Hereford United Football Ground) to Widemarsh Common, a short distance from Hereford Leisure Centre and Racecourse. To the south a direct connection was made to the entrance of Haywood School in an attempt to encourage children away from major roads. At the Hunderton Bridge across the Wye two flights of steps dropped 5.5m to riverside footpaths and cycle ways and these, as well as other measures to make roads more cycle and walker friendly in the 1980s and 1990s, anticipated national policies seeking to cut pollution and congestion by encouraging people away from the use of four wheels.

In 1991 a transportation study carried out on behalf of the city promoted a scheme to use part of the route as a bus-way, associated perhaps with a Park and Ride service, but no action has been taken on the proposal.

Other main roads
In 1965, when the first stage of Hereford's inner relief road was about to open, the number of cars and commercial vehicles in use on United Kingdom roads was given as 10.4 million. Just 35 years later, as earlier prospects of an outer by-pass were officially dashed, the total count was over 24 million. There is every reason to believe that traffic numbers in the city and county have increased at least in the same proportion and one can only guess about the state of the city at the end of the 20th century had it not been for the drastic measures carried out in the 1960s. Many roads have been upgraded since 1965, notably parts of the A4103 Roman Road, on the northern boundary of the city. As part of the historic route from Gloucester and the Midlands to Brecon and South Wales (originally through the walled town of *Magnis*, today's Kenchester), it was hoped that the entire length could be widened to serve as an outer relief road between Aylestone roundabout at Burcott to the east and Stretton Sugwas to the west. By early 1967 two sections east of the Leominster Road at Holmer were completed and preparatory land acquisition and design had also commenced in respect of a substantial length between the A49 and Tillington Road to the west. Despite designation as an A road it was very narrow and lacked a footway, often required

expensive repair and was a constant source of danger for pedestrians and motorists. Because of design gradients and property driveway levels it was necessary to realign the route through Church property along the Bobblestock section between Aylesbrook and Canon Pyon Road, and many smaller parcels of land were also acquired and new boundary walls and fences agreed. By 1971 it was hoped that the entire scheme would be included in the Ministry of Transport's 'Firm Programme' for 1972, with a view to the city length from Holmer to Tillington Road being commenced in 1973. Local government reorganisation put an end to that prospect and the prepared city portion was eventually commenced by Hereford and Worcester County Council in 1991, and this was followed by a further short length leading to Aylestone roundabout, over a new bridge at the derelict Hereford and Gloucester canal. Attention to all remaining sections was delayed, chiefly because of considerations surrounding the Department of Transport's 1987 proposals for a Hereford By-pass. It was revived in 2000 as argument continued to rage about the best ways of dealing with Hereford's traffic problems.

A49/A465 Hereford By-pass
After the pre-war Ministry of Transport decision to opt for an inner relief road was confirmed in the early 1960s, ambitions for a by-pass were hardly mentioned. Every few years there were references in local newspapers about how much easier the traffic problem would be had the new bridge and road been built much further west, somewhere on the longitude of Breinton, but there was no organised pressure for such a road from within Hereford. It therefore came as a surprise when, in early 1986, it was learned that a scheme to solve the trunk road traffic problems in Hereford had been added to the government's national trunk road programme in June 1985. Part of a series of improvements on the important A49 trunk route between Warrington, in Cheshire, and Ross-on-Wye, the proposal would allow Hereford to join the list of other major towns on the route,

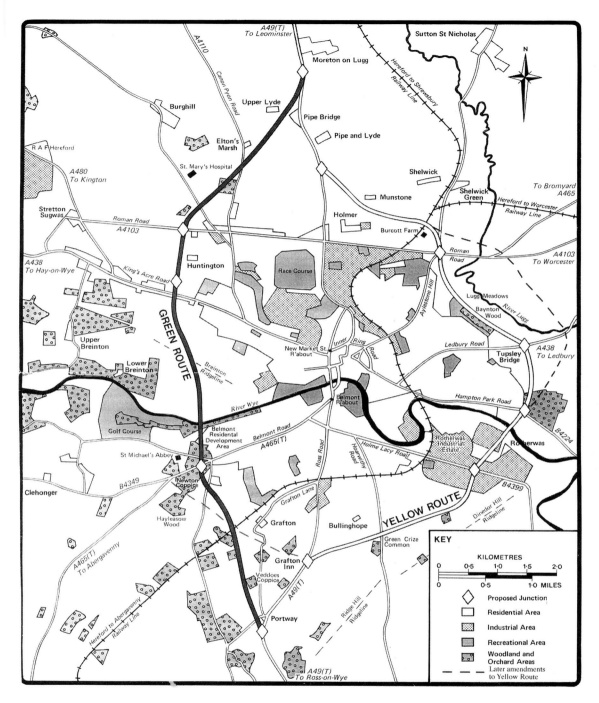

The 1987 consultation plan of the alternative Yellow and Green by pass routes, with the subsequent amendment to the Yellow route added on. The Yellow route was estimated to cost £14.5m, the Green £13.7m. Main intrusions into the landscape along the favoured Yellow route, before amendment, were to be: deep cutting between Holmer and Munstone; embankments to the rail bridge, between the hillside at Bayton Wood and Lugg Meadows Nature Reserve, and to the Wye crossing near Rotherwas Chapel; and a deep cutting in Green Crize Common. The course of the amended Yellow route from the A49 south of Hereford to the the A438 has subsequently been safeguarded by Herefordshire Council such as Leominster, Ludlow, Shrewsbury, Whitchurch and Tarporley, which had existing or planned by-passes.

From 1986 various alternatives were considered, including an internal relief road through the city, making use of parts of Great Western Way on the former railway line. This soon proved to be impracticable and after much deliberation two alternative by-pass routes were chosen and put forward for public consultation in July, 1987. These were referred to as the Green and Yellow routes (see previous page).

The Green Route formed a western by-pass of Hereford and extended from the A49 at Portway, to the south of the city, and rejoined the trunk road south of Moreton-on-Lugg to the north. Intermediate junctions were proposed where the route crossed the A465, A438 and A4103.

The Yellow Route formed an eastern by-pass extending from a point on the A49 near Grafton Inn to the south and rejoined it south of Pipe and Lyde to the north of the city. This route proposed intermediate junctions at the B4399, B4224, A438 and A465/A4103.

The Green Route was put forward as the better option but after an exhibition and consultation exercise,which produced 4,507 responses, the 13.6 km (8.5 miles) long Yellow Route attracted the stronger support at 56%. This concurred with the opinion of local authorities and the route was adopted on the grounds that it would provide better traffic relief and better value for money (though more expensive), be less environmentally intrusive (despite its impact on the Lugg meadows), adversely affect less residential property and farmland and provide better connections to Rotherwas Industrial Estate.

At this stage in the process an extension was added at the southern end between the A49 and A465 in order to give additional traffic relief and further enhance access to Rotherwas. In August 1988 it was announced that it was now the 'preferred route', and this, with a further modification in the Aylestone Hill area, provided the eventual scheme to go before a public inquiry in 1991 and 1992.

It was intended to start construction during 1993, with anticipated completion in early 1995, but this was not to be, for the inquiry inspector advised ministers against the submission. He further took the unusual step of recommending an alternative route to the west. In March 1993, ministers, in a decision reflecting the difficulties of providing an environmentally acceptable by-pass for Hereford, upheld refusal of the Yellow Route, but did not accept that a western alternative would be preferable.

It was back to the drawing board. A government-promoted new-style Hereford Traffic Conference met during the winter of 1993/94 to debate and seek to reach consensus on possible new approaches, following which a new £40 million eastern route was announced in April 1995 by the Transport Minister. Based in part on suggestions by Herefordshire Nature Trust, who with many others had been vehemently against anything which would hazard the ecologically treasured Lugg Meadows— as the former Yellow Route had gravely done—this passed to the east of the Lugg between the Worcester and Ledbury roads before crossing the river, just clipping a small portion of the Meadow upstream of Lugwardine Bridge. Environmentalists remained militant and further studies of a package of complementary transport measures within the city were proposed. The scheme remained on the National Priority 2 list and no firm timetable was indicated for the start of construction. Soon government attitudes were again changing and in early 1997 it was announced that: 'Whilst the Hereford bypass remains in the Trunk Road Programme, it may well be some considerable time before it is built'. Two years later even that sounded positive and encouraging, for by then a completely new government had brought in programmes and policies removing all prospects of a by-pass approach towards Hereford's through traffic problems—producing also an end to some 14 years of debate, waiting and untold wastage of everyone's time and money.

Chapter IV
Industry and Skills

By the beginning of the 18th century a wide range of industrial manufacture was being undertaken. The processes involved were revolutionised from the 1760s by the combined resources of machinery, transport and power, the harnessing of steam being the fundamental achievement of the early industrial revolution. But Hereford's transport problems, as highlighted in chapter III, meant that until the arrival of the railways, coal prices in Hereford were considerably higher than in most other towns and cities in Britain, hampering any local industrial development.

Over the years industries which did not require coal-fired power had been attempted. As early as 1668 Lord Scudamore had bequeathed £400, free of interest, to anyone who would establish a woollen manufactory at Hereford to find employment for 'the industrious poor', but it took until the end of the 18th century before 'a manufactory of flannel', employing between 20 and 30 hands, was set up in King Street with some assistance from the fund. However, these efforts to re-establish a woollen industry from the abundance of available raw materials and labour came to nothing. Attempts to establish a speciality in glove manufacture bore fruit for a while, but the returns were nowhere near enough to sustain the economy of the city on their own. Cider making, the raising of hops, flax dressing, the collection of bark for tanning and the making of hats and even cutlery all provided some employment.

At the start of the 19th century, its population stuck at little more than 6,000, Hereford remained isolated from the industrial revolution, though it did retain its local role as a provincial market town. Its trades and industries were occupied in processing the produce of local farming, grinding corn at Eign, Scutt, Widemarsh and Castle Mills and tanning skins and hides at Hatton's yard in Barton Lane, Crowes at Above Eign and a third nearly opposite the Coningsby Hospital. Due to the strong smell of the raw hides, the tanyards were situated as far away as possible from the built-up area and close to an abundant supply of water—which afterwards fed into the nearest ditch! Their busiest times were during the May and October Fairs when skins and bark were bought to begin the 12-month tanning process.

Tanners with their tools at Hatton's Yard in Barton Lane, c.1896

Many of the 72 boot and shoemakers in the city and others from the surrounding villages would also attend to buy in their supplies for the year.

By the middle of the 19th century other local raw materials were being processed by a wide variety of trades such as fellmongers (dealers in skins and hides), curriers (who finished leather to make it strong, flexible and waterproof), dyers, straw bonnet makers and woolstaplers. But as the population reached 12,000 there was still little sign of any manufacturing activities. Malting was carried out to some extent—there were 17 maltsters in 1851—and there was brewing, whilst brickmaking across the county gave employment to some 200 men and boys.

The Hereford Brewery was founded in Bewell Street by J.C. Reynolds in 1834 and bought by Charles Watkins in 1858. He transferred his business from the rear of the Imperial Inn in Widemarsh Street and in the 1870s added Bewell House and its garden so that the brewery came to cover a large area extending from Bewell Street to Wall Street. At one time it included St. George's Hall, built as a skating rink but afterwards used as a hop and ale store. A supply of pure well water contributed very largely to the fine quality of the beer, mineral waters and high-class temperance drinks. Subsequently acquired by the Hereford and Tredegar Brewery Limited, the business was extended and modernised in 1907; on building a pump house for a new artesian well, an inscription was found on the foundation wall which read 'Well, 71 Feet, 1724'. This was thought to refer to the renowned Bewell Spring, of some historical significance and certainly a source of water with crystal clearness and great purity. The firm established over 200 agencies and owned more than 70 tied houses for the sale of their beverages, which included Mild Ale, India Pale Ale, Export Pale Ale, Old Hereford Ale, National Household Pale Ale, Watkins' Cream Stout and Porter. The aerated and mineral water range included Orange Champagne, Soda, Seltzer, Lemonade, Lemon beer and Lemontina but undoubtedly most famous of all was Watkins' Golden Sunlight Ale, which was awarded the only gold medal at the

Victoria tile works, Holmer in 1970

International Exhibition in 1886 and received 'the encomiums of many of the highest medical authorities' (although there is no record then of what it was said to be good for!).

Mr. R. Pritchard of Stone Bow produced bricks, tiles and pipes in the early 1840s, boasting 'a windmill to prepare his clay in a superior manner' for his clientele of 'the Nobility, Gentry, Clergy and Agriculturists'. Of the three brick and tile makers listed in 1858, Thomas Tunks had succeeded Thomas Beech of Worm-hill brick and tile yard at Holmer. He was followed in 1863 by Ralph, Preece, Davies and Company. The renowned Holmer bricks produced at their Albert Steam Pipe, Tile, Pottery, Building and Artistic Brick Works at Roman Road were used in large numbers by the railway companies for building Barrs Court, Moorfields Goods and other stations and some of the works on the second Dinmore Tunnel. Of great density, strength and durability they were also specified for the Hereford County College (later the Teachers' Training College and now the College for the Blind), St. Mary's Hospital at Burghill, the new Council Gas Works at Widemarsh and the Water Tower at Broomy Hill as well as many stately homes.

Their roofing tiles were adopted by Messrs. Godwin and Hewitt for an extensive range of buildings and workshops at the Victoria Tile Works, College Road, which they took over from the Hereford and South Wales Manure Company

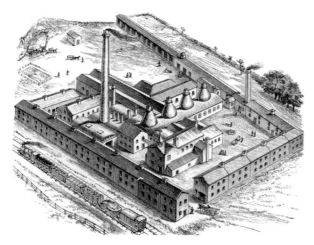

Victoria tile works, Holmer in 1892

in 1884. The superior red claybeds enabled them to achieve early fame with their enamelled and embossed tiles, made in every conceivable design and colour and employed in tile fire-places, mantels, fenders and countless other uses (their slip tiles were specified in 1965 for the walls of the two pedestrian underpasses at Victoria Street and Newmarket Street on the inner relief road).

In 1909, Mr. H.S. Thynne and Mr. G.A.C. Thynne formed a tile company and built up an extensive business at home and abroad until 1959 when work ceased, except for the production of tiled fireplaces, storage and retail sales of tiles. The property changed hands in the 1960s, to

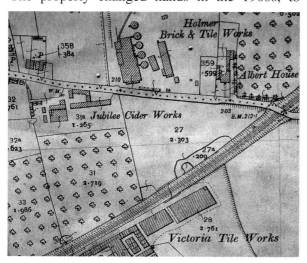

OS map of 1904 showing the concentration of businesses on the northern edge of Hereford

become the Holmer Trading Estate, and planning consent was granted to HRD Estates for a complete three phase development of the 11 acre site. None of the permissions was taken up, however, and the old buildings, originally constructed for tile-making purposes, became occupied by a variety of small industrial, storage, service and retail businesses. Relatively low rents made them suitable for start-up or 'nursery' use and changes to the former slabbing block made for some improvement of accommodation and appearance near the estate entrance off College Road. By the end of the 1990s the estate catered for the needs of 60 companies, employing over 300 people, but despite initiatives to try and realise the maximum employment potential of the estate the condition of most buildings continued to deteriorate. The road and car-park areas were sub-standard, the circulation arrangements rudimentary and the site entrance and exit far from satisfactory.

The Hampton Park Brickworks was founded as a small concern by a Mr. Wilson and in 1891 was taken over by Mr. W.E. Britten's Hereford Brick and Tile Company. Such was his success that the fires for the new continuous kilns were not extinguished once lit in 1892 until 1915 (when they probably required repair and maintenance), as they produced over five million bricks a year, together with many other clay products. The raw material at Hampton Park was suitable for making the finest machine pressed 'cherry red' facing bricks 'of a texture very similar to terra cotta'. Ordinary common and wire cut building bricks were turned out in millions, and moulded bricks, red flooring tiles, roofing tiles, land drain pipes, chimney pots and many other products were manufactured for wide distribution. In 1990, many years after operations ceased, the Hampton Park Brick Pit (Tupsley Quarry) was declared a Local Nature Reserve and recognised as a Special Wildlife Site due to the habitat value of what had, by then, become a diverse area of scrub and wetland and an important wildlife reservoir.

In 1834, the same year as J.C. Reynolds first built the Hereford Brewery, Captain Radford, R.N. built an iron foundry in Friars Street, but shortly after a race to introduce the first steam engine in Hereford, both concerns shut down and were derelict for 17 years until Charles Watkins bought them. At the foundry he built and equipped a new flour mill with six pairs of stones until, by 1882, new roller mill plant engineered by his son, Alfred Watkins, was installed to become the first of its kind to operate in Herefordshire. (The mill was lighted with incandescent electric lamps served by a dynamo from St. Georges's Hall which had inaugurated electric lighting in the county in 1879). Many other innovations were to follow as new ideas in milling were developed and Watkins Flour Mills maintained a leading position until the second half of the 20th century, purchasing grain direct from farmers and taking their flour and Blue Peak brand of animal compounds to ever expanding markets. Following a fire, all the buildings were demolished and the site is now awaiting redevelopment.

However, not all the early industries relied solely on the agricultural or rather more limited material resources of the county and the large wool scouring and leather dressing works oper-ated by G.R. Herron and Son at Monkmoor Mills, with its necessary abundance of water, obtained their raw material from as far away as Australia. Their main purpose was to cleanse and prepare the partially scoured wools for the manufacturers of yarns and woollen materials and the raw skins for the glove cutters of Yeovil, Worcester and other specialist centres.

Herefordshire cider had long been renowned, owing much to the spirited exertions of Lord Scudamore of Holme Lacy during the 17th century. The firm of William Evans and Co. was established near Widemarsh Common in 1850 and was subsequently purchased by Mr. W.F. Chave. He turned it into a private limited company in 1898, just as Mr. H. Godwin was opening his cider works at Tillington Road in Holmer. Both had ceased trading by the second half of the 20th century. Rather more modestly, Mr. H.P. Bulmer, younger son of the Rev. C.H. Bulmer, Rector of Credenhill, heeding his mother's advice to make a career in either food or drink 'because neither ever goes out of fashion', had tried making some cider from apples in the

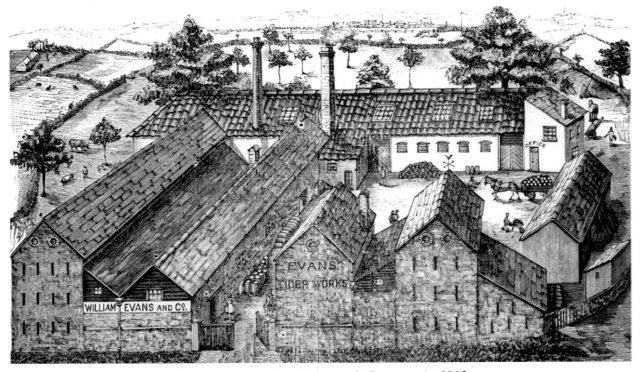

Evans' cider works, Widemarsh Common in 1892

94

Rectory orchard. Percy Bulmer's efforts were so successful that a year later, in 1888, he engaged in cider-making on a larger scale. Starting in Maylord Street he then took an acre of land in Ryelands Street, Hereford where he was joined as marketing manager by his brother, Mr. E.F. (Fred) Bulmer. The business grew steadily, more land was purchased in Ryelands Street and then at Moorfields and eventually the factory sites covered over 80 acres. With almost a 60% share of the total UK cider market, Bulmers are clear leaders at home, whilst international business in over 50 countries accounts for over a fifth of the Group operating profit. Outside the city, Bulmers has planted 5,000 acres of bitter-sweet apples and also contracts out a similar expanse of Herefordshire farmland. Such large scale orcharding ensures that the county maintains its lead in the production of cider fruit and the importation of whole French apples has ceased. However, the huge output of cider in Hereford is such that there is still a need for foreign juice concentrate.

In the eyes of some, planting on this scale, combined with the thousands of acres of potato and oil-seed rape crops, has been at a high price in terms of biodiversity with the loss of ancient unimproved grasslands, wildlife and other irreplaceable features of the county's distinctive landscape.

Unlike cider, gin is not a beverage which one would readily associate with Hereford, but one of the few distilleries outside London was established in East Street by William and John Pulling in 1813. A large range of underground vaults was constructed not only to deal with the products of the stills but also to bottle and store spirits, champagne, port, sherry, claret and most other wines, whilst on the opposite side of the street there was the bond, consisting of a three-storied red brick building. This contained the blending vats for whiskies and other spirits and a bottling department and stores, all under the eye of Excise officials. Pullings were eventually taken over by Tanners of Shrewsbury, equally venerable independent wine merchants dating from 1842. Through them they maintain a presence in St. Peter's Square as the longest established extant business in Hereford, still offering the highly regarded Pullings Hereford Gin, now made to the original recipe in Dundee, Scotland.

Industries reliant on the resources of the county also include Davies Brook and Co. Ltd., formed from an amalgamation of the businesses of Davies and Co., established in the early 1870s,

Label for Pullings' Hereford Gin

Distillery premises in East Street, since converted into nos. 1-5 Pullings Mews

95

The lines at British Canners, Bewell Street, now part of Tesco's car park

and Kemp and Brook who started in 1900. Incorporated in 1910 at Coningsby Works, like the brewers and cider makers they drew on artesian well water for their wide range of still and carbonated soft drinks. They later held franchises and licences for the sale of most nationally known drinks, including wines and spirits, and ventured into the pickled food market with onions, eggs, beetroot and cabbage. After well

over a hundred years of increasing congestion in Coningsby Street, the company moved to a site equally well blessed with abundant water at Moreton-on-Lugg.

A food preservation business had been established near the city centre since the late 19th century and, as British Canners, had grown from a small jam making and fruit bottling factory into a modern cannery and preserve manufacturer employing up to 1,000 people. A substantial proportion of the many thousands of tons of fruit and vegetables handled at the works was grown locally and sold under their trade name Wye Valley. In 1966 they were joined by T.W. Beach and Sons at Tillington Road, who also produced preserves, canned fruits and vegetables, often from locally-grown supplies. Egg packing and milk concentration provided for further employment. Herefordshire timber was used by Greenlands in connection with the manufacture, repair and restoration of furniture in their large factory at Foley Street.

For a short while, there was surprisingly also some ship building. Mr. Easton, of the Castle Quay, Hereford, is recorded in *The Hereford*

The Water Witch, *a steam vessel built at Hereford in 1834. It has been reported to be still in service along a river in South Africa at the end of the 20th century*

Journal of 13 February, 1823 as having launched a sloop named the *Hereford* from a timber yard opposite the Castle Green. It was 47ft. long and 15ft. 3 ins. in the beam, and in the following year he launched a brig of 170 tons with a keel of 61ft. and a beam of 20ft. and another, the *Helen*, of 122 tons and capable of carrying 180 people. By 1832, Mr. Easton had built his eighth ship at the Hereford yard — the schooner *Collinoque* of 140 tons burthen. For a number of years other ocean-going ships were built in Hereford and sent as hulks to be fitted out downstream. All had been built below the Wye Bridge and on 26 April 1834, the *Water Witch*, a steam vessel of 80ft. length and 23ft. width built by Captain Radford, was launched for fitting out at Chepstow. Smaller builders were also at work; in 1844 James Proust of St. Martin's Street advertised a new sailing boat and several rowing boats for sale. There is no later record of shipbuilding at Hereford, but it continued downstream at Brockweir for a further few years.

But in the absence of any significant manufacturing activity, agriculture continued to serve as the backbone of industrial life in the city and in the 19th century there were numerous small scale trades and crafts which supplied the needs of the surrounding countryside (see pp.19-20).

Rotherwas

The Rotherwas estate at Dinedor, the seat of the Bodenhams for well over three centuries, comprised Rotherwas House, an 11-bay mansion built on the site of an earlier mansion by Charles Bodenham to the designs of James Gibbs in 1732,

Rotherwas House, demolished in 1925

and over 2,500 acres of land on the south side of the River Wye. After the death of Count Louis Bodenham-Lubienski in 1912 it was broken up into 76 separate lots and sold. The house was demolished in 1925 following a fire, leaving only the chapel. At the auction just prior to the War, Herefordshire County Council bought an area of 185 acres overlooked by Dinedor Hill and bordered by the Wye meadows as part of a scheme to provide smallholdings. But the land quickly turned out to be unsuitable and seemed likely to become a costly 'white elephant'. It was, however, well served by the Hereford, Ross and Gloucester Railway and could draw on an ample water, gas and electricity supply. In 1916 it was acquired by the Ministry of Munitions as a site for a factory for filling shells with lyddite, made chiefly from fused picric acid, and amatol, an explosive mixture of ammonium nitrate and TNT, as an insurance in case of accident or mishap elsewhere. Production started in November 1916 and quickly built up, especially after the appointment of Winston Churchill as Minister of Munitions in July 1917. During one week soon afterwards, the lyddite section filled a record 50,892 shells of 6in. calibre. The amatol section went into production with the filling of its first shell in June 1917 and was heavily involved with 6, 8 and 9.2in. and 60 pounder shells. The factory also came to fill 50 and 230 pound aerial bombs, chemical shells and manufacture amatol block charges. At the height of its activity in October 1918, there were 5,943 employees, 1,966 of them men and 3,977 women. To help feed them, some of the land was found suitable for cultivation and grazing, and as a result the factory canteens were kept well supplied at an economical cost.

After the signing of the Armistice huge stocks of ammunition were left over and the Hereford factory was given the task of safely breaking it down. A recovery plant was erected for removing ammonium nitrate and although only a small proportion of the original workforce remained, mostly men, very satisfactory profits were made. However, during 1920 the factory was transferred from the Ministry of Munitions to the War Office

The munitions factory at Rotherwas in 1998, an immense open plan area where shells were moved through the filling process slung from overhead rails

and closed, leaving a large number of the men unemployed. There was also a wide range of specialised buildings, shelters and blast walls, wooden rails and sidings within the 5 mile perimeter of the factory, which also seemed destined for redundancy.

Barely 20 years later, ammunition and bombs were once more being filled at Rotherwas, again mostly by women. By the autumn of 1940 some 3,700 were employed at what was then the Royal Ordnance Factory (at a basic wage rate of £1 12s. [£1.60] for a 47 hour week) and work continued throughout the war, but this time not without tragedy. Early on 27 July 1942, in Hereford's only German raid of the war, a lone aircraft dropped two bombs, the first exploding on impact killing 19 workers and injuring many more, whilst the other travelled some distance before penetrating the factory perimeter fence and killing all but one of the occupants of the police superintendent's house. Three workers had already been killed and six injured by an accidental explosion the previous September and on 30 May 1944 a 2,000 pound bomb exploded in a filling house which set off other munitions. The filling house was demolished, a sheet of flame shot 2,000ft. into the air, two people were killed and another 30 injured. Action by emergency services and employees at the factory in averting a major catastrophe led to the exceptional award of five George Medals and many other bravery decorations.

For a further 20 years after the end of the war, Rotherwas reverted largely to its former 'white elephant' state—until it was considered with other sites in the Lower Bullingham area for expansion of Hereford's sewage disposal system, then based at the Eign Works across the Wye. The Rotherwas option was finally chosen after a full appraisal of flood levels and foundation conditions and the complicated scheme commenced in January 1973, only being substantially completed during 1977 at a cost of £6.1 million. Designed to serve 60,000 people in Hereford and 6,000 in the surrounding countryside, it also catered for all industrial effluent, bringing the equivalent population capacity to between 250,000 and 300,000. The new works were formally inaugurated on 14 September, 1978, by the Mayor, MP and other notables, in true 'Clochemerle' ceremonial, by which time much else was starting to happen within the nearby estate. Of a suitable total of just over 300 acres, Herefordshire County Council had purchased about 230 acres of Ministry of Defence land and this time, with much better prospects than before, they began a phased programme of industrial development which was continued and expanded upon reorganisation of local government in 1974 by Hereford and Worcester County Council. New roads and services were installed, selective demolition and conversion of existing munitions buildings was undertaken and new factory units built, ranging in size from 500 to 10,000 sq.ft. Serviced land was sold and leased and private sector development also made great strides. By the end of the 1990s, 127 local and international companies occupied working space and gave employment to over 2,000 people.

Thorn Lighting was the largest firm, having acquired the factory and lighting interests of A.E.I. as long ago as 1964. Changing the name to Smart and Brown Lighting, they were the largest firm of lighting engineers in the county, employing between 650 and 700 people. Mainly occupying former ordnance factory buildings, they manufactured fluorescent lighting fittings for the Atlas, Mazda and Ekco brand names, street lighting lanterns for British Lighting Industries and a specialist range of flameproof fittings used in the petro-chemical industry. In October, 1972, the company undertook what was believed to be the biggest lighting scheme then known on a European motorway when they installed 5,000 lights to illuminate a 38-mile stretch of the M1 from Watford to Newport Pagnell. They subsequently gained the Queen's Award for Achievement in Industry for their development of the Haline Tungsten Halogen Floodlight, and also the Queen's Award for Export. The majority of streetlighting installed at that time was made at this factory, as was the floodlighting equipment for Hereford Cathedral and the Hereford United football ground. But in 1999 the workforce was greatly reduced and, amidst great local surprise and distress it was announced that the Rotherwas factory was to close down, with the loss of more than 300 jobs. A few former workers set up their own businesses at Rotherwas, with financial and practical support from Herefordshire Council, the Chamber of Commerce and other agencies. Early the

following year the former 40-acre factory complex was sold to Pontrilas Developments, a family business that had already converted the former Whitestone tile works into a business park. The new Thorn Business Park comprised 270,000 sq. ft. of buildings and small sites of 10,000 to 40,000 sq. ft. were offered for occupation by small firms.

Next to Thorn in size were Rexam Plastic Packaging with 275 employees, IMI Mouldings with 250 and Technical Rubber Products with 160 on their payroll. Between them, all 127 companies produced a total annual turnover estimated to be some £300 million—and a volume of road traffic which included approximately 500 truck movements each working day. To this was added the weight of an estimated extra 90 vehicles a day, varying from light goods to big bulk waste carriers, operating from a new 'waste transfer station and materials reclamation facility'. Based in Chapel Road, this was designed to receive and transfer up to 80,000 tonnes of domestic and commercial waste each year from the city and surrounding areas.

However, even more business and investment would have been catered for easily at Rotherwas, had it not been for the loss of the one-time crucial rail link with the main line, and the severe limitations of very poor B road access to the A49 and A465. This road not only passes through a dense residential suburb, but is subject to a rail bridge height limitation of 15ft. and is at times flooded and impassable. The only alternative for wide, tall or other abnormal roads is under police escort along narrow, tortuous country roads through the village of Holme Lacy to the modest weight-restricted Holme Lacy Bridge and thence via Mordiford. Little wonder that some firms on the estate have to struggle to keep competitive! Many industrialists cherished hopes that the construction of an eastern Hereford by-pass would have provided a highly desirable link to the main-road and motorway network.

Following the 1998 local government re-organisation, Rotherwas Industrial Estate, still with over 100 acres of available developable land, was transferred to the new Herefordshire Council. This body was committed to the well-aired eastern route for either a bypass or relief road, but also impressed with a 'considerable logic' in looking west as well, in ways which would assist other major employers to gain better access to main radial routes.

Major manufacturers North of the Wye

Without Rotherwas, most of Hereford's manufacturing and related industries would be within the city boundary north of the river—not ideal from a traffic point of view with so many people living to the south. The earliest significant development in this area was Hereford's second gas works at Holmer (replacing the first one in Commercial Road), extended and improved in 1930. During the uneasy years between the two World Wars a few firms started to appear and widen employment opportunities. Painter Brothers Limited, founded in 1920, became internationally known in the field of steel fabricating, hot dip galvanising, shotblasting and paint spraying: one of the prominent features on their skyline from

1928 was an electro-mechanical testing station equipped to handle the full scale testing of structures up to 36.5m. in height, which was later extended. Jeffrey Tiles started manufacturing fireplace and wall tiles at Barrs Court Road in 1926 and became H. & R. Johnson in 1958 as the result of an acquisition by one of the largest manufacturers of ceramic tiles in the world. Aeroparts Engineering was founded as a private concern in 1937 and, located on the former gasworks site in Commercial Road, became widely known in conjunction with its associated company, Westland Motors, for both car body work and components for the aircraft industry.

By 1951, however, with the city population at 32,490, only a very small percentage of the employed population was engaged in manufacture. For the county as a whole, for every 1,000 people in employment, 266 were engaged in catering, domestic service and distribution trades, 220 in agriculture, 153 in public administration and defence, and well under 100 in what could in any way be described as manufacturing industry. This was not to be the situation for much longer.

The Wiggin factory from the air in 1980

Growth of Manufacturing Industry

In 1950, the Ministry of Supply, wishing to disperse strategic production supply, selected Crossway Farm at Holmer as a site for the development of a new generation of metals for the aircraft industry. Over a century before, in 1835, a Birmingham partnership between a Mr. Evans and Mr. Askin began the refining of nickel and the manufacture of German Silver (an alloy of nickel and silver much used at the time for cutlery), and were joined in 1842 by Mr. Henry Wiggin, who later gave his name to the firm. With great foresight they concentrated on nickel alloys, in due course producing resistance wires for the newly arrived age of electricity, and by the early 1950s were well placed to join in the Ministry exercise at Hereford and established the Wiggin Works. The first melt was produced in 1953, the trade named NIMONIC* alloys were created, the Whittle jet flew and a new era of civil and military aviation opened up. The company later centred a massive modernisation and concentration programme on the Hereford works, in 1962 withdrawing from their older heavily developed sites in Birmingham and Glasgow and acquiring the Ministry of Supply factory and land. The whole process was broken down into three stages, involving firstly the melting and machinery functions, then the finishing departments such as cold rolling and drawing and finally the hot-working departments including hot rolling and extrusion functions. A workforce of over 3,000 and their families in the late 1960s accounted considerably for raising Hereford's population to 46,500 by the 1971 census, an increase of 43% in 20 years. Since then Inco Alloys, the parent firm and the world's largest producer of nickel, has based its European headquarters and manufacturing and research centre at Hereford. The Wiggin factory joined in producing the many different nickel alloys found in aircraft jet engines, chemical and process plant, offshore oil and gas engineering, industrial furnaces, domestic electrical appliances, power stations and in many forms of electronic and telecommunications equipment. By the end of the century the name of the company had changed again, to Special Metals (Wiggin) Limited, and due to a lengthy sequence of major production and management changes a high level of output was being achieved by a much reduced workforce.

Just as Hereford industry was boldly entering the jet age, a group of local farmers was embarking on another of the county's most remarkable success stories. Two of them, Colonels Corbett and Phillips had been involved in producing laying hens and joined forces to provide for the broiler industry, building a new hatchery at Shobdon. Business boomed and led to the need for breeding farms, feed mills, growing farms, a processing factory and an integrated broiler operation involving other breeders and growers. Six of these (known as the 'Hereford Half Dozen') formed Sun Valley Poultry in 1961 and opened its first factory at Westfields, Hereford on city council land acquired for industrial uses preferably allied to the farming industry. When fully equipped the factory was designed to process up to 100,000 birds a week and by the end of the year it had already achieved 50% of its target. Selection by Marks and Spencer as its main supplier soon led to adoption by other major 'household name' retailers and to keep pace with the growing demand from these as well as for its own brands Sun Valley expanded its production capacity, by the end of the 1960s producing 300,000 chickens and 20,000 turkeys each week. Further diversification in the 1970s made the company a leading supplier of cooked poultry and 20 years after its creation, Sun Valley became a member company of Cargill Incorporated. This American company invested more than £20 million during their first six years, leading to the building of a new factory (called the Corbett Block in honour of the colonel who had played such a large part in the success of Sun Valley) and this was followed in 1986 by an ultra-modern extension to the cooked products plant in Yazor Road and further works at the hatchery and Tram Inn feed mill. On 6 September 1993, Sun Valley suffered a serious setback when the Corbett Block burnt down and two firefighters, John Davies and David Morris, lost their lives. The company managed to retain its market leading position among the largest 100 food companies in the UK and from an initial workforce of 100, the company payroll at its plants in Hereford, Abergavenny, Blaenavon and Wolverhampton grew to 4,000 by the end of the 1990s. A £100 million cash injection to redevelop existing plants and a new plant to house its Marks and Spencer recipe dish and McDonald's business went a long way towards consolidating Sun Valley's brand position for the future. By then, combined with H.P. Bulmer and Inco Alloys, Sun Valley accounted for about 57% of city manufacturing employment, a category which had grown to 40% of all jobs in Hereford—a considerable change on 1951.

To cater for the red meat trade, and to complement the modernised livestock market, the city council built an abbatoir next to the poultry processing factory on its Westfields industrial site. Replacing a much outdated and inefficient slaughter house at Stonebow Road, close to the County Hospital, its facilities eventually included 6,000 sq. ft. of covered lairage, slaughter, gut, hides and skins, fat, casualty and chilling rooms and refrigerating plant. Leased to G.H. Bowkett's of Tenbury and subsequently redesigned to meet E.E.C. Standards, in 1978 it accounted for 17,276 cattle, 220 calves, 55,837 pigs and 67,272 sheep, but annual 'throughput' subsequently fell away. This was due to a variety of challenges and changes in requirements for the domestic and export meat industry and led to Bowkett's withdrawing to their base at Tenbury. No-one could be found to take their place and the entire installation was disposed of by the council to Sun Valley who cleared the site and incorporated it into its territory.

The Westfields site was just one of a number in the city which provided land for a range of industrial enterprises. Phillips Buildings started in Belmont Road in 1949 as a small company which manufactured farm buildings and after rapid expansion was the first to move to Westfields Trading Estate, specialising in portal frame structures of up to 150 ft. span. In 1963 they recognised the potential of galvanising and became pioneers of hot dipped galvanised structures for agricultural use and became associated with Hereford Galvanisers, established a year later.

Their neighbours, Excelsior Plastics, commenced in the business of manufacturing low density polythene film in 1964 and grew to be one of the leading specialist extruders of polythene film in Europe. Supplying the food and drinks industry with shrinkwrap it was also a leading supplier of refuse sacks in the UK and Europe and, as Gelpack Excelsior, became one of Herefordshire's top 50 businesses in employment terms.

Saunders Valve had been associated with the city since the late 1940s. Originally at Blackfriars Street, the firm moved in 1966 to a 6.5 acre site adjoining Westfields at the former Evans Cider Works at Widemarsh Common. The considerably larger 60,000 sq. ft. of factory floor space enabled them to increase their workforce, occupied in the design and manufacture of Sabal ball plug valves, from 30 to about 300. Used throughout the world, the valves were made in a variety of materials to control the flow of fluids ranging from corrosive chemicals to the smoothest of whisky. In a relatively short while, however, the factory closed down and the land was cleared to make way for Chave Court, a housing development.

Coming fourth on the 1999 Herefordshire 'Top 50' list of businesses with nearly 500 employees was Denco of Holmer Road, a member of the AMEC group. Leading manufacturers of precision air conditioning equipment they were pioneers in catering for the heat generated in early computer rooms. Subsequent advances were designed for precise control of temperature, humidity and air quality in applications such as telecommunications suites, data centres, clean rooms and laboratories. A full design, supply, installation and commissioning and aftercare service was available. The company also offers a wide range of centralised lubrication systems for the many complex production techniques employed in modern industry throughout the world.

Many smaller companies were provided for at industrial parks or estates, some of them on sites formerly occupied by much larger concerns. The Aydon Industrial Park was established near the former main entrance to Henry Wiggin, further up Holmer Road, and comprises 11 small businesses as varied as fire and safety suppliers, refrigerator sales and servicing, parcels delivery and window installation.

The Beech Business Park occupies the site of the previous canning factory at Tillington Road, which had itself succeeded the cider works built by Mr. H. Godwin in 1898.

T.W. Beach and Sons a member of the Allied Suppliers group of companies, arrived in Hereford in 1966 and concentrated on the production of preserves, canned fruits and vegetables, bakery jams and soft drinks. During the soft fruit season a considerable tonnage of strawberries arrived daily at the factory (the majority from Herefordshire growers) for washing, inspecting, grading and canning. Not all the local residents enjoyed the pervasive cooking smells and sounds at the busy times and often let this be known. Eventually the factory was closed and in due course the site and some buildings were adapted and extended to cater for a range of service industries as diverse as farm equipment, tile sales, wholesale meat and renal dialysis.

The Three Elms Trading Estate is centred on a long established government cold storage depot and acts as the depot for all Yeoman Canyon Travel buses and coaches and as a venue for items ranging from chilled and frozen foods to motor parts and industrial tools, equipment and clothing supplies. Another former government food store site off Grandstand Road serves a wide range of similar needs in units at the Grandstand Business Centre, as well as providing the Department of Transport with a facility for commercial vehicle testing.

In a special initiative at a time of high unemployment, the city council converted underused allotments in Plough Lane into a range of serviced industrial building plots—with the aim of offering them on appropriate terms to firms prepared to employ only local people. After a slow start most were taken up, one of the first by Spink and Sons, manufacturers of windows, doors and conservatories. The Plough Lane Trading Estate eventually flourished and, with the adjoining older Sweetmans Yard Estate, became an address for businesses and trading outlets providing services as varied as building, plumbing, joinery and 'do it yourself' trades, furniture, business systems, signwriting, steel framed buildings, engine reboring and vehicle repairs, welding and paint spraying. One of a number of car main dealerships which moved out from inadequate garages nearer the city centre took a plot in Harrow Road—whilst the widened and improved Plough Lane also provides access from the A438 Whitecross Road to H.P. Bulmers' head offices and much of their cider factory.

The Victorian flour mill in Bath Street, at one time the home of *The Hereford Times*, was developed in 1985 as the Berrows Business Centre and provides a home for 26 very different commercial enterprises. Other small industrial sites near Barrs Court Station, at Rockfield Road and at the former Greenlands Furniture Factory at Foley Street all added their own significant share to the total range of businesses within the city.

Employment in all the various service sectors, including distribution and transport, retailing, hotels, catering, financial and professional business, accounted for another 40% of all jobs in Hereford during the early 1990s. Unemployment followed regional and national trends, rising from 4.9% in November 1989 to 11.5% in August 1992, before falling slightly towards the middle of the decade. Domination of the manufacturing sector by a small number of large firms (the destinies of some of them controlled from outside the city and country) continues to be a source of concern and further widening of this productive base is seen to be very important in the interests of a balanced, diverse, healthy and secure local economy.

A local strategy therefore set out a number of business development programmes aimed at publicising the many investment attractions of

Hereford and encouraging and assisting the growth of viable businesses. This involved a survey of suitable land and it was clear that amounts within the city boundary were severely limited due to the extent of existing development and the proximity of houses and other sensitive uses to otherwise promising sites. Top quality agricultural land also needed to be protected and consideration given to landscape and wildlife conservation. Less than 20 acres were forthcoming, at Holmer Playing Field (a source of local controversy and opposition), Legion Way/College Road (which throughout the 1990s failed to attract any takers despite being opened out with a new access road, other than from a car main dealer) and land at the former School of Farriery and police traffic department, Newtown Road (which has now become a retail park). However there were substantial stocks of undeveloped land at the Rotherwas Industrial Estate extending to just over 300 acres.

At the start of the 21st century this former pre World War One 'white elephant' land seems to provide much of what is needed (except, crucially, for good road communications), to guarantee the future business and industrial growth, and essential viability of the city and much of the county, for many years to come.

Chapter V
Hygiene and Healthcare

When Speede drew his map in 1610, and for long afterwards, the city was poverty stricken. The streets were in a ruinous condition and heavily polluted with every kind of refuse. The courts were regularly obliged to deal with 'present-ments' of offenders who emptied their household utensils either out of windows or doors: there were occasions when parishioners of All Saints had to be restrained from throwing 'mucke, dunge, duste, rubble or any other filth at the end of the Church or against the wales thereof'.

The town was supplied with water from wells and pumps (often called 'plumps') and these were regularly and wantonly abused. For example in 1658 several residents were 'presented' for:

> Causinge Certaine Annoyances to bee made & don abouts the plumpe at the head of Bewalls streete within our said Warde by throwing out, or causing to bee throwed out certaine filthly styncks both by Emptying pissepotts, and other stinking excrements to ye great annoyance of the neighbours there.

There was no provision for any form of concerted action to bring about a change despite a growing urge in many quarters for something to be done. The Mayor and city council did not apparently have the political will or initiative, nor indeed did they have sufficient powers to deal with all the acute physical conditions met during these unwholesome times. These only came about with the 1774 Paving, Licencing and Lighting Act. The improvement commissioners appointed under this Act worked alongside the city council in reasonable harmony in what amounted to the start of public environmental health awareness. There was little, however, that they could do about the indescribably squalid living conditions in privately owned courts, 'stews', cottages and houses in the poorest, most congested parts of the city. Created by infilling, many quarters were badly built, cramped, airless and dark and often obliged to share primitive water and sanitation provision. An inspector of nuisances in the early 1850s reported that up to 12 cottages in St. Owen Street shared two privies, in Friar Street there were from 20 to 30 houses to one privy and he was aware of a dozen other instances where there was not more than one privy to ten or 12 cottages. Mr. Dalton, a draper, spoke of Barnard-court, a yard then leading off Bye Street, where 'one privy in the middle of his premises, but not belonging to him, lay in front of the ten cottages it served and anyone entering it must be seen from the cottages and even from the street'. Chief among dwellings in the worst and most miserable condition were houses and courts in Eign Street, Bewell Street, Church Street, King Street, Berrington Street, Bridge Street, St. Owen's Gate, Commercial Street, the east end of Castle Street and Widemarsh Street. All stood out in the Register of Births, Deaths and Marriages as being the most unhealthy in the city in terms of deaths from disease.

Added to this, a system of common lodging houses provided cheap makeshift accommodation for vagrants and 'trampers'. Generally in filthy condition and subject to little control, they were often grossly overcrowded—the superintendent of police on one occasion reported that 117 lodgers had been accommodated at night in ten modest-sized houses, when only 86 were normally allowed! Although he could not offer information about the incidence of sickness in any of the houses, it was inevitable that they would be the foci of many forms of contagious disease in view of their state—and that of their 'casual lodgers'.

Throughout human history, the topmost cause of premature death has been the contamination of water supply where sewage was not separated from what people drank. As in most other towns, typhus, diarrhoea, smallpox, typhoid and other infectious fevers had been very much a part of everyday life in Hereford and were suffered almost with resignation. Throughout Britain, life expectancy was short, often depending on location and circumstances. In a rural city such as Truro in Cornwall from 1837 to 1840 it was 40 years of age for professional classes or gentry, 33 years for those engaged in trade and 28 years for labourers, artisans and their families—whereas in 1840 corresponding figures for Liverpool were just 35, 22 and 15 years. Life expectancy for children had reached the point where, of those born to the labouring classes in Manchester, more than 57% died before they reached five years of age, and although infant mortality in Hereford was not of that order, Victorian parish registers nevertheless reveal a very sad story, alongside a not unrelated high proportion of births. The figures might well have been a lot worse, for in 1831 an epidemic of Asiatic cholera struck Britain for the first time and became endemic, flaring up again in the late 1840s and in 1853. Miraculously it did not reach the city but it helped to concentrate minds everywhere and frightened people so much that pressure built up for legislation to be framed to deal with the national problems of dirt, disease and poor living conditions.

Previously only a small number of sanitary reformers had been concerned and they had met with considerable obstruction and opposition from landlords, speculative builders and a great phalanx of other vested interests. *The Times* in August 1854 which, although generally supportive of reform, preferred 'rather to take our chance with cholera and the rest than be bullied into health'—having proclaimed in 1848 that 'Cholera is the best of all sanitary reformers'.

Ten years before, the trio of very different sanitary reformers, Dr. Southwood Smith, Dr. James Kay and Dr. Neil Arnott had prepared reports dealing with the physical causes of fever in London and such was the effect on the government that an urgent investigation was ordered for all parts of Britain. In 1842 the secretary of the Poor Law Commission, Edwin Chadwick, presented to the House of Lords his monumental *Report on the Sanitary Condition of the Labouring Population of Great Britain*. Six years of resistance and controversy ensued before royal assent was given to the resulting Public Health Act of 1848—even then limited to an experimental life of five years. A main provision was the establishment of a national Board of Health which could create local Boards of Health, either where the residents asked for them, or where the annual death rate was 23 per 1,000—just above the national average. (By the 1990s, barely four generations later, it had settled at between 11 and 12 per 1,000).

In Hereford, returns revealed a seven years average between 1846 and 1852 of 27 per 1,000 and 'the attention of the Honourable Board having been drawn by communications from certain residents in Hereford to the unsatisfactory nature of the sanitary arrangements of that city', a preliminary inquiry was accordingly arranged before a superintending inspector, Thomas Webster Rammell, Esq.

Report to the General Board of Health
Rammell opened the inquiry at the guild-hall in Hereford on 5 January 1853, and for the next four days heard evidence, each afternoon inspecting

various parts of the city and surrounding district accompanied by some of the witnesses and other interested gentlemen (there was no question of any women being present). He intended to find out about the sewerage, drainage and supply of water; the state of the burial-grounds; the number and sanitary condition of the inhabitants; the local Acts of Parliament in force within the city for paving, lighting, cleansing, watching, regulating, supplying with water, or improving the same; and any other relevant information.

Mr. Parry, representing both the paving commissioners and city council, raised concerns about the likely financial implications of being placed under the control of the Board of Health, 'Hereford not being a very rich city' and 'unable to pay heavy expenses'. It was explained that the provisions of the Act of 1848 were only permissive and that the General Board had no power to compel a local Board of Health, should one be formed following the inquiry, to undertake works which they did not think proper. Only the power of dismissing the appointed surveyor and appointing a medical officer required the direct involvement and sanction of the General Board. This would seem an obvious weakness.

After hearing evidence on Poor Relief, land tenure and flooding, the inspector heard from Dr. Henry Bull, one of the principal witnesses. Bull had lived and practised at Harley House, St. John Street since 1841 and through a wide sense of public spirit and many interests had become intimately involved in many aspects of life in the city and county. He was also one of a number in the medical profession to become closely involved in researching the social basis for disease. He had received his training as a doctor at the highly regarded University of Edinburgh medical school, as had doctors Southwood Smith and Kay.

He first presented an analysis of deaths in the city for the years 1846 to 1852, tabulating all causes, as they were then understood, dividing epidemic, endemic and contagious fevers from 'sporadic diseases'. All told there had been 256 deaths in the seven year period from a catalogue of infectious diseases which included typhus,

Dr. Bull

typhoid, smallpox, whooping cough, measles, chicken pox and dysentery. These not only hit hard in the cramped quarters of the city but were suffered throughout Britain, even in the highest abodes of wealth and power. For months in 1826 the seven year-old Princess Victoria was a source of acute anxiety with a fever, thought possibly to have been dysentery, whilst years later, in 1861, Prince Albert, then her husband and consort, having been 'greatly out of sorts', died at Windsor Castle from what is thought to have been typhoid attributed to the drains. Just ten years later their son, the Prince of Wales, came close to death due to an illness blamed on the bad sewerage at Sandringham, where the queen had hoped for healthier conditions.

Dr. Bull's tables showed an even greater number of diseases of respiratory organs, including tuberculosis and pneumonia, which of a city population of about 12,000 accounted for almost 600 deaths during the seven years of analysis. Over-crowding in dark, unventilated, damp homes and the undernourished, debilitated state of those living in squalid poverty, each contributed to the high death rate. Whilst infectious diseases led to an annual average of 1 in 300 of the population dying, chest diseases accounted for 1 in 140 and were accepted almost as a matter of course, receiving no mention anywhere in the inspector's final conclusions or recommendations.

The inspector heard there was no public provision for the supply of water but that there were many private wells, driven 10 to 15ft. into drift bed deposits of gravel throughout the water-bearing formation found in most of the city. At earlier times there had been seven public wells but they had been closed except when needed for fire-fighting purposes. All delivered exceptionally hard water which was not very good for washing and soap economy, for which many inhabitants used rain water collected in tubs, butts or cisterns. River water was far softer and it was commonly sold throughout the city at the rate of a halfpenny a bucket. One expert witness reckoned to make four cups of tea with Wye water for only three cups of equivalent strength and inferior flavour from the High Town well—a difference of 25% on the cost of tea leaves! The well water was still regarded as being wholesome in most other respects, except when it was polluted by impurities draining through the soil from cesspools and sewers, or impregnated with lead from pipes and pumps.

Lavatories were in indoor or outdoor privies mostly connected to cesspools, or bogholes as they then were often termed. Many were situated in house cellars and all had to be emptied when they were full or overflowing. The time for removal of this elegantly termed 'nightsoil' was fixed for between midnight and 6 a.m., and arrangements could be made for it to be done at an average cost of £1 per cesspool through Mr. Andrew Rowan, an enterprising local chemist. He dealt with between 40 and 50 cesspools a year and produced a manure for farmers at his factory behind the Commercial Road gasworks (somewhere in the area of the 1990s Safeway supermarket). Rowan thought that about one fifth of the total amount was dealt with in this way, the rest either being removed inexpertly for nothing by farmers or buried in a hole in another part of the garden. In some instances a whole succession of cesspools was constructed in one garden or yard. All were sunk to the level of the gravel, generally 6 ft. or so above the lowest levels of the wells, and were normally 'open-steined' using dry stone or brick to allow water to percolate through the joints. The surrounding ground showed obvious discolouration and it was felt that any well within 18ft. would usually be polluted to some degree.

The sewerage of about a third of the houses and other properties was connected, improperly or otherwise, to flat and often badly clogged drains and culverts and disposed of to one or other of the streams which surrounded the city. There were no cesspools at the town gaol, built only nine years before in 1844, and a drain serving nearly 30 officers and prisoners discharged directly to the adjacent brook.

'The most glaring evil', reported Dr. Bull, 'is the Castle Mill-pond [alongside Britons Street, later Mill Street], which receives the drainage of St. Owen's Street, Widemarsh Street, Eign Street and the line of houses on either side of the Town Brook, throughout the extent of nearly a mile round the city'. St. Owen's Gate was, in his opinion, the most unhealthy part of Hereford, with poor houses and an overcrowded burial ground immediately adjoining the offensive open drain. In 1848 there was an outbreak of typhus, smallpox in 1850, diarrhoea in 1851 and scarlet fever from 1852. He considered that the state of the Castle Mill-pond was one of the contributing causes to the unhealthiness of that quarter and was also worried that further to the south it was only some 60 to 70 yards from the boundary wall of the Infirmary.

He feared that 'the emanations from the pond' would be prejudicial to the health of the patients, and like most doctors and others at the time believed that 'malaria', or bad air, was responsible for many of the prevailing diseases. It was only in 1854, during the second cholera epidemic, that Dr. John Snow demonstrated empirically for the first time that the disease was in fact communicated through the water supply. Although it took many more years for the connec-

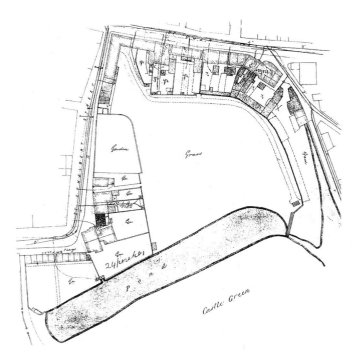

Part of the Castle Mill-pond area which received drainage from much of north-west Hereford, as surveyed by Timothy Curley

tion to be proved, the long standing belief that 'miasmas' or smells were the cause of so many infectious killer diseases had to be reconsidered by Edwin Chadwick, his medical colleagues and the entire public health movement.

It was not until the 1870s and 1880s that there was full acceptance that disease was caused by bacteria and, as he heard further evidence in the winter of 1853, Rammell could only imagine and worry about the effects of the foul and deadly atmosphere over Hereford. He was told by Inspector Wainscott that it was the practice for every butcher to have his slaughterhouse adjoining the shop, that there were numerous pigsties in the heart of the city and in Maylord's Lane there was a most filthy leather currier's establishment close to 30 houses. Dr. Bull referred to the weekly cattle market held in one of the public thoroughfares of the city which greatly added to the excrement of the daily horse traffic in all the streets and in undrained stables. And Mr. Watkins, a watchmaker, passed on complaints about candle manufactures, two in Bewell Street

and one in Packer's Lane (later West Street): 'The fat deposited in the warehouses on Saturdays and remaining there till Mondays stinks abominably. In the summer fishermen get their maggots from these tallow warehouses'.

Until 1791, when the city population was just 6,000, the only burial ground in the city had been in the cathedral precincts but, as John Davis the verger stated, they had become exceedingly over-crowded well before then. Subsequently the 11 parish and chapel grounds in the city, although enlarged in some cases, had also filled up and become overcrowded, often requiring gravedig-gers to use a crowbar to detect positions and condi-tions of coffins. For example at the burial ground of All Saints, consecrated in 1791 at Above Eign (later Whitecross Road), nominal space for 1,133 graves had been required to accommodate 2,623 burials, in some cases with resultant ground cover of only 2ft. By the middle of the 19th century it appeared that two thirds of the inhabitants of the city were totally unprovided with a decent and proper (and hygienic) burial ground for their dead. The Hereford Cemetery Company's proposals for a six acre site in the parish of St. Nicholas at Broomy Hill were firmly opposed by the bishop, apparently on the grounds that 'it would be injurious to the interests of the see and of the church to alienate the landed property of the see, and especially that adjacent to the city'.

The evidence gathered in, Rammell drew up his report. In his General Conclusions of 20 July 1853, he urged that the comfort and health of Hereford's inhabitants would be promoted, and their condition improved by a number of measures, namely:

An improved system of surface drainage, and the lowering of the water level by the removal of the mill-dams on the brooks in the immediate vicinity.
A complete system of refuse drainage.
An abundant supply of pure water.
Increased privy accommodation and the filling-up of all existing cesspools.
Improved ventilation and other sanitary arrangements to the dwellings of the poor.
Increased burial provision.

He accordingly recommended that the 1848 Public Health Act's provisions be applied and that the city council should become the local Board of Health.

The Hereford Improvement Act, 1854

To its credit the council acted swiftly on the Rammell Report and set about finding expert advice. They did not have to look far, for working as agent to Messrs. Dennis and Logan, contractors for the Newport, Abergavenny and Hereford Railway and the Junction Railway at Hereford was Mr. Timothy Curley, a professional civil engineer. On 3 November, 1853, he was appointed 'to make plans and estimates for the construction of a new cattle market, a cemetery, water works and drainage for the city'. That same month the council passed a resolution to apply for an enabling Act of Parliament and by 31 January 1854, Curley was putting the finishing touches to what was one of the most exhaustive and frank reports ever presented to the city.

Prefaced by a comment about 'most exaggerated and unfounded statements industriously circulated throughout the city, many from misapprehension, others from an habitual feeling of opposition to all sanitary improvement and a few from motives of a more selfish character', he produced a budget estimate of £43,225 'at an average return of more than £5% per annum on the whole of the works'. He noted that 'during one of my visits, I witnessed such scenes of filth and uncleanliness in this city, as I did not before believe could exist in a civilised community ... [and] ... the back streets and courts are in a most filthy state, the floors of several privies being inundated by the semi-fluid contents of the cesspools; in some cases they are too filthy to be entered'.

He pulled no punches and was particularly scathing about conditions near *The Hereford Times* printing offices, a large school and many superior private houses in Maylords Lane all close upon 'the pestiferous sources of zymotic [infectious] disease that were to be found in a stagnant pool behind the White Lion, the property of Hereford Town Council'!

Timothy Curley

His recommendations formed the main basis for the enabling Bill laid before Parliament and, despite further controversy, not least about the £1,862 promotion expenses, the Hereford Improvement Act of 1854 received royal assent on 2 June that year. Following upon the Municipal Corporations Act, of 1835, it gave very considerable powers to the reformed city council, including those which had been exercised for 80 years under authority of the Lamp Act.

The 1835 Act had brought about a change to the former system of self-perpetuating, exclusive and non-accountable appointment to the city council. Members of the resulting elected council were not too comfortable about continuing to work alongside the unelected 'top men and leading citizens in public positions' who comprised the 57 commissioners created under the 1774 Act—especially after they had declined to hand over their functions, as the new law of 1835 would have permitted. Some tension between the two bodies was inevitable and no further improvements of any substance were achieved by either until the commissioners were finally forced by the 1854 Act to hand over all their affairs to the council.

Sanitary Revolution

The scope of the new Act's duties showed through in the titles of the six standing committees appointed to supervise the general business of the city. Formed in 1859, these were the Waterworks, the Markets, the Paving and Streets, the Police and Courts, the Gaol and Fire and the Watch, Finance and Sanitary Committees, their activities subject to council control at quarterly meetings. Meanwhile, on 3 May, 1855, the council's seal was placed on an agreement that Mr. Curley should undertake his proposed sewerage works.

The sewers were to be laid at such levels as to drain every house and be capable of extension to serve further development. All street drains would be accommodated and the sewers inclined so that they were self cleansing, with any curves constructed at the greatest possible radius. The principal sewers would be egg-shaped with the small end downwards (producing faster flows during dry weather than round pipes laid at the same gradient), and constructed of radiated bricks in cement mortar. The outfall was to be removed as far as practicable from the town, and accessible 'manure tanks' would be placed in such a position as not to be a nuisance. Curley planned three different sections, made up of a 'southern group' discharging into the Wye opposite Hinton Cottage, a 'middle group' which would discharge into the river at Quay-lane, and a 'northern group' comprising the drainage of the principal part of the city. Sewerage from this section would pass to a field behind Tupsley Cottage, where the only manure settlement tanks were planned, whence the effluent would flow alongside the mill stream to the bridge near the Whalebone Inn into the River Wye. It was promised that after leaving the tanks, and following further precipita-

tion with lime, the sewerage water would be 'as clear and free from any disagreeable smell as the mill stream alongside' (which probably was not saying much). The total length indicated on the Parliamentary plans was 12.75 miles, estimated to cost £14,021 plus £2,933 for the tanks, but with an initial phase of only 8 miles.

In June 1855 a contract was let with a Mr. Moxon for the drainage and sewerage work, and instead of the sewage entering cesspits, ditches and open pools within the city, pipes discharged large volumes of partially settled or wholly untreated effluent straight into the River Wye. More than 100 years would pass before, in the 1970s, all discharges of untreated, albeit diluted, sewage were finally stopped and the overflow pipes sealed.

Such river pollution was rapidly becoming a national problem; in the hot summer of 1858, during the 'Great Stink of London', the stench from the Thames outside the House forced Parliament to rise and quickly disperse, leading the government to press ahead with Sir Joseph Bazalgette's vast scheme of intercepting sewers, pumping stations and holding tanks. During the next 30 years many miles of sewers were built in towns and cities throughout Britain, and by 1900 the number of deaths from cholera and typhoid had decreased 500-fold.

In 1876 the Rivers Pollution Act was placed on the Statute Book and in Hereford 81 acres of land at Tupsley were bought at a cost of £15,652 with the idea that sewage gravitating to a site at Eign Mill could be pumped there for treatment before being discharged into the Wye. After the land had been purchased it was concluded, rather late, that the cost of pumping large volumes over Eign Hill was far too high and the scheme had to be abandoned. At the time the new acquisition was branded as wasteful and it was only many years later that the city benefitted from this investment at Corporation Farm, providing as it did for many local authority and private sector homes.

The sewage treatment and disposal topic continued, and from 1881 was to be a leading preoccupation of John Parker, the new city surveyor, who remained in office until after the First World War. He prepared designs for treatment works for a site at Eign near Park Street and, in November 1885, work commenced on a steam-driven pumping plant, five precipitating tanks, 100 sq. ft. night flow storage tanks, and 6.5 acres of filter beds. Sewage sludge was compacted in two filter presses, and afterwards tipped on the site. Partly due to a change in the main contractors, the works were only finally commissioned in May, 1890.

In 1897 a refuse destructor was erected at the sewage works at a cost of £800. Capable of burning 5,000 tons of refuse per annum it produced a saving in an annual coal bill of at least £250, relieved refuse tips of 8 tons of refuse per day and produced valuable clinker for road foundations and other works.

Further expansion of the city and many new sewers greatly added to the load to be treated at the works but it was not until 1924, when the population had increased to over 23,500, that any alterations or additions were carried out. Electrically driven pumping plant was introduced and grit removal and screening facilities were added to the system. After the Second World War it was thought necessary to design works to cater for a population of 50,000, as well as for an increasing volume of industrial effluent, plus an enormous 2.3 million gallons per day of ground water which was entering at the joints of defective and ageing sewers (a longstanding problem—a daily infiltration of 1.5 million gallons had been recorded as long ago as 1890). After a public inquiry the original proposals were modified, not least by the reduction in the number of biological filters from 23 to 14, and the £600,000 scheme was completed in 1952.

For the next 10 years various expedients had to be adopted to accommodate increasing loads and in the early 1960s a large diameter northern sewer was provided to relieve the existing sewerage system, to provide for future development and also to provide a temporary storm water overflow to the Wye via the Eign Brook. By this time it was evident that a further expansion of the works was necessary, for whilst the resident population had increased to over 40,000, the city also attracted half as many again during working, business and leisure hours.

In 1963 the city council commissioned consultants to submit proposals for further extensions to the works. A site at Rotherwas was finally selected, flood levels there being significantly lower that those at Eign and ground conditions favourable for the planned heavy structures. Existing plant at the Eign works would be modified to treat one third of the proposed dry weather sewage flow and all storm flows, the rest being piped to Rotherwas. The new works, costing some £6.1 million, was formally inaugurated on 14 September, 1978.

In 1978 internal reorganisation of the Welsh Water Authority, based on what was termed the 'hydrological cycle', led to Hereford becoming the headquarters of one of seven new multipurpose divisions based on river catchments. Subsequently the 1989 Water Act led to the creation of a privatised water industry, the resulting Dwr Cymru Welsh Water becoming a part of the Hyder Group. The sewerage responsibilities within the city were shared between the company and the city council whilst the sewage treatment works at Eign and Rotherwas were placed under the direct control of the new company. By early 2000, Hyder were reportedly in danger of collapse, with debts of £1.9 billion.

Meanwhile, the National Rivers Authority took over water resources, pollution prevention and control, recreation and conservation until, in 1996, all statutory powers, duties and functions were transferred to the government's Environment Agency.

A Good Water Supply
Hereford has never been short of water for its needs; the problems have been those of distribution and control, abuse (leading to pollution and disease), and wastage. As long ago as January, 1695, the city council resolved 'that this House thinks that water works, as pipes, engines, cisterns, etc., may be erected or set up for conducting, conveying, carrying, or bringing up of the Wye water to the inhabitants of the said city, for the

common good and benefit of the same'. Other than fetching it for themselves, however, the only way inhabitants would receive the soft river water for their domestic needs for the next 150 years was by buying it by the bucketfull from water-sellers. It would not always have been crystal clear, often carrying flood sediments. Added to this, during the summer months the river, generally flowing at about 170 million gallons per day, suffered from heavy algal infestations.

By October 1856, the Hereford Improvement Act had conferred the necessary powers for the council to instruct Timothy Curley to proceed with his proposals for waterworks, mains and services. These consisted of an intake at Broomy Hill, about one mile upstream from the Wye Bridge, which led to a pump well and '20-horses' steam engine driven pump' which lifted the raw water to a 9 million gallons reservoir standing 95ft. above the adjacent summer level of the river, so providing a constant supply sufficient for 25 days of use at the rate of 30 gallons per person per day. In cases of fire, the drop allowed a strong jet of water even for the highest buildings. After standing in a reservoir of 24ft. depth it was expected that all 'animalculae' would be destroyed and any earthy matter held in suspension would be deposited at the bottom. The water would also pass through slow-sand filters before entering the mains and reaching consumers. There were to be 130 hydrants or fire-plugs positioned throughout the city, and in the summer fire hoses could also be used to water the streets and wash public buildings, 'considerably promoting the health and comfort of the inhabitants'. His estimated construction cost amounted to £15,271 and a nett annual income of over £1,000 could 'be safely calculated upon', to be produced through a charge of 2½d per week from each house to be served. Another £100 per annum could come from brewhouses, malt-houses, cow houses and stables, and at least £200 per annum from the newly arrived railway companies who required water for their steam locomotives.

New suburbs, principally in the Whitecross, Aylestone Hill and Hampton Park districts, quickly brought the need for a second pump. This was also useful in cases of breakdown and an identical beam pumping engine and well were installed in 1862.

By 1880, it had become necessary to consider other additions to improve supplies and pressures to higher parts of the city and these included a 34m. tall water tower at Broomy Hill. Completed in 1886, it housed pumps to raise water into its high 45,000 gallons (200,000 litres) storage tanks. At the start of the 21st century this landmark tower is a listed building that has a new use as a mounting for security cameras and an aerial carrier in the chain of Dwr Cymru - Welsh Water's extensive radio system.

At the end of the 19th century the two pumping engines were wearing out, and in 1895 Messrs Worth McKenzie of Stockton-on-Tees were appointed to install a highly versatile 'Inverted triple-expansion double-acting condensing engine' in a new bay of the waterworks (then in the forefront of technology, it now survives as the only working engine of its type at the Waterworks Museum). Capable of pumping at the rate of 1 million gallons every 12 hours, this became the main source of Hereford's water supply until 1914, when it was superseded by electric pumps. But eventually storage capacity at Broomy Hill became no longer adequate, and for continuity of supply it frequently became necessary to depend on pumping. Without added high-level storage reservoirs this was an unsafe

A familiar Hereford landmark—the tower of the Broomy Hill waterworks

expedient for coping with the ever increasing demand, for the distribution pumps became incapable of meeting requirements and booster installations were necessary to meet water demands in higher outlying districts. Even this system had no safeguard against power failures and it could not provide flexibility for meeting peak demands. Only high-level service reservoirs would provide the real answer and in 1906 the Westfields neighbourhood of the city became the first to benefit in this way. A constant supply was provided by the council from a 20,250 gallons service reservoir at Roman Road, Bobblestock, to replace temporary tanks in Highmore and Westfield Streets. By the 1960s direct pumping had been taken to the limit, and the only possible solution was to build very much larger high level storage reservoirs to serve the entire distribution system.

The Herefordshire Water Board came into being in 1960, covering a much greater area of supply than just the city, and as an interim measure carried out an augmentation scheme. Satisfying needs for the next two to three years, this provided another one million gallons of water per day. In the meantime, a comprehensive scheme had been prepared for new waterworks, trunk mains and service reservoirs to the north and south of Hereford to serve both the city and surrounding rural areas. After being put in hand by the board the work was continued from 1974 by the Welsh National Water Development Authority and completed in 1977. After filtration the water flowed to an underground 3 million gallons treated-water storage reservoir close to the Breinton Road works entrance, ready for distribution to the Hereford ring main. A high-lift pumping station delivered water to the 3 million gallons capacity reservoir at Ridge Hill south of the city. Here additional pumps moved water to a higher reservoir at Aconbury Hill, whence it could gravitate in the Ross-on-Wye direction. Another large main ran northwards to a 3 million gallons reservoir at Upper Lyde. This was later to be doubled in capacity, supplying consumers to the east of the county, including Withington and the Ledbury area, whilst water was also pumped

onwards to a reservoir at Dinmore Hill to serve Leominster. The two large reservoirs stood high over Hereford and the surrounding area to serve both domestic and commercial consumers. A small number of major water users, such as Davies Brook (until they moved to Moreton on Lugg), Sun Valley and the market and associated lorrywash, continue to rely principally on their own artesian wells or boreholes. Such wells also provide watering for the turf at Hereford Racecourse and the adjacent golf course greens, to the envy of gardeners who from time to time suffer hosepipe and sprinkler bans.

Much of the supply network in Hereford had become old, and as minerals built up in the many cast iron pipes, corrosion lowered water quality, produced leaking and reduced pressures and flows. Modernisation and refurbishment operations were intensified and by the late 1990s underground pipework in a high proportion of streets in the city had been replaced to some degree. Much costly digging and subsequent reinstatement has been involved, but in some cases it was possible to employ the 'bursting' method. This uses either compressed air or hydraulic methods to burst the old pipe and then pull new blue polyethylene pipe into the space that is left. Traffic disruption is greatly reduced—although not as much as by the third, 'relining', method which scours fairly sound pipes of corrosion material and inserts a very strong resin lining.

Burial Grounds

Just under three years after the delivery of Thomas Rammell's report, the town clerk received a letter from the General Board of Health in London, enquiring politely what the council intended to do about their inherited problem of overcrowded churchyards. His reply was that they proposed to carry out the stipulations of the Act of 1854 as soon as was possible. The Mayor promptly organised a public meeting, where one suggestion was that the Anglican parishes should be responsible for acquiring land for their own burial grounds, as and when they needed it. Finally a proposal by Dr. Bull, that the council should assume its statutory responsibilities and buy the land for the benefit of all citizens, won the day.

The Church of England had owned a great amount of land in and around the city since its earliest days and soon afterwards the new bishop of Hereford made an offer to donate 8 acres of sloping meadowland off Breinton Road. There would be no cost, on condition that use was confined to the Anglican parishes of the city. The council did not approve, and responded with an offer to buy the land for £1,200 without such a restriction. Not everyone understood why that amount of public money should be 'wasted' when the land could otherwise be obtained at no expense; excluded 'dissenters', on the other hand, naturally took a different view. In the event procedural difficulties prevented purchase. In 1858 Bishop Hampden conveyed a first acre of land at the site to the vicar and parishioners of All Saints, to be followed by similar plots for the parishes of St. Nicholas, St. Peter, St. Owen and St. John Baptist. Forming a United Parish Burial Board that year, all combined to lay out the ground with roads, paths and walls and mark out grave positions. A chapel that could hold some 40 people, with its spire, cost £470, and £150 was spent on a two-bedroomed lodge alongside Australia Gardens Lane (afterwards Westfaling Street). The total cost of £1,050 was divided among the five parishes and the charges liquidated through their rates. Bishop Hampden consecrated the ground on 28 May 1863, after all previous church burial grounds had been closed. By the end of the 1990s, only those of St. Peter's in Commercial Road and St. Nicholas' in Victoria Street survived and could be visited — All Saints' in Whitecross Road, St. John's in Belmont Road and St. Owen's in Bath Street had been 'redeveloped' for new buildings or roadworks.

In 1903 a further 2 acres and 20 perches was distributed by the Ecclesiastical Commissioners among the five parishes, shared by the parish of Holy Trinity, which also had legal use of the burial grounds.

The case for a public cemetery for citizens of all shades of belief and opinion was still being made, partly as a result of special representations from the parish of Holmer Within, and in 1908 the city council bought additional land from the Church, which was then laid out and drained, with special provision for Roman Catholic and other denominations. A mortuary chapel was built, special arrangements were made for joint working with the grounds of the United Joint Burial Board and the City Cemetery was opened for interments on 1 September, 1909. During the early 1920s the council took over responsibility for the adjoining Parochial Burial Grounds and subsequently extended the cemetery westwards along Westfaling Street. In 1956 a crematorium was opened on the site.

Environmental Health
When Thomas Rammell set out his six proposals with the aim that 'the comfort and health of the inhabitants would be promoted, and their condition improved', he had no inkling of what would develop from them. His recommended improvements in water supply, sewerage and drainage, housing conditions and burial arrangements certainly represented a great step forward, and out of them came a gradual but distinct quickening of interest in public hygiene.

During the 27 years which followed the passing of the Public Health Act of 1848, almost 30 national sanitary measures were enacted and this led to much confusion. In 1866 all towns were obliged by the Sanitary Act to appoint sanitary inspectors and after 1872, public health and the poor law were placed in the hands of a Local Government Board. 'Sanitary Areas' were defined throughout the country, each having to appoint a Medical Officer of Health. In 1874 Disraeli became Prime Minister and in the following year another Public Health Act finally consolidated all previous legislation. It is this statute which has formed the main basis of all subsequent health measures, covering a wide range of activities, as diverse as street lighting, lodging houses, water supply, drainage and disposal of sewage, provision of pure food, public parks, new housing and public toilets.

For its part, Hereford City Council had formed a Sanitary Committee in November, 1873, and had appointed Dr. Vavasour Sandford at £125 per annum as its part-time Medical Officer of Health, in addition to an Inspector of Nuisances. Mr. H.C. Moore followed Dr. Sandford in 1889 and in 1908 Dr. J.W. Miller was appointed as the first full-time Medical Officer of Health, Medical Superintendent of the City Isolation Hospitals and Medical Officer of the Education Authority. By 1910 he was able to report 'that the death rate is the lowest ever recorded in the city'. From 27 per thousand of the population just 60 years before, the ratio had fallen by almost 50% to one of under 15, thanks to determined sanitary measures, greater public hygiene, a measure of improvement in housing conditions for the less well-off, and significant advances in medical science.

The Sanitary and Foods and Drug Inspector, Mr. Protheroe, was described as 'the eyes and ears and nose' of the Medical Officer of Health and it was his duty to discover and report the nuisances of the city. There was no doubt about his being a full-time job. He had to examine the drainage, water closets and privies, inspect both inside and outside of dwelling houses to check for smoky chimneys, defective windows, dilapidated pantries, dangerous cellar windows, ill-paved back yards and general adequacy and fitness for human habitation. Working in partnership with Dr. Miller, he also needed to be sure that all food and drink sold in the city was fit and safe to consume.

Sixty years later, and 100 years after the passing of the Public Health Act of 1875, Mr. Attfield, the then Chief Environmental Health Officer, had been reinforced by a staff of 22 officers to share in a much broader task of overseeing the health, safety and welfare of the citizens of Hereford. By his time the worst of the unfit and sub-standard housing in the city had been eradicated, but even in this field much work remained to be done. Too many of the 8,416 properties in the private sector were in an unsatisfactory state of repair, lacked basic amenities, were in multiple occupation or grossly overcrowded. For example in the 19th-century Moorfields neighbourhood,

12 dwellings still lacked sanitary accommodation, another 84 a suitable bath, 86 a proper hot and cold water system and 91 an inside water closet. In particular cases like this, General Improvement Areas were declared. These had the purpose of creating a partnership between owners and the local authority, which not only worked to modernise the houses but also provide co-ordinated improvements to roads, car parking arrangements, open spaces and other features of the wider environment.

In the realm of environmental health there was a greater duty than ever to look out for and eliminate 'nuisances' and hazards. By 1975 there had been a substantial reduction in infectious disease in the city, measles remaining as the most common at 202 out of 224 notifications. These still required investigation, in collaboration with the Area Health Authority and the Public Health Laboratory Service, and in appropriate cases a disinfection service was provided by the department.

An eye was kept on water supply standards, sewage treatment, refuse collection and disposal and other health related services and a monitoring, inspection and disposal service was operated to keep down rodent and insect infestations. A third of the staff of the department was occupied in meat inspection at the abbatoir and at the Sun Valley poultry processing plant. During 1975, 132,879 animals and over 15 million birds were slaughtered for human consumption and inspectors had to guarantee them to be free from disease, that hygiene standards were observed and that all animals and birds were slaughtered humanely. It all seemed a far cry from the days, just over 120 years before, when the inquiry inspector had to visit city centre slaughterhouses which were in 'a filthy and unwholesome state'. It was then not unknown for beasts to be drawn by rope through the streets from fasting pens to the butcher's shop and slaughtered there, sometimes at the front door in full view of everyone. Earlier practices and sights in Butchers' Row were said to be even more horrifying and hazardous to public health. During the reign of Elizabeth I, it was found necessary to order that all offal and waste from the slaughtering of animals be 'carried away in the night and taken to Wye Bridge, there to be cast in at the place accustomed, between eight and nine o'clock in winter, and nine and ten in summer'.

Nor could easy comparison be drawn with former working conditions. The year 1975 saw the introduction of the Health and Safety at Work Act of 1974, which imposed heavy responsibilities on both employers and employees to observe stringent work practices and demanding safety measures. In 1853, assistants at Brunsdon and Gurney in High Town, Webb and Bosley in High Street and many of the other shops used to work long hours in poor conditions without any legal protection.

Although much had been achieved in the removal of waterborne forms of pollution since 1850, little was done about harmful air and noise levels. There were no agreed standards for clean air until well into the 20th century, although regular monitoring of sulphur dioxide and carbon particle levels, both regarded as representative indications of atmospheric pollution levels, was being carried out at selected sites. The blight of noise pollution had increased generally over the years and 'good neighbour' approaches were attempted to minimise rowdy domestic activities and disputes.

Healthcare

Before 1800 medical practice was greatly hampered by a lack of knowledge about the causes of disease, with treatments depending on long established theories and practices, some not too removed from the ministrations of witch-doctors. There was no help from any form of equipment, and conditions requiring surgery usually led to patients dying; either due to professional ignorance, or from infection caused by a complete lack of hygiene, or from surgical shock as there were no anaesthetics—apart from alcohol or opium. Complicated operations were not possible and surgery was usually confined to amputations, the removal of kidney and bladder stones and a few minor procedures. Consequently

the few hospitals of the time were regarded as places of last resort.

In the belief that many ailments were produced by an excessive volume of blood in the system, the commonest form of medical intervention for centuries had been by blood-letting. This was carried out in various ways, including 'cupping' which drew blood to the surface of the skin before removal, and by the employment of leeches. Generally doctors had little influence over the course of any illness or disease and much usually remained in the hands of nature. Traditionally, practitioners of medicine had comprised physicians (who were able to practise after licencing by the Royal College of Physicians, formed in 1518, and who might be compared with later consultants); surgeons (who were part of the Company of Barber Surgeons until 1745, when they formed the Company of Surgeons, becoming the Royal College of Surgeons in 1800): and apothecaries—the poor man's doctors—who charged the least and by the mid-18th century dispensed medicines, provided medical advice and practised surgery.

By the start of the 19th century, the divisions between the three professions were changing as the pace of medical reform quickened following the impact of the industrial revolution, a wider discussion of public health and hygiene and the advances in surgery as a result of wars. A new kind of doctor emerged, in some respects a successor of the apothecaries but far better trained and motivated, and the closest equivalent of the later general practitioner. From 1858 all doctors were expected to be qualified in medicine, subject to professional rules and have their names placed on a Register.

For a place of its size, Victorian Hereford came to be well served by the profession, one of its more prominent members being Dr. Henry Graves Bull. He quickly became highly regarded as a doctor not only among his paying patients, but also by poorer people who attended for free consultations at his home each Saturday morning. He threw himself into local philanthropic activities, was involved in pursuit of public health and hygiene improvements in the city, volunteered his services at the Hereford Dispensary and in 1864 became physician to the Infirmary. As if this was not enough, he made a particular name for himself in the subjects of fungi and local cider apple lore, his daughter Edith, joining him as a major contributor to the authoritative volumes of *The Herefordshire Pomona*, produced in 1884. At the time of his death, a year later, he was one of some 15 physicians or surgeons (and the same number of chemists and druggists) listed in the city.

Many doctors also took part-time appointments as Poor Law Union medical officers in the city and the Burghill, Fownhope and Dewchurch Districts. Here their chief duty was to attend paupers and vagrants, including patients at the city's workhouse (later part of the County Hospital buildings). They were expected to provide medicines when necessary and to lead in attempts at preventive medicine, all under the watchful and sometimes heavy control of the relieving officer whose duty it was to administer the poor law provisions.

A dispensary was first established in 1835, during the early days of the Reverend John Venn's philanthropic ministry, from St. Peter's church, and was supported by annual subscriptions, donations and voluntary effort. Its purpose was to provide free advice, relief and medicine to 'deserving' sick patients of city and country parishes who were not ill enough to require hospital care. At first its work was undertaken at doctors' houses, and afterwards at a house in Commercial Street. In 1881 accumulated legacies enabled a stone building to be erected in Union Street. Local family doctors, initially including Drs. Bull, Hanbury and Morris, acted as honorary physicians or surgeons, making home visits when necessary. Not long after this new and spacious dispensary opened, a provident branch was set up to enable the thrifty poor to help themselves, of which membership stood at 536 in 1912. From an initial attendance of 178 patients in 1835, the annual total by then had reached over 3,000. Still treating 1,500 patients a year, it closed when the NHS came into being. With its ornamental

stonework, the dispensary building remains standing into the 21st century as a warehouse for Chadds which is on the opposite side of the street.

By the beginning of the 20th century there was a considerable improvement in the essentials of public health in Hereford. Much purer, and softer, water was being pumped from the river instead of from polluted wells, there was proper sanitation and sewage disposal and a spacious new cemetery, whilst regular livestock sales no longer took place on city centre streets. Pollution produced by horses was also reducing, whilst exhaust fumes from motor vehicles had not yet become a problem. Also there had been some improvement in housing conditions as the council commenced a pre-war programme to replace some of the worst slum property. On the scientific front, the chief 'killer' infectious diseases—

The old Dispensary building in Union Street before restoration in 2001

smallpox, typhus, typhoid, cholera and diphtheria—were being largely overcome: the crude mortality rate of the population had halved during little more than half a century. And yet the health of many people was far from robust, when compared with later standards. This showed in many ways, as when a large percentage of volunteers for military service in the Boer War had to be rejected as unfit. In 1911 David Lloyd-George, in the face of much adverse pressure, brought in a measure aimed at further raising standards of health by providing for a widely available medical service. Lloyd-George himself felt that the measure was an 'ambulance wagon', as he described it in *The Times*, but in some respects it would herald the Welfare State which would be introduced by a minister of a different colour some 37 years later.

'Panel' doctors

The 1911 National Insurance Act aimed to 'provide for insurance against loss of health and for the prevention and cure of sickness', and it was to apply compulsorily to all workers of between 16 and 70 years of age earning up to £160 a year (increased to £420 by 1942). A weekly contribution of 4d. was augmented by 3d. from the employer and 2d. from the state, arousing a much trumpeted political boast of 'Ninepence for Fourpence'. Limited sickness, disablement benefits and approved medical treatment from a general practitioner were provided for the contributor, who was able to choose who he wanted from a 'panel' of doctors. However, no hospital costs were met, other than at tuberculosis sanatoria, and wives and children were not normally covered, the sole family provision being limited to a not overgenerous maternity grant of 30s.

Until 1948 little could be done for many, especially the unemployed and the majority of women and children. They had to choose between running up a bill or further stinting on already inadequate food. The cost for even a few calls or bottles of medicine could easily exceed any earnings, and no amount of kindly 'doctoring' of accounts could help those in the greatest poverty.

Inevitably some people died just because they could not afford to pay, while others only called the doctor for emergencies. Many sufferers were taken in by quack remedies, or looked to their own tried and trusted home cures. It was very common for damp and badly ventilated homes to be the cause of a variety of 'chesty' conditions every winter and in many households there was a jar of goose-grease or hen-fat to apply liberally to chest and back, in some homes as a 'brown paper vest' with the paper left on until it rotted—the resulting aroma often causing the young patient to be sick, so bringing up the offending phlegm! Smelling much nicer were the great expanses of 'Thermogene' wadding which were pinned to countless small vests, back and front, at the first sign of a cough. For kidney irregularities, great trust was placed in pearl barley, spoons of cod liver oil were a well-hated tonic, and syrup of figs, brimstone and treacle, senna pods or, in extreme cases, ipecacuanha or soap suppositories, were supposed to work all kinds of wonders.

District Nurses, financed by a subscription to the District Nursing Association, dealt with many medical needs, including dressing wounds and, as there were few hospital births, often acted as midwives. The doctor was usually only involved in difficult cases, sometimes when surgery was needed. He would carry out a range of minor operations, either at the surgery at his house or in the homes of patients. It was not unknown for small children to be parted from their tonsils on a kitchen table, although it was more usual, and certainly safer, to carry out the operation at a hospital. For many years, countless youngsters, the luckier ones bribed with promises of soothing ice-cream, lined up to have the troublesome organ snipped—until it was realised that they were often unnecessarily losing an important part of their immune system, and so the procedure was dropped. Measles, chicken pox and whooping cough cases were usually isolated at home, but those with dreaded infectious diseases such as diphtheria and scarlet fever were removed to the Tupsley isolation hospital, and afterwards an enclosed yellowy-brown vehicle would be sent by the authorities to remove bedding and other articles for fumigation and disinfecting.

Other ailments, including many associated with sight, hearing and mental illness, would be beyond the scope and expertise of the general practitioner and he (and it was usually 'he' until well towards the end of the 20th century) gradually became able to diagnose and refer such cases to a new and growing breed of specialist hospital physicians, surgeons, nurses and other carers.

Hospitals

The first hospitals to appear in Hereford were founded by charitable bodies or individuals during the Middle Ages and were closer to being homes for 'deserving' old and frail people rather than places for medical care and treatment. But from the 18th and early 19th centuries attention turned to the foundation of hospitals for tending and administering to the sick, and no fewer than 154 new hospitals and dispensaries were established in Britain between 1700 and 1825. Voluntary effort towards establishing a hospital in Hereford was led by the Rev. Dr. Thomas Talbot, Rector of Ullingswick. At his third attempt, the publication of a ponderous 'Address to the Nobility, Gentry and Clergy of the County of Hereford', (said to have been partly 'ghosted' by a supportive Dr. Samuel Johnson), and a personal opening donation of £500, he finally prevailed. With 80 subscriptions and legacies of amounts ranging up to £5,000 and the gift from the Earl of Oxford of a fine Wye-side site (which he dedicated to 'the sick, lame and diseased persons by whatsoever name or names called or known') it was possible to start.

The enterprise began in a modest way when a temporary infirmary was opened for patients in March, 1776 at a house at No. 42 Eign Street. This was used rather in the nature of a cottage hospital for over seven years, dealing with fractures, wounds and simple needs. (Renumbered as 162 Eign Street, and coincidentally opposite the headquarters of the current Herefordshire Health Authority at Victoria House, this not unhistoric scrap of Hereford's health history continued to minister to special human needs more than two hundred years later, in the role of an 'outpatient' Chop Suey Bar!).

Work on the General Infirmary started in 1781 and by the time the first patients were admitted in August 1783, hospitals had already been established at Shrewsbury, Gloucester, Worcester and Bristol. Providing 55 beds in 1785, the Infirmary was to be the most westerly institution for the care and treatment of patients for another quarter of a century. (There would be no hospital in Wales until 1807, when one was built at Denbigh in the north, and in the south a further ten years would pass before Swansea Infirmary was founded.) No distinction was drawn in the wards between medical and surgical cases, or even highly infectious diseases. Despite this, the early honorary medical staff, consisting of two visiting surgeons and two physicians, with the resident house-apothecary, matron and nurses, managed well enough.

The land donated by the Earl of Oxford was sufficient to allow for expansion, though this was heavily dependent on responses to fund-raising and appeals for donations and legacies. The first Hospital Sunday Collection in 1861 produced £681 and by 1868 it was possible to spend a large sum on improvements to internal arrangements, lighting, ventilation and drainage. A donation of £1,000 by Mr. Francis Hawkins provided a boost to funds in 1882, and thanks to the Hutchinson family the Victoria Ward for children was opened in 1887 as a memorial of the queen's jubilee year, raising the number of hospital beds to almost 100. The site of the former Castle Mill was added by the city council in 1865 in order to accommodate a lodge and additional garden landscaping.

After much discussion regarding the distinction between the title 'infirmary' and many so-called 'hospitals' (which were really almshouses), the arguments for change prevailed and from 1900 it became known as the Herefordshire General Hospital. The First World War created a pressing need for the treatment of crippled veterans and in 1919 a Physiotherapy Department was opened. This was followed in 1927 by an open air orthopaedic unit for 20

The Infirmary when newly constructed on the banks of the Wye

patients, named the Hewat Pavilion, built with much support from Mrs. Hewat in memory of her husband and son, who had both been lost in the war. A new Ear, Nose and Throat Department functioned jointly with the Worcester Royal Infirmary and further expansions followed.

For a voluntary hospital the outlay created great financial worries and all kinds of money-raising activity, even a beauty contest, became essential. In 1926 a countywide contributory scheme was launched, calling for 1s. a head per month, and this rapidly attracted 15,000 contributors and an annual revenue income of £9,000, amounting to nearly one-third of the hospital's running cost. A further £3,000 a year was raised from treating private patients. Despite the nation-wide economic difficulties of the 1930s, the hospital was enlarged to 11 wards, capable of receiving 150 patients, together with an isolation block and facilities for a few private patients.

The Second World War brought many new demands and extra room was quickly required for 58 new folding beds in the wards as part of an emergency scheme to cater for 14,000 evacuees. Help with much of the extra work often came from medical staff at R.A.F and Army bases at Credenhill, Bradbury Lines, an ambulance train based for a time at Barrs Court station and evacuated London doctors. The introduction of sulphonamide drugs had already revolutionised treatment of wounds, whilst penicillin, the first antibiotic, arrived at the hospital in 1944, before the D-Day casualties arrived.

The hospital had also been involved in the establishment of the City Lunatic Asylum. This was erected as a result of public subscription in 1799 to cater for up to 36 patients 'of mixed classes, private and pauper'. Lying to the north-east of the main infirmary building, it was built of brick on a part of the land given by the Earl of Oxford. Leased out by the main governing body of the infirmary to a city surgeon as a 'private madhouse', it closed in 1853 when remaining patients were transferred to the joint 'lunatic asylum' at Abergavenny. With ever increasing demand there was soon overcrowding and in 1867 a committee of justices chose a site for a new asylum at Burghill. The Hereford County and City Lunatic Asylum was designed in Italianate style by William Griffiths, a Stafford architect. The red and yellow brick building, with its two almost obligatory Victorian towers, was commenced in 1868 and completed at a cost of £87,873 in 1872. Two further blocks were added in 1900, bringing the total accommodation to 11 wards. These contained approximately 300 beds for women and 250 for men, and in addition the asylum had a chapel, dining hall, bakehouse, kitchens, a wide range of domestic offices and other facilities. The asylum farm and gardens

The rear of the Infirmary in 1899

covered about 100 acres and provided work and therapy for many patients, whilst workshops and kitchens helped others to try their hands, and become skilled as cobblers or in baking bread. Women tended to work in the laundry. Despite all the distress and upset around them, many ex-patients of St. Mary's Hospital were nevertheless able to remember it as 'a place of safety and security; an asylum in the best sense of the word'.

The Herefordshire and South Wales Eye and Ear Institution was established in 1882 in a small Commercial Road house (on land partly in front of the subsequent Baptist Church) by Mr. F.W. Lindsay, a local surgeon. Supported by private subscription, its need was soon proved and calls for treatment and help quickly outgrew the accommodation. Funds were then raised for a purpose-built hospital in Eign Street to the design of Mr. E.H. Lingen Barker, a Hereford architect. The Victoria Eye and Ear Hospital opened in 1889, but rapidly became too small, so more land was bought and there were extensions, a new ward and an enlarged common room until, in 1923, the hospital was fully reorganised as the Victoria Eye Hospital and confined to eye treatment. During the years leading up to the Second World War it provided for 20 in-patients and,

including out-patients, treated an average of 4,500 people each year. From its foundation the hospital was a voluntary institution, supported entirely by contributions from individuals and businesses throughout the county and beyond. By 1948, it had gained a glowing reputation extending well beyond city and county boundaries, that year treating 5,525 out-patients and undertaking 150 operations with just one, part-time, surgeon.

Hereford Municipal Borough Infectious Diseases Hospital was erected at Gorsty Lane, Tupsley in 1893 with initial provision for 12 patients, expanding to 24 in 1898. In 1902 this was followed by an isolated smallpox hospital, built of corrugated metal in a field to the east of Hollywell Gutter Lane. Its 12 beds were rarely used, the final time being in 1929, and it eventually closed in a state of some neglect in 1948. Hereford Rural District Isolation Hospital was erected at Stretton Sugwas in 1904, initially for up to 12 patients but in 1933 it was extended to cater for 36 beds.

Holme Lacy Hospital was established in Holme Lacy House. Bought in 1919 by Mr. Noel Wills (of Wills Tobacco Company), his widow presented the house to Herefordshire County

The early Herefordshire and South Wales Eye and Ear Institution, 1883

medical scene in Hereford, is given by the author Catherine Cookson, a voluntary patient for six weeks, in her biography *Our Kate*).

Despite a world financial crisis, the General Hospital continued to expand during the Thirties. A pathology department was established under a salaried pathologist in 1934, the first member of the medical staff to be paid, and that year a blood transfusion service was started. After registration and grouping, the names of 100 volunteers were entered in a small black book in the department. Suitable donors were usually fetched by taxi when needed, taken to the anaesthetic room and the blood went straight to the theatre. As a reward they were allowed to 'peep in' to see the patient. Transfusions increased from 23 in the first year to 55 by 1939.

Finance was, as ever, the biggest problem and the growing demand for hospital services was compounded by anxiety about the needs of the sick at the Union Workhouse. This had become the responsibility of the council and renamed the Public Assistance Institute (P.A.I.) and in 1935 the authority voted to build a new hospital, to be called 'The Herefordshire County Council Hospital', soon shortened to 'The County Hospital'. The decision was far from unanimous, whilst the local trades council considered that 'an isolation hospital in the middle of the city was obnoxious', (seemingly having no qualms about the central abattoir and piggeries). The governors

Council. In 1933 a scheme was put forward for converting the building into a hospital for the treatment of ladies 'suffering from nervous or mental breakdown' and this went ahead in 1935 with provision for about 100 patients. (A vivid wartime account of life there, and of part of the

Tupsley Hospital in 1898

of the General Hospital and the local branch of the B.M.A. also objected, fearing encroachment on their preserves, and there were two years of wrangling until, in 1937, Queen Mary laid the foundation stone of the three storey '1930 block'. At an estimated cost of £68,835 (about £2.5 million at year 2000 values), there was to be provision for 115 beds, including 12 for TB patients, eight for complicated maternity cases, eight for children and three for venereal disease. There would be no operating theatre and no provision for acute cases—in deference to the roles of the General Hospital.

But before the new hospital was ready, war came and altered everything. The Emergency Medical Service (E.M.S.) set up by the government in early 1939 proposed 10 extra hutted wards for evacuees, each providing for 36 patients (the scheme as ever facing objections—in this case at the loss of market garden space bringing in over £200 a year). These 'Canadian' huts were intended to last for 10 years, but were still in use for patients 60 years later, even living on into the 21st century as part of a new 'state of the art' District General Hospital. The new '1930 block' opened in stages during 1941—and most is soon to be demolished to provide space for the new hospital access. The County Hospital ended the war fitted out for general medical and surgical work, and with a larger number of beds than the General, but for both the future was uncertain until the advent of the National Health Service Act in 1946.

Up to the start of the NHS, and in the 1950s, the senior doctors working at the hospitals were, for the most part, GPs in the city who also had special interests in surgery, medicine and ear, nose and throat treatment. They were gradually superceded by consultants trained in the various specialities and although the hospital facilities were poor, many set a very high standard and took a lead in improving services. As a result, Hereford was early in developing resuscitation facilities, an intensive therapy unit, isotope services and many other new treatments, together with modern teaching methods and in providing good accommodation for junior staff. Most importantly,

contact and co-operation between hospital doctors and GPs was of a very high order.

From 4 July 1948, the County, General, Victoria and all other remaining Hereford hospitals became the responsibility of the Ministry of Health and formed part of a comprehensive approach for the general improvement of mental and physical health in Herefordshire. To achieve this they were integrated with specialist services, family practitioners for medical, dental, ophthalmic and pharmaceutical functions, maternity and child welfare, ambulance and community health services.

National Health Service
The massive reform provided that all medical, optical and dental treatment would be available for everyone without charge, the costs being met from taxation. Doctors, most of whom initially opposed the changes, could continue to offer private treatment, but those who decided to enter the service became—as they had dreaded—salaried servants of the state. And instead of benefitting upon retirement from a traditional system of selling the goodwill of medical practices they would receive a state pension.

In 1948 a District General Hospital was proposed for Hereford by the new Birmingham Regional Hospital Board. Only the County Hospital had sufficient room for what was in mind and was selected for future provision of a modern establishment with 560 - 600 beds, to cost an estimated £1 million. There was no prospect of that amount becoming available for a long time and great efforts were required to rationalise the respective services at the two existing hospitals. The E.N.T. and fracture and orthopaedic departments were developed at the General Hospital, but it was to take another 20 years before the Casualty Department could be combined there, despite the risks taken during emergencies when the service was divided between two hospitals. The County Hospital became the centre for obstetrics and gynaecology, a nurses' home was built in 1954 and in 1956 two huts were converted into a paediatric department and the remaining six into medical, geriatric wards and staff dormitories. Modern twin operating theatres were promised 'far out along the corridor, where the long-promised District Hospital was to be'. This was generally welcomed but surgeons at the hospital could not at first contemplate using it because of the distance for patients coming from wards in the main hospital. Eventually agreement was reached and the deluxe theatre block was built in 1967 at a cost of £150,000—and then stood unused for a year until a further £60,000 had been spent on upgrading the adjacent 27 year-old hutted wards 9 and 10. With support from the Regional Hospital Board and generous donations a postgraduate medical centre was opened in 1968.

By 1970 over £500,000 had been provided by the Regional Board for building and improvement works in Herefordshire, but there was still no sign of the new hospital recommended in 1948. There was, however, much unseen, rather slow-moving, activity behind the scenes. Notwithstanding the considerable investment in the long selected County Hospital site—a new pathology block was added in 1974 and an acute psychiatric unit in the early 1980s—there was a new government directive for the Regional and Area Health Authorities to undertake studies to find out if there were better options. As the estimated project budget passed £20 million, one of the first alternatives to be examined was the building of an entirely new acute hospital at St. Mary's, Burghill, three miles from Hereford. Another was to consider a suitable 'green-field' site for development. Further studies examined the possibilities of enlarging the County Hospital site, possibly by attempting to add the adjacent Ravenhills property, the bus station and even allotment land on the other side of the railway line (which would be linked through a tunnel to Ledbury Road).

By 1973 the County Hospital contained about 385 beds, mainly for acute patients (generally meaning those capable of responding quickly to treatment) and from the 1950s approximately £800,000 had been spent on improvement and modernisation. At the General Hospital there were 156 beds, also for acute cases, with plans for it to become a major accident centre, orthopaedic unit, with added provision for ear, nose and throat and geriatric patients. At Tupsley, 25 of the 31 beds were allocated to geriatric patients, the remainder for TB and chest cases, but this hospital later closed and a satellite GP Surgery and Pharmacy was established on part of the site. The Victoria Eye Hospital continued to be fully used as a separate unit with 25 opthalmic beds.

In the meantime some patients from the 505 mental illness beds at St. Mary's were transferred to Holme Lacy whilst improvements were carried out. Afterwards all patients were transferred to Burghill and in April 1981, the NHS returned Holme Lacy to Herefordshire County Council; it is now a hotel managed by Warner Holidays.

The improvements to St. Mary's had also made room for pre-convalescent and terminal care services and this led to the closure of Stretton Sugwas Hospital, and eventually to its use as a private nursing home. By then, the days of Victorian long stay asylums were coming to an end with new approaches in psychiatry. This led to many mentally ill residents being resettled under less institutionalised conditions under the 'care in the community' policy that included group homes and hostels. The Stonebow Unit had already been built at the County Hospital, on the site of Stonebow Road car park, council houses and the Red and White bus garage, and provided the necessary number of acute psychiatric beds. In 1993 St. Mary's was closed, leaving only a small rearguard of patients at Acorns, a rehabilitation unit in the house of the former Medical Superintendent. Before the end of the 1990s the site was being developed for housing as St. Mary's Park. It was hoped that the two prominent towers of the original chapel and hall could be preserved as part of the layout, but they were found to be too unstable and had to be demolished. Some of the original hospital blocks were converted into 18 modern flats to integrate with an arrangement of 70 new houses and seven refurbished cottages.

By 1993, only three of the original eight hospitals in Hereford and the surrounding area remained, but in May, 1974 a new form of acute hospital had opened in Venns Lane.

Private Healthcare and the Nuffield Hospital

It was not long after the introduction of the National Health Service in 1948 for it to be appreciated that the cost was going to be far greater than had been budgetted. The suppressed extra demand from millions of people who previously had not been able afford attention, many of them women, children and the elderly, soon led to a need for savings and reductions in expenditure on services. By 1951 Aneurin Bevan had resigned over the introduction of charges for prescriptions and spectacles and within many parts of the service pressures had developed which could not adequately be managed. Waiting lists quickly formed.

The National Health Service was still the best and only source of attention for emergencies and seriously ill cases, for which waiting lists did not apply, but there could be long waits to see a specialist for non-emergency conditions, let alone obtain a bed. In Herefordshire, in April 1999, there were about 3,300 patients waiting for surgery, a small number of them for over 15 months.

An absence of prompt medical attention for hernias, hip/knee replacements, hysterectomies, and cataracts could inevitably produce prolonged pain and discomfort, inconvenience, loss of earnings and domestic upsets. For some needs, varicose vein removal for example, there was virtually no chance of ever receiving any attention from the NHS. All such treatments, and many others, fell readily into the realms of private healthcare, and soon became their 'bread and butter'. The Wye Valley Nuffield Hospital was built in 1974 with the help of funds raised by the local community through donations and subscriptions and provided 20 private bedrooms, a three bedded high dependency unit, two operating theatres and a wide range of medical resources. With a staff of over 80 (including the doctors and consultants also working in the NHS) it offered a comprehensive range of specialist services and high standards of care. The *en-suite* rooms, unrestricted visits, varied *à la carte* menus and choice wine lists created an atmosphere more akin to that of a 5 star hotel, but with advanced medical facilities! Most of its patients are those with 'acute' rather than on-going 'chronic' ailments. Payment is either through private medical insurance or corporate cover provided by employers but it is also possible to arrange advance fixed prices direct with the hospital. Terms can also be quoted for a range of outpatient services, not calling for the involvement of a general practitioner, including sports injury physiotherapy, pre-emptive health screening and many forms of complementary therapy.

But no private hospital or medical insurance healthcare package could begin to embrace the needs covered by the National Health Service. The duty to arrange and supervise the provision of all these was soon placed squarely with Herefordshire Health Authority.

Herefordshire Health Authority

After a bewildering range of policy and organisational changes brought about by 12 different governments and many more health ministers in the 50 years since the introduction of the National Health Service, responsibility for meeting the health needs of the people of the city and county from April 1996 fell to the new 'stand alone' Herefordshire Health Authority. Within boundaries to be shared with the subsequently created Herefordshire Council, its role was to assess the health care needs of the local population and develop integrated strategies for meeting them. This duty was to operate in partnership with general practitioners and involved close consultation with the hospitals and members of the public. In its first Health Improvement Programme the new authority focussed on some of the major health problems in Herefordshire, notably high levels of heart disease, strokes, diabetes and cancers. A study of special problems arising from mental illness extended to an assessment of increasing local misuse of drugs, especially heroin. County road accident levels compared unfavourably with numbers in other parts of Britain. The arguments in favour of improving dental health by fluoridation of public water supplies were once more pursued, guided by unfavourable comparisons of pain and dental decay suffered by Herefordshire children. Communicable disease still required great vigilance, especially in the maintenance of immunisation programmes among children, and so did matters of food safety and a widened range of sexually-transmitted diseases. Inequalities in health and higher levels of deprivation observed in the South Wye wards of the city compared with rural parts of the county are prompting the authority to give priority to approaches which will produce health improvement in Hinton, Belmont and St. Martins.

With the split between 'providers' and 'purchasers' of services before 1996, there came into being the Hereford Hospitals NHS Trust, Herefordshire Community Health NHS Trust and the Hereford and Worcester Ambulance NHS Trust. From its inception Hereford Hospitals NHS Trust provided healthcare for a community of approximately 200,000 residents of Herefordshire, a significant area of Powys and peripheral areas of Gwent/ Monmouthshire, Gloucestershire, Worcestershire and Shropshire. In some surgical specialities, particularly opthalmology, the catchment extended to 220,000 people. During a typical 12 months, in-patients amounted to 18,069 emergency, 5,651 non-emergency and 10,172 day cases and there were 122,125 out-patients and 38,396 accident and emergency cases.

Faced with a mounting demand for acute care, the Trust functioned from the three split sites at an annual budget of over £44 million. Despite all handicaps it was still able to enhance services, often through voluntary donations, bequests and appeals, with most people still hoping that one day there would be a modern new District General Hospital, all under one roof. There were few encouraging signs. Dr. Philip Brooks, the Director of Public Health and Planning for Herefordshire, in his 1990 Annual Report felt able to confirm that development of a new acute hospital had been agreed for the St. Mary's site at Burghill. Unfortunately this was not scheduled to start until 'the turn of the century', and as the years progressed unpromising government declarations on public sector health spending moved expectations still further onwards. It was only when a slight prospect arose of the use of the Private Finance Initiative (PFI) being considered for the building of hospitals that hopes began to revive.

District General Hospital

Hereford duly provided one of 13 PFI hospital projects authorised across the country by the government in a large scale testing of the model. Once more detailed planning was undertaken, this time with a chosen private consortium, and one of the first decisions was to return to the County Hospital site as the preferred location, even accepting that it was too small, difficult of access with local lack of car parking and that additional adjoining land would not be acquired. It required three further years of planning and negotiations before, in April 1999, Herefordshire Hospitals NHS Trust and Mercia Healthcare Limited announced that Herefordshire was to have a new £65 million 'state of the art' District General Hospital.

The private sector consortium comprised three partners: Alfred McAlpine Special Projects was responsible for construction, WS Atkins Healthcare undertook design and certain non-clinical services and Gardner Merchant acted as the support service company, undertaking functions such as house-keeping, catering, portering, managing car parks, linen and laundry. From a former capacity of 390 beds in the County and General hospitals the design of the new, smaller hospital would provide for a total of 250 beds, supported initially by a further 90 from refurbished hospital stock at the 'Canadian' huts.

There was much concern among GPs, consultants, other health workers and the general public that this would not be enough to meet demands.

Model of the new hospital

Local representations from Dr. Jonathan Sleath, a GP from Kingstone, Dr. Adrian Eyre, secretary of the Herefordshire Local Medical Committee and Dr. Eric Barton, consultant radiologist and chairman of the Hospital Medical Committee appeared in the letters columns of the *British Medical Journal*. Dr. Kevin Ilsley, of Bromyard, writing to *The Hereford Times* on behalf of the Hereford branch of the British Medical Association, asserted that the system was not working even with the larger numbers of beds still available in early 2000. He said that on several days during that winter GPs who had tried to admit emergency cases were told no beds were available. Patients had to wait for several hours for a vacancy or be cared for inappropriately at home. In a response through the columns of the newspapers, the Medical Director of the Trust, Dr. Frank McGinty, explained that 'in Hereford [we] are implementing a county-wide healthcare system, not just running a new hospital ... Our strategy embraces recent changes in technology and management, including better use of community facilities, improved links with social services and more home care within an NHS led by primary care. Consequently fewer beds are needed'. In support, the directors of public health with Herefordshire and Worcestershire Health Authorities, Drs. Mike Deakin and Brian McGloskey, said in a joint letter published in the *British Medical Journal* that critics had not acknowledged 'the real shift of emphasis towards primary and community care that had happened in recent years'. It was this shift 'that had caused health authorities to agree long-term health strategies based on increasing investment in services, not beds', they asserted.

Construction of the new main building started in September, 1999, with a target completion date of April, 2002. In place of the traditional long hospital wards of 20 or more beds, there are to be four-bedded rooms and a high proportion of single and double rooms, all equipped with *en-suite* shower/WC facilities. The modern wards were to be arranged to allow greatly improved flexibility for nursing and effective management and comfort of patients. The three existing operating theatres will be integrated with an additional four suites. There is to be space for a helicopter, a multi-denominational chapel and facilities for patients' relatives. Observation of district general hospitals serving other areas of high car dependency suggests that the proposals for 'up to 400 vehicles' will leave many staff, patients and visitors with the problem of finding parking space elsewhere, including neighbouring streets.

Artist's drawing of the approach to the new hospital

Many parts of the existing County Hospital are to be retained, including the pathology laboratories, the former P.A.I. buildings—which will be refurbished for rehabilitation and 'age care' services, most of the 'Canadian' huts—for a further 'few' years, the nurse training centre, hospital doctors' and nurses' residential accommodation, the John Ross Post-Graduate Medical Centre and the Charles Renton cancer unit. In due course both the General Hospital and the Victoria Eye Hospital sites will be decommissioned. A final phase saw the demolition of the '1930 block' in 2002.

From July, 1999, some 400 former non-clinical employees of the Trust transferred to contracts with the Mercia Healthcare Partnership, mostly with Gardner Merchant. Medical and Nursing services remained with the National Health Service and would be part of the establishment of Hereford Hospitals NHS Trust.

Under the Private Finance Initiative the hospital is paid for by private money and leased back to the Trust for 30 years. Allowing for income from the disposal of the General and Eye Hospital sites, the full development cost of the new hospital (including fees, financing and interest charges) are estimated at £85 million by the time it opens. The ultimate overall cost during the rental period is expected to reach an estimated £470 million.

From April, 1999 the Herefordshire Primary Care Group replaced the short-lived GP 'fund-holding' system (which ran alongside the Health Authority and NHS Trusts 'purchaser'/'provider' split) and was intended to give the medical profession a major role in deciding how primary care services should be provided. Covering all Herefordshire practices, its committee comprised six general practitioners, two community nurses, a Social Services and a Health Authority non-executive member, a lay representative and a

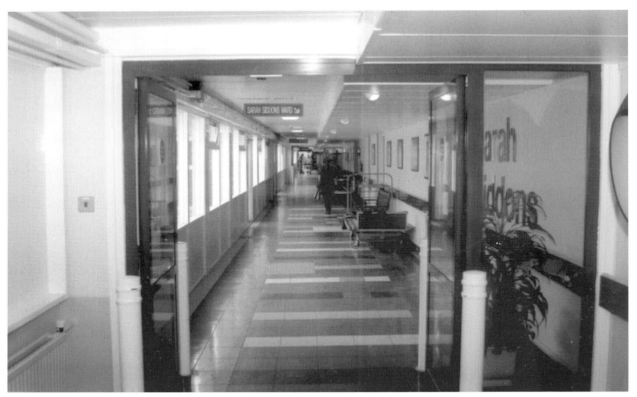

Erected in 1940 to last for 10 years, Sarah Siddons and Arkwright hutted wards are to receive a facelift and new names, Monnow and Leadon, in 2002 as part of the new hospital

Primary Care Group chief executive. The Group is now responsible for forming policy and buying all community services for its patients, as well as acute services from the hospitals. On 1 October, 2000, it became the Herefordshire Primary Care NHS Trust, the first to achieve this status in the West Midlands, when it merged with the Community Health NHS Trust, taking on its 1,000 members of staff. In addition to buying nearly all health care for Herefordshire's population, it thus also became responsible, as a 'provider', for the community hospitals, community nursing and a wide range of services including child care, mental health care and support to those with learning disabilities.

Chapter VI
Housing and Town Planning

Every year, from 1728 to 1753, the brothers Samuel and Nathaniel Buck travelled to different parts of England and Wales, gradually preparing a series of detailed panoramic views of the 'cities, seaports and capital towns'. Hereford was one of the earliest places they visited, and as they settled themselves with sketchboards at Aylestone Hill (not far from the much later Churchill Gardens), they faced a view of the city which was essentially as it might have looked to John Speede, the cartographer, more than a hundred years before, and to countless travellers during much of the Middle Ages.

Another visitor in the early 18th century was Daniel Defoe, who was researching for his guidebook, *A Tour through the Whole Island of Great Britain*, a skilled and detailed study of early 18th-century Britain during the period immediately before the industrial revolution. Compared with many other places which he visited along his way, Hereford was then 'large and populous'. It was 'the chief city not of [this] county only, but of all the counties west of Severn'. But he saw it also as 'truly an old, mean built, and very dirty city', containing little worthy of note except the cathedral, which was in need of repair, and the college of celibate vicars choral.

Such run-down state as it suffered was due largely to the continuing economic after-effects of what the Buck brothers in 1732 were to term 'the late Civil Wars', as well as the damage to

trade caused in the reign of King Henry VIII. This state would remain, with much of the medieval and 'unmodern' appearance as well as considerable poverty, until the early 19th century.

Until the beginning of the 18th century the principal building materials used in Hereford had been sandstone and timber from the forests to the west. Oaks abounded, and were called 'the weeds of Herefordshire', but through heavy use for house building, shipbuilding, iron smelting and mining, their numbers dwindled. Fewer timber-framed buildings were built after the closing decades of the 18th century. Local sandstone, varying in colour from grey to red and dark brown, became less expensive and was more widely used for main structures and in the form of very durable roof tiles. (After almost 400 years, the Coningsby Hospital of 1614 still retains its original stone-tiled roof at the beginning of the 21st century.)

Because of fire risks, there was caution about using thatch for roofs in built-up areas; as one precaution in 1212 there was a requirement that it should be white-washed. Bricks had been used for chimneys since the 15th century and sometimes to replace old wattle and daub panels of timber-framed houses. There was no shortage of suitable fine marl clay near the city for the making of bricks, and there were abundant and inexhaustible supplies of water, but no suitable fuel for firing could be found anywhere in the

Top: Coningsby Hospital
Middle: Price's Almshouses
Bottom: The brickwork on the top storey
of the Mansion House

county. Hopes for a source of coal near Widemarsh Common were once raised with the discovery of a bed of peat, but searches came to nothing. Brushwood and loppings provided a poor alternative in the kilns and only small quantities of bricks could be produced until after 1662, when the first cargoes of Forest of Dean coal started to arrive by barge up the Wye.

Early bricks were distinctively shallow in depth and first appeared in Hereford in the construction of the upper storey of Price's Almshouses at Above Eigne (later Whitecross Road) in 1665. The Mansion House, erected in Widemarsh Street for Dr. William Brewster in 1698, also displays the attractiveness and high quality of its distinctive narrow brickwork—sound after 300 years, despite being lodged between grossly misplaced modern shopfronts—and a fine enriched (and lately conserved) eaves modillion cornice.

As brick became more plentiful and fashionable from the late 17th century, the face of the city began to change and be substantially rebuilt. Slowly it lost its ancient outward appearance, although it remained difficult for some time for loads of hay to pass along parts such as Widemarsh Street and High Street due to projecting upper storeys of the numerous timber-framed houses.

Metamorphosis

Isaac Taylor's map of 1757 includes good contemporary drawings of major buildings and riverside scenes and tabulates results of his own census of the 5,592 inhabitants and their 1,279 houses within the walls and in the suburbs.

Much of the modern townscape dates from that era, but the pace of change accelerated after 1774, following the passing of Hereford's Lamp Act. The city gates and sections of the wall were demolished, overhanging and run-down timber buildings along the streets trimmed back and much of

High Town was cleared. Some main streets, such a St. Owen Street, were completely rebuilt but little was done about all the cramped 'courts', cottages and houses packed within former yards, gardens and other spare land lying behind buildings alongside parts of the surviving medieval road network. Such areas were initially of little concern to the city councillors or improvement commissioners, and even the early public health legislation did little for the people living here except improve sewerage arrangements and purify their shared water supply. There was nothing in Rammell's 1853 report to the Board of Health that even touched on the squalid, unsafe and unhealthy state of the actual dwellings in which men, women and children had to live in poverty and frequent ill health. Three-quarters of the 19th century would have to pass before public attitudes started to change towards the living conditions of the working classes, partly prompted by Benjamin Disraeli in his novel, *Sybil*, on the theme of the great social divide between the lot of the rich and poor.

At the start of the 19th century, Britain had been at war with France for seven years and after peace was restored in 1815, the combined effects of demobilisation and agricultural depression created increased deprivation and unemployment. These contributed to migration from the countryside and a need for more low cost houses in towns such as Hereford. By the start of the Victorian era the city population had reached over 10,500, an increase of 3,670 since the first national census of 1801. Many must have crowded into the already densely packed dwellings of the walled city, but there was also a noticeable outward movement as more spacious houses appeared on the outskirts. The attractions of 'Ailstone Hill' had already drawn some of the well-to-do in the 18th century and a ribbon development of substantial brick houses continued further outwards, and along Holmer Road (later Venn's Lane) and Folly Lane. To the west, Clarence Place, Moorfield Place and Richmond Place appeared beside Portfield Street (later Edgar Street) in the 1830s, and impressive

terraces were built in St. Martin's Street, St. Ethelbert Street and other parts of the city. A block of 30 acres of land was purchased at Above Eign by the Freehold Land Society and Oxford Street, Bedford Street and Guildford Street were set out to provide building sites for new residents appearing in the lengthening directories of trades and professions. Changes in business and retailing practices in the central area were also beginning to produce further demands for new homes, as the more prosperous professionals and traders started to move from quarters over the shop to more spacious and comfortable houses and villas in the suburbs. Their former rooms were used for staff accommodation, storage or even left empty.

By the middle of the 19th century the population had reached over 12,000, more than double the number counted by Taylor almost a century earlier. At 2,420, the number of dwellings had increased almost in the same proportion and there was shortly to be a surge under both headings. This came with improved market arrangements and the general mid-Victorian boom which also saw the health benefits brought about by better sanitary arrangements and uncontaminated piped water, as described from p.111. In 1871 the population had increased by a further 50% to a total of more than 18,000, partly due to the arrival of the labour-intensive railways, and further new houses started to appear along the main radial routes and on intermediate sites. Allotment land in the Moorfields area was cleared and Railway Terrace was built (later to be replaced by Brunel Court). Sturdy artisan houses in Moorfield, Walmer, Richmond and Canonmoor Streets, in the Portfields and other quarters of the city, bear 1850s and 60s name and date plaques. Meanwhile, the slopes of Aylestone Hill, Hafod Road, Hampton Park and Broomy Hill provided spacious and leafy sites for the desirable residences of richer Herefordians. Design of their Italianate and Tudor-gothic villas gave architects scope for embellishment with the high quality products of The Albert Steam Pipe, Tile, Pottery, Building and Artistic Brick Works at Roman

One example of the wealthier homes built on the slopes to the east of the city

Road, Holmer, the nearby Victoria Tile Works off College Road and, from 1891, the Hampton Park Hereford Brick and Tile Company.

However, little had yet been done to assuage the deprivation and misery of people in the 'stews' of Bewell Street and other infill slum properties in the city. A certain amount of private enterprise led to the construction of low-rent cottages in Hereford, such as those in Coronation Road (later Moor Street), to meet the requirements of poorer families. But despite comparable efforts throughout the country, it became increasingly clear, not just to sanitary and housing reformers, that this would not be enough. In 1874 the mood was not lost on Benjamin Disraeli and he introduced seminal legislation which consolidated and greatly expanded all previous provisions governing sanitary matters.

Aspects of the impact of The Public Health Act of 1875 on Hereford have already been

The 'Stews' off Bewell Street in the centre of the city, which date to the 16th century and were demolished just after the First World War

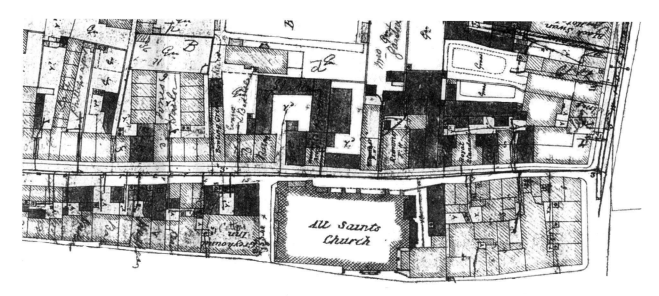

Curley's survey of 1855 which shows properties crowding together in the Bewell Street 'Stews'

covered in chapter V, but it also included important implications for housing, establishing a code which formed a basis for the regulation of all house-building until well into the 20th century. The sanitary authorities which the Act established exercised control over standards of building construction, the sufficiency of space between and around buildings, the layout of streets, and a great many other matters relating to new development, through a system of bye-laws and inspectors. It brought to an end the creation of any further cramped streets and unhealthy 'courts'. New nationally required street widths (of 24ft. at the front and 15ft. at the back) discouraged further 'backland' development, but in design terms resulting new developments lacked variety and flair. For many years afterwards, Hereford, with everywhere else, was to see the growth of dutiful 'bye-law housing', in the form of monotonous and unimaginative terraces placed along uniform and featureless streets.

Nevertheless, the Act produced much healthier and more comfortable homes, but the new laws did very little to improve conditions in existing areas of sub-standard housing. The city council's new health committee, formed in November, 1873, did, however, make a start with the appointment of an inspector of nuisances. He soon dealt with over 40 cottages which were totally unfit for human habitation, lacking water, drainage or other sanitary accommodation. By the turn of the century the Bewell Street, Friars Street, Cross Street, Turk's Alley and St. Owen Street precincts were well in course of being 'swept away as unhealthy and unwholesome areas'. During a period of three years over 70 houses were demolished, 68 others closed or altered and another 40 buildings were under observation.

However, more than a hundred years would pass before, in 1975, the chief environmental health officer was able to report that 'the worst of the unfit and sub-standard housing in the city had been eradicated'. In efforts to preserve the strong social links of affected communities, his officials took care to determine which unfit or dilapidated dwellings warranted renovation (with encouragement in the form of various improvement grants), and which should be closed, demolished or adapted for some other purpose. For tenants dispossessed in the process there was, from the beginning, the need to produce better homes to go to and the mechanism for local authorities to achieve this came from conclusions of a Royal Commission on Housing in 1884.

Council Housing

The ensuing Housing of the Working Classes Act of 1885 was based on the assertion that:

> It is totally impossible that private enterprise, philanthropy and charity can keep pace with the present demand. Economic forces and population have outstripped their endeavours, hence lists accrue. But what the individual cannot do, the state municipality must seek to accomplish, for it alone possesses the necessary power and wealth.

An Act of 1890, under the same title, empowered local authorities to deal further with unhealthy areas and purchase land for housing but, like most legislation of the period, it was not compulsory and not many councils took action until after the First World War. One exception was Hereford. Under the leadership of Councillor E.F. Bulmer, the statutory powers available through the Act of 1890 and a further similarly titled one of 1903 were used to enable the council to buy land at Barrs Court, construct roads and sewers, plant trees and other landscaping, and define general conditions for the building of suitable houses upon the new estate. As part of this novel initiative it then leased the land to Hereford Co-operative Housing Ltd., a registered industrial society. After securing a government advance and other forms of assistance and appointing Hereford architects, Groome and Bettington, this body constructed 85 cottages which provided accommodation for over 400 people.

The layout adopted was also quite new, based on principles pioneered by Ebenezer Howard and the Garden City movement in 1898, indeed the title was adopted for the scheme at Barrs Court, which became known as the Garden City, (not being self-sufficient, like Letchworth of the same period and Welwyn later, it was more accurately a Garden Suburb).

No part of the estate was built at a density of more than 12 houses to the acre and a total width of 70ft. was allowed between houses on either side of 15ft. wide roads and 5ft. wide footpaths. Arranged in 15 blocks of five and three houses and eight blocks of semi-detached houses, each

house with its three bedrooms and two living rooms was built of brick with its upper storey covering of rough cast and a roof of red Brosely tiles. There was an inside W.C. and coal-store in all the houses, an upstairs bathroom in 16 of them and an iron bath in the scullery in others. Weekly rents, including rates, ranged from 4s. 9d. for 32 of the houses, between 5s. and 6s. for another 35 and from 6s. to 7s. 6d. for the remaining 18. When the formal opening took place, amid much excitement, the bishop of Hereford expressed a hope that it was 'but the beginning of a great social reform'. And so it turned out!

The first keys were handed over in 1909, at a time when a provincial 'Study of Town Life' had been evaluating the cost of sustaining a typical family of husband, wife and three children at a minimum level of 'physical efficiency'. Assuming a rent of 4s., food costing 12s. 9d. and clothing, lighting and fuel amounting to 4s. 11d., the essential weekly income came to 21s. 8d. In Hereford a bleak economic climate produced many workers who were paid not much more than this amount

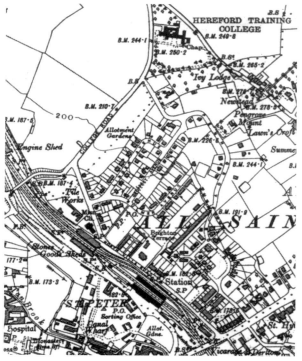

OS map of 1904 showing the street plan of Hereford's garden suburb on the then fringes of the city

Artist's impression in 1909 of one of the houses in the garden suburb

Modern photograph of the same houses(?) in the garden suburb

each week, and some were earning less. (The weekly cash wage of an agricultural labourer was 14s. 8d., although this could usually be topped up with perquisites, allowances in kind and extra pay at harvest time). An old age pension of 5s. had just been introduced, but only for 70-year olds and over. In many households the rents, although very reasonable when translated to end-of-century levels in the city, cannot have left much for contingencies, savings or any 'little luxuries of life'. Certainly there would be no hope of a working-class tenant finding £160 and running costs for one of the exciting new Ford Model T 'Tin Lizzies' which were due to leave Manchester's Trafford Park production lines two years later. Perhaps it was just as well, for demands of the First World War would very shortly call up most private cars for military duties.

Few local authorities provided social housing until after the war, despite further powers granted by the Housing and Town Planning Act of 1909. To its credit as a housing authority, Hereford had built 67 new homes between 1902 and 1914, most of them at Eign Mill, Green Street, St. Owen's Gate, Canonmoor Street, Edgar Street and Greenland Road. They were to form part of an eventual total of some 8,550 dwellings to be built for sale or rent by the city council during the next 80 years.

In the aftermath of the Armistice, a great housing need, especially 'Homes fit for Heroes', became one of the most pressing issues facing the Lloyd George government. A succession of major Housing Acts was passed from 1919, culminating in the 'Wheatley' Act of 1924. This reaffirmed local authorities as major providers of working-class housing (subsequently, at one period during the 1960s the city council came to own more than one third of all the houses in Hereford), whilst also encouraging private enterprise.

Early post-war council houses appeared in Portfields, Breinton Road, Ross Road, Hunderton, Link Road, Westfields, Mostyn Street, College Road and Stonebow Road, amounting to over 550 in all. From 1930, more than 500 houses and 64 flats were built at College Hill, 391 homes at Hinton Court and 16 aged persons flats at St. Owen's Place, a grand total of approximately 1,600 since the first council house tenancy in 1902.

In 1944, shortly before the end of the war, the council's housing programme restarted with the erection of 100 'Tarran' two-bedroomed prefabricated bungalows on the College Estate, Eign Mill, Hinton and Westfields. Described as 'temporary' and intended to last for about ten years, they generated a considerable attachment and affection among tenants. Although many of

Area Plans and House Styles over the years

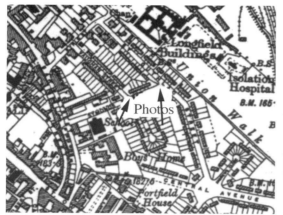

Left and above: Portfields. After buying land to construct a profitable corn mill in 1847, the Hereford Society for Aiding the Industrious (p.180) went on to acquire more and sold some of it in 1874 to enable a Working Boys' Home to be built. About 45 years later it helped to meet a great need for 'Homes for Heroes' after the Armistice by selling more again to enable the council to build over 200 houses by the mid-1920s

Bottom left and below: Close to the site of St. Owen's Church, demolished during the Civil War, and to Turk's Alley and other slum properties in St. Owen's Street, 16 'model dwellings' were built in St. Owen Gate in 1914, to the design of John Parker, city surveyor. (The council tenants soon had close access to Hereford's first real cinema, 'The Kinema', in the former chapel building next door (see p.187)

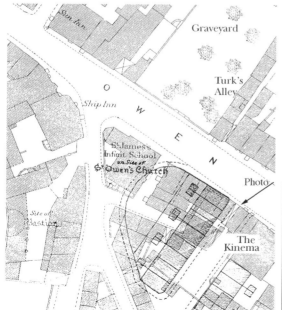

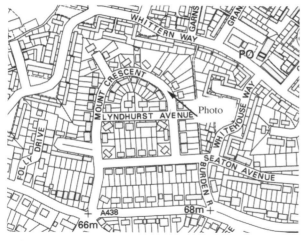

Top left and above: Tupsley. The Mount Crescent/Lyndhurst Avenue private sector houses at Tupsley were built not long before the outbreak of the Second World War. It would be another 25 years before Whitehouse Farm and Prospect Farm were built on, eventually with nearly 500 council houses, served by the new Whittern Way spine road between Folly Lane and Ledbury Road

Left: In the 1950s and 60s the council built 1,230 Cornish Unit homes, using prestressed reinforced concrete components. By the 1980s these, and 66 Unity homes and 91 Tarran bungalows, displayed defects requiring expensive reinstatement. Former tenants who had exercised their 'right to buy' suffered mortgaging and other difficulties and in special hardship cases dwellings were repurchased by the council

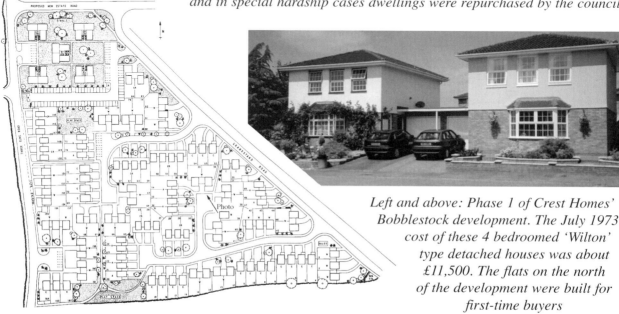

Left and above: Phase 1 of Crest Homes' Bobblestock development. The July 1973 cost of these 4 bedroomed 'Wilton' type detached houses was about £11,500. The flats on the north of the development were built for first-time buyers

139

these prefabs were eventually demolished to make way for new housing, the rest were modernised with new doors and windows, improved insulation and central heating, designed to extend their useful lives even longer (by 1997 at a weekly rent of £30.86). Others were bought by devoted tenants and lavished with external brick cladding and further enhancement.

Despite many post-war shortages and difficulties in a building industry recovering from the hostilities, a vigorous programme saw the building of over 1,800 new homes of many descriptions, including numbers of pre-fabricated 'Cornish Units', during the next ten years. The largest developments were a first phase of 464 houses and flats at Newton Farm, 471 at New Hunderton, 146 at Redhill and 216 at Holme Lacy Road, whilst ten other schemes, varying from between 2 and 94 units, were undertaken at Crossfields, Hinton Road, Mortimer Road, Oak Crescent, Panson, Putson, Ross Road, Templars Lane, Whitecross and Winston Road. The programme continued to gather pace during the late 1950s, the '60s and '70s as further phases of rented accommodation were added at Newton Farm and Redhill, and new estates formed with the building of 431 houses and bungalows at Green Lanes, 537 units at 'Whitehouse' and 'Prospect' Farms at Tupsley, 200 houses and 80 four-storey maisonettes and 25 warden-assisted flats at the 'Moor' Farm, north of the White Cross. Here, the listed 17th-century timber-frame and brick farmhouse was carefully restored and converted into two flats.

One of the earliest collaborations with a housing association arose at Drybridge House, St. Martin's Street. Built in 1733 by Benjamin Bird, the listed house had been purchased by the council in 1959 to be left empty and increasingly wrecked by vandals. A proposal was finally worked up in 1975 for the erection of old-age pensioners' flats, warden accommodation and a day centre. Anchor Housing Association took over the project in 1976 and the result was a scheme of 37 new flats, built on land to the rear, together with refurbishment of the old house that included a careful 'facelift' to restore its impres-

Drybridge House

sive facade to St. Martin's Street. The Haywood Foundation Charity Trust contributed over £100,000 for the financing of a day centre for elderly people on the ground floor, equipped with a luncheon club and WRVS meals on wheels service. A short distance away an even older building was brought back into beneficial use. Originally a 15th-century hall house, Pool Farm in Belmont Road had been largely reconstructed in the 16th century, except for the central hall, whilst a porch was added in 1624. The building was acquired and in 1977 was converted into four flats, providing housing for 11 people (winning a *Birmingham Post* 'New Lease of Life' award in the process). Because of increasing flooding problems, it acquired a further lease of life in 2001 — as a base for the South Wye Regeneration Partnership.

To the east of the city, 95 council houses, 30 flats and 12 bungalows were built at Hampton Park, on part of the land at Corporation Farm that had been purchased many years previously as an unavailing site for Hereford's main new sewage disposal works. Many smaller developments also occurred, often to cater for special housing needs, such as warden-assisted flats at Ballinger Court, Bryngwyn Close, Richard Weaver Court and Southgate Court, and warden-assisted bungalows at Freda Pierce Close and other parts of Hillside. The council's housing stock was further enlarged with the separate purchase of some 550 extra homes, notably at Belmont, Newton Farm (Sherborne Close) and Redhill. In addition, almost 1,000 houses were built for sale, 216 of them at Hampton Park, another part of Corporation Farm, along with 142 at Whitehouse and Prospect Farms, 126 at Green Lanes and groups of from 2 to almost 80 at various sites throughout the city.

The need for a range of local shops at the larger new estates led to the construction of a total of 36, some with integral flats or lock-up garages, at Newton Farm, College Hill, Whitehouse and Prospect Estate, Whitecross and elsewhere. The increase in car ownership was not anticipated, and the 1,648 lock-up garages included in blocks on the estates, were not only wrongly located, but insufficient, leading to congested roadside parking in later years.

Because of constantly changing national and local policies, standards of design and arrangement of local authority housing varied considerably over the years. Some developments reverted to a high-density approach of dull and monotonous rows of terraced blocks and other unattractive forms, whilst others stood up well to, and eventually surpassed, the high standards set at Barrs Court in 1908. There was wide agreement that many later house types and layouts compared very favourably with their equivalents in the private sector, but in achieving this, successive housing committees had to overcome many challenges.

Few were as demanding as those of the 1950s and '60s, when efforts to attract additional industry to Hereford resulted in the arrival of Henry Wiggin with employment for up to 3,500 additional people. According to National Census Returns, a 1951 city population of 32,490 was theoretically expected to reach 33,545 by 1961 and 34,050 by 1971 but actually became 40,431 and 46,503 respectively. The differences were due chiefly to the arrival and expansion of the company, and the council had to take steps to build houses for imported workers and families from Glasgow and Birmingham. Through agreements with the employers, over 700 extra council dwellings were provided for key workers before the end of 1967. By this time housebuilding by the local authority had produced a rent roll of almost 6,000 dwellings, more than a third of the total housing stock of the city. The proportion fell to a quarter during the 1980s due to the vicissitudes of changing national and local housing policies and particularly to the practice, started in the mid-1950s, of selling the stock to tenants at a discounted price. Before this opportunity was made compulsory in 1985, up to 100 homes were being sold every year, not surprisingly in large part from the council's better properties. Between 1980 and 1989, sales totalled over 1,200 homes. Owner occupation in the city over a similar period increased from 54% to 66%, whilst the supply of private rented housing showed a considerable decline. This was reflected in a lengthening waiting list, more homelessness and a growing inability of the council to deal with the problem. In April 1990 the list showed 1,735 households as seeking rented homes, 749 of them with, or expecting, children and 126 comprising deserving elderly or disabled applicants. A desperate situation was exacerbated by a list of 137 households presenting themselves as homeless and accepted as being in conditions of priority need. Of the new lettings for all categories of those in need, some 39% were taken up by homeless families.

Throughout this whole period one important strength was that elected members of all political colours were united in their approach to the unacceptable housing conditions in the city. This was especially marked in the housing committee, where a fruitful liaison between Labour and Conservative chair and vice-chairmen was, after a change of control in the early 1980s, followed by a succession of initiatives by equally constructive Liberal and subsequently Liberal Democrat post-holders.

New national legislation saw the council becoming an 'enabler' rather than a direct 'provider' of housing. In this role it promoted a newly established Hereford Housing Association by donating land worth some £3 million for future development (as a way of helping to attract additional capital for the construction of houses on the land); financed several Housing Association developments from council funds; reduced land values to Housing Associations, in some cases to nil; discounted other land to provide low-cost home ownership in partnership with the private sector; provided 'very sheltered' accommodation and assessment units for the frail elderly, in partnerships with other organisations; provided temporary accommodation in conjunction with a local convent and took short leases of vacant and sub-standard private sector accommodation to house the homeless; and worked with the county council to achieve 'care in the community' arrangements.

Typical of the many initiatives in this enabling role, was the development of a brownfield site at Canonmoor, to the west of Edgar Street. Fourteen acres of the former G.W.R. Worcester Sidings site were bought from British Rail by the council and added to its own five acres, once mainly the site of the municipal refuse incinerator. There had been much deliberation about the best use for the land, wavering between a residential or industrial outcome, but eventually it was agreed that the entire area should be redeveloped for residential use involving a diversity of dwellings and tenure. A portion was allotted to the county council, who built 72 dwellings and a 'very sheltered' housing unit that was managed by its social services department. Approximately one acre was sold to the Railway Housing Association and Benefit Fund, who built Great Western Court, 32 flats for the elderly alongside the route of the former main line. To provide a balance of accommodation it was agreed that more housing for families was required. Harden Housing Association already managed the flats integrated with the Maylord Orchards shopping scheme in the city centre and old age pensioners' bungalows at Venns Lane and Barrs Court Road, and they were chosen to provide 28 two-bedroomed flats for rent and 14 family houses for 'shared ownership'—accommodation that is part purchased and part rented. Funding of approximately £1 million was provided mainly by the government's Housing Corporation, a very useful injection of resources for the city. The development also included a new park and children's play area behind the Nell Gwynne Theatre (later to be rebuilt as The Courtyard Centre for the Arts), its roads named impartially after former statesmen and politicians of all the major parties.

The council often joined in owners' attempts to make better use of wasted upper storeys of premises in the city centre, many of them listed, which had once been the living quarters of shop owners before customs changed. The council duly restored accommodation over shops on the west side of Widemarsh Street and produced nine flats and eight bed-sits for homeless families. After a long period of dereliction, another prominent block in Union Street was totally rehabilitated, providing further homes whilst also helping towards restoring domestic 'life' to the city centre after shop hours.

The housing programme increasingly concentrated on providing for the elderly and disabled and a need evolved for arranging emergency help, particularly for people living on their own. This led to the introduction of a 24-hour community alarm system, manned from a communication centre at Garrick House. Those in distress could make easy contact by pressing a portable button and there were links with all local care services. By March, 1987, 1,077 properties, including

Great Western Court

142

600 private sector and Housing Association contributors, were connected to the system.

Building the right type of accommodation for the elderly (in areas where they were not isolated but could remain very much members of a broad community) had produced the added benefit that larger properties were likely to become available for family needs. It was therefore frustrating that the council gradually had to reduce new house building during the 1980s due to changed funding priorities at central government level. Waiting lists grew of people who, because of a shortage of rented private properties and insufficient income to buy their homes, could not be housed in any other way than through the council or a Housing Association, though the latter still managed some developments utilising Housing Corporation finance. Of the original 8,550 homes that had been built over the years, the number still remaining under direct management of the city council stood at 5,007 in 1990, the others having been sold under various provisions to sitting tenants or first time buyers.

By the beginning of the final decade of the 20th century, not all the homes within the city were fully habitable, 304 council and private dwellings being classified as 'unfit', 598 in need of renovation and 1,276 officially 'designated' and thus in need of reinstatement. Approximately 450 dwellings were found to be vacant.

Private Sector Housing

By April, 1990 the total number of dwellings in the city amounted to almost 21,000, of which 75% were in private ownership. This showed a four-fold increase since the beginning of the 20th century, when all homes were still in private hands, although then chiefly rented. In 1900 much of the city still retained a medieval air, and whilst something of a 'late developer', Hereford did not really deserve the withering remark attributed to George Bernard Shaw that it was 'three glacial periods behind the [other] cities of England'! Like most it had acquired new Victorian suburbs.

In common with much of Britain during the 1850s and 60s, the population and economy of Hereford were expanding at a strong rate and some of the more affluent middle class citizens were starting to leave crowded parts of the centre for the suburbs. An annual income of £150 could provide for life in a pleasant small villa, and the prospect of admission to the socially significant servant-keeping class, possibly with the services of a daily maid-of-all-work (until the First World War there were almost 1.5 million people, mostly poorly paid women, in service).

To the west, many large houses were being built from the 1850s along the White Cross Road, from which a generally mixed development, including semi-detached houses (an invention of the 19th century), extended southwards to Whitehorse Street. These contrasted with the tight-knit standard terraced and smaller houses in areas such as Chandos Street, Cotterell Street, Clifford Street and Cornewall Street. These catered more for artisans who might be earning up to £2 per week, of which 3s. or 4s. went on rent. A further number of larger houses later appeared between Baggallay Street and Ranelagh Street to the north.

From 1920, the increased use of the motor car led to the growth of classic 'ribbon development' extending beyond the White Cross along King's Acre Road towards the long established (in 1785) nurseries close to the junction for Credenhill. Ribbon development also took place along the east side of Canon Pyon Road beyond the municipal boundary, as it did for some distance along the north side of Roman Road.

It is not possible to move very far in or around Hereford without meeting with a Church of England property interest and this is certainly so to the north-west in the township of Huntington and at Holmer. Some 80 acres of church farmland existed at Bobblestock in an area approved primarily for residential purposes in 1960 and intended for municipal housing. After some discussion this was amended in 1969, clearing the way for the Commissioners and developers, Crest Homes, to propose a private sector housing scheme covering the entire acreage up to the south side of Roman Road, which would include a primary school, shops, a public house and open space. Separate discussions explored opportunities for the introduction of other facilities, including a Roman Catholic church, but came to nought.

It was considered impractical to develop the whole site at once and in 1973 the developers put forward plans for a first phase of 164 homes on a triangular portion of land bounded by Three Elms Road, Grandstand Road and the Wiggin Sports Ground. A need was identified for single bedroomed flats to serve as affordable first homes, and for retired people, and a total of 60 was built in five blocks of three storeys, selling on a long leasehold basis for £6,250. All were taken up immediately after being put on the market, indicating the shortage of that type of accommodation at a time when house prices were starting to move dramatically upwards. During the second half of 1972 there had already been a very steep rise, averaging more than 25% nationally, and although abating a little in 1973, due mainly to mortgaging difficulties, it was to resume to a degree which reverberated for the remainder of the century. House prices in Hereford were close to the national average, but earnings were only about 80% of the average in 1973 and first-time house buyers had great difficulty in obtaining a mortgage. There was little available at much less than £7,000, except a limited number of old two- or three-bedroomed terraced houses. Many were forced to stay with parents, in-laws or friends whilst joining the council's waiting list and searching for privately rented accommodation.

The rest of the first phase comprised three and four bedroomed detached houses, having 'individually varied Georgian-style elevations and a quiet air of elegance', as the sales details proclaimed, and laid out at a high density, incorporating short cul-de-sacs, two small play areas and pedestrian linkways. They were offered to those who could then afford between £10,950 and £11,500.

The remainder of the Bobblestock Estate was developed in tranches and included many house types, sizes, densities and prices according to the state of the market. After ten years enough land still remained for almost 400 dwellings, providing also for a wide strip south of Roman Road for a new A4103 carriageway together with a wide tree and shrub margin. By the time all the houses were completed in 1988, the area included a small supermarket and two lock-up shops near the Three Elms Road junction, but nothing came of the original proposals for a school or a public house and the amount of open space was hardly as 'considerable' as had been anticipated.

As employment levels at Henry Wiggin reduced to one third of their former peak, use of the bowling green, tennis courts and other facilities at the company's sports ground, next to the Crest estate, fell away. Eventually this land was granted planning permission for approximately 120 private houses and a public recreation ground. Before this could happen the approval of the county council was required because of the 'departure' involved from the statutory Development Plan and Town Map. This was classified as a 'windfall' site, making it a significant contribution to the city's land supply, saving a need for an equivalent area of new greenfield land such as that at Bobblestock. Another 'windfall' arose at Yazor Road in 1988 when Crest Homes obtained permission to build 120 dwellings on land which, until then, had been designated for secondary school use in connection with Whitecross School. In planning parlance both areas differed from brownfield sites, such as the former railway sidings at Canonmoor, but all reduced the need to invade valuable farming land.

Except for the immediate vicinity of the city centre, land directly to the north lacked any real amount of private housing, being zoned and used for industrial and open space. Older houses in Mortimer Road, Perseverence Road and Burcott Road were among those regarded as liable to suffer from being too close to the effects of businesses such as the gas works and Painter Brothers, and so no further planning approvals were issued there other than for compatible uses. Only on the Roman Road outskirts were suitable sites available, at Glenthorne and as far west as Aylesbrook on the south side, and on the north between Orchard Close and the former golf driving range near Old School Lane.

Building of the Penn Grove estate off Aylestone Hill had commenced soon after the arrival of the first passenger rail service but until 1886 low water pressures from Broomy Hill Works had hampered development at much greater heights. These problems eased, at least for many years, once tanks in the tall new water tower were filled. As a result, there were seven substantial dwellings in Venn's Lane by 1900 and others were being built as far as Hampton Park during the immediate pre-war years. Most of the houses which appeared in Tupsley and the suburb served by Ledbury Road, Hampton Dene Road, Gorsty Lane and Hampton Park Road during the inter-war period were usually smaller but generally solid and built to a good and lasting standard. By 1939, added to the provision of local authority social housing, they brought the estimated total number of city dwellings to over 7,700.

Shortages of materials and skilled labour (and a bulge in the birth rate) in the immediate post-war years produced many challenges as the building trades started to expand again. As the Churchill government from 1951 set its trumpeted target of 300,000 a year, local planners estimated that almost 2,000 dwellings would be erected in Hereford during a five year period from January 1951. A high proportion of the private sector building took place in Tupsley, chiefly in the area south-west of Hafod Road, between Old Eign Hill and Ledbury Road; south-west of Church Road and south-west of Folly Lane. From 1956 to 1971, land north east of Hafod Road, north of Upper Ledbury Road and between Venn's Lane and Aylestone Hill was developed at a time when the Wiggin impact was being felt. House completion rates reached their peak between 1962 and 1966; in 1963 alone, 572 new private and local authority houses were completed, to be followed by 509 in 1964. The building rate for all new housing was, however, easing towards the end of the 1960s, partly as a result of various government 'squeezes'. Between 1971 and 1981 it fell away to a rate little more than half its former level, averaging only 262 per year.

Social and economic changes had meanwhile changed the tenure of the older large Victorian and Edwardian villas. Following the close of the Upstairs/Downstairs divide with the emancipation of most domestic servants, floors from kitchen basements to the attics acquired new uses. These were usually residential, but one of the exceptions was Penn Grove, no.3 Venn's Lane, the impressive home of Dr. Wood Power which, with extensive grounds overlooking the city was purchased by the city council for museum and public recreation purposes. A gallery was added to exhibit the work of the Hereford artist, Brian Hatton, who had been killed during the First World War. Nearly opposite, Elmhurst was converted to serve as a nursing home and day centre for the elderly and much of its grounds developed as the Nuffield private hospital. Other large houses further west (towards artist David Cox's thatched cottage of 1817) were also converted into nursing homes. Several large houses on Aylestone Hill were adapted to educational uses and Carfax at No. 50, once home of the Carless family, became the Judge's Lodging for the period when the 'red judge' (from the High Court in London, and named after his red robes) was sitting at Hereford Assizes, and then a grand official residence for the chairman of the county council. On the opposite side of the Folly Lane junction, the Three Counties Hotel, originally The Elms, built by Charles Anthony—founder of *The Hereford Times* and six times mayor—relinquished its striking location overlooking the city towards the Black Mountains, making way in 1972 for a cul-de-sac of new 'executive' houses. Large houses further along Folly Lane became associated with the nearby Art and Technical Colleges, or were demolished to provide for new housing projects. Many large houses in Bodenham Road were converted into flats and some particularly large gardens were divided into building plots or laid out with modern flats. One exception was at No. 49, where planning permission was given for a change of use to offices for the Wye River Authority, later succeeded by the Welsh Water Authority. Another non-residential use was established in 1947 (the year when legislation was passed creating new town and country planning powers) in the grandest house in Hafod Road—No. 35, the former home of Mr. W.J. (Billy) Bowers, one of the chief builders of the new Hereford. Under Mr. Freeman Newton, Chief Constable of both the city and county police forces (see chapter VII), Brockington became the police headquarters for many years, then the offices for South Herefordshire District Council and its successor Herefordshire Council.

In Hampton Park Road, not far away, one of many large Victorian houses to be subdivided into flats was Plas Gwyn at No. 27. In 1904, the year of his knighthood, Sir Edward Elgar rented the property and lived there with his wife, Alice, and daughter, Carice, for the next eight years, during which time he became the dominant figure in the British musical world, receiving countless world celebrities. He composed much of his greatest music whilst living there, including 'The Introduction and Allegro for Strings', the first and second symphonies, the violin concerto, 'The Kingdom' and the two 'Wand of Youth' suites. It would have been surprising, therefore, if at least half a dozen drives, closes or places had not been named to mark his association with the city, although it was well after the end of the Second World War before the first, Elgar Avenue, appeared off Old Eign Hill. Later still, Nimrod Drive was grafted to Gorsty Lane to provide for a safer junction with Hampton Park Road and to act as a boundary for Sinclair Drive, Alice Close and other quarters linked with the famous musician.

By then, most available building sites of any size had been taken up and in a three years period from 1985/6 dwelling completions had averaged just under 400 units each year. An increasing proportion of these were in the private sector, in 1987/8 taking place on a total of 28 widely differing sites. By 1991, 73% of the 20,829 houses in the city were privately owned, 24% managed by the local authority and 3% by Housing Associations. These increases in the city's housing stock did not, however, lead to a commensurate increase in population, since average household sizes had fallen from 3.07 people per dwelling in 1971 to 2.47 in 1991.

Nearer the centre of the city, some of the inter-war housing stock was improved by rehabilitation, others were demolished through slum clearance programmes. Limited new building was also undertaken. Most prominently, in October, 1934, the John Venn Building in Bath Street was provided by the Hereford Dwellings Company, comprising 28 flats 'for poor persons'. Designed by H.E. Bettington and years later classified by Hereford Civic Trust as 'a unique example of the early "Modern Movement" worthy of "listing"', it stands on the opposite side of the main road to Venn's Close. Interestingly, the houses here were designed by his father, E.J. Bettington, in an altogether different 'Tudoresque' style.

Equally convenient for shops, surgeries, churches and other city centre facilities, flats designed for 'third age' citizens were erected during later years of the century at Ferrers Street and city gate locations at St. Owen Court and Deen's Court, Greyfriars. As a further means of encouraging people to return to live in or near the city centre, 21 flats were included at first floor level in the design of the Maylord Orchards shopping scheme and a brownfield site at Coningsby Street was used for a high density 'affordable' housing development. For those seeking a truly spiritual ambience, a good opportunity was provided in East Street not far from the cathedral, where part of Pullings' former early 19th-century gin distillery was imaginatively converted into 5 mews dwellings. Others, preferring an association with water, had the prospect of a new house on the site of the former Victorian treatment tanks at Broomy Hill, made redundant by more modern filtering plant and equipment. This development did not proceed before the 20th century had ended and, with only a relatively small amount of infilling, that part of the city remains with mostly large houses.

Chapter VII
Public Institutions and Social Development

Although depicted by Defoe in 1725 as 'large and populous', the bulk of 18th-century Hereford was barely half a mile across in any direction. Apart from the cathedral, three surviving medieval churches (two others had been destroyed during the siege of 1645), the market-house and guild-hall, the Tolsey and the city gaol, there were few other public buildings plotted on Taylor's map of 1757. At a time when hospitals were generally charitable institutions caring for the poor and elderly, rather than the sick, there were Badhams, St. Ethelbert's, Trinity, Symonds and Weavers hospitals lying within the walls and Coningsby's, Giles, Williams', Lesley's, Lyngens and Prices' outside, the oldest founded as long ago as 1225. One unique but missing building was shown in vignette form by Taylor as a 'View of a Chapel now taken down'. Built on two floors, of early

Taylor's illustration of the chapel of Saints Katherine and Mary Magdalene, taken down between 1737 and 1746

Norman date and older than the cathedral, the double chapel of Saints Katherine and Mary Magdalene was pulled down between 1737 and 1746 on the instructions of Bishop Egerton. Only the north wall remains, now incorporated into the south wall of the bishop's cloister, when, allegedly, all could have been restored for £20! Indeed, John Price, writing in 1796, thought that Hereford did not 'boast a great number of public buildings'.

The main public building, the cathedral, had a long pedigree and just before the end of the 18th century underwent enforced change. The fabric had suffered long centuries of neglect and abuse, not least when the chapter house roof was stripped of its lead by the Royalists during the Civil War and the building left partially in ruins until it was finally demolished in 1769. The western range of the bishop's cloister was demolished in 1762 to make way for a new school-room—before it was realised that the stability of the west end of the cathedral would be compromised. On Easter Day 1786, the west tower collapsed, taking with it about half of the Norman nave and aisles. After much debate about restoration, the dean and chapter decided to curtail the nave by one bay and James Wyatt, designer of Belmont House and a widely renowned architect, was engaged for the work.

It was not altogether a happy choice and he was much maligned, unjustly some felt, for his

Hereford Cathedral after the collapse of the west front, by Thomas Hearne, c.1786

at All Saints Church. In 1843 some Three Choirs Festival performances were also held there, but by the time of Hereford's next turn in 1846 the cathedral nave was once more in use. Not before time, the tower foundations were strengthened in 1841 but sadly the work could not be done without removal of the six and a half centuries-old stone choir screen. It was replaced by an ornate structure of iron, copper, brass, tinted glass and polished stones in time for a thanksgiving service marking the reopening of the restored cathedral in 1863. Designed by Gilbert Scott for an International Exhibition in London in 1862, it was made at Coventry by the metalworking firm of Francis Skidmore, (the Dean and Chapter afterwards securing it at half its £3,000 cost). *The Illustrated London News* described it as 'the grandest achievement of modern architectural art'—but the artist rather disapproved, feeling that his design had been treated 'somewhat aberrantly', making the screen 'too loud and self-asserting'. He was not alone in this view, but the screen remained at the cathedral for just over a hundred years. Finally, condemned as 'out of place and out of date', it was dismantled in 1967 amidst a great local and national outcry and sold

austere west front and for what he did in unnecessarily replacing the surviving Norman triforium and clerestory. He also removed what was left of the nave vault, substituting his own creation made of wych elm. Between 1840 and 1863 the cathedral required extensive restoration and was closed from 1841 until 1850, choral services being held

Hereford Cathedral's restored screen on display in the V&A in 2001

148

The west front of the cathedral: Wyatt's design on the left, and the current design by John Oldrid Scott

in some 14,000 pieces to the Herbert Museum, back in Coventry. It was presented to the Victoria and Albert Museum in 1983 and 11 years later a successful appeal was launched to 'save a rusting chunk of Herefordshire's artistic heritage'. The V&A's largest ever conservation project cost over £800,000, restoring the screen to its former gilded and brightly painted splendour. From May 2001 it reappeared on permanent display in the Ironwork gallery above the main entrance of the museum to coincide with a major exhibition — 'The Victorian Vision: Inventing New Britain'.

There had been disenchantment with Wyatt's west end for over a century and, to mark the death of Queen Victoria in 1902, a new memorial window was installed there, subscribed by women of the diocese. Dean Leigh followed it with energetic fund-raising for a new western facade to the nave. This was built between 1904

and 1908 to the design of John Oldrid Scott, son of Sir George Gilbert Scott, but is not of his best work. Many find it difficult to quarrel with George Marshall's judgement in 1951 that it 'is fortunately not seen in close juxta-position to other parts of the cathedral; for it fits against the nave, as seen from either side, as if it were an entirely separate creation pushed against it without any attempt at incorporating the earlier work. It would have been better had it been built of a local stone, such as was used in the Norman period, and not of the red stone from Hollington in Staffordshire. It is irregularly overloaded with ornament, the sculpture is good in some instances, but in others had better be passed over in silence'.

Until the early 1930s it was largely screened from the west by buildings fronting Broad Street, but its long enclosure was then significantly reduced when they were demolished. Later railings were subsequently removed to be melted down towards the war effort. Within the cathedral a significant liturgical step was taken during the 1980s when a raised sanctuary was built below the tower, and in 1992, in memory of Bishop John Eastaugh, an 18ft. by 9ft. oval silver gilt 'corona', like a chandelier set with candles, was suspended high above it. Designed by Simon Beer, it was the first corona to be installed at an English cathedral for a century. In the Autumn of 2000 there were celebrations at the restoration of the 700 year-old shrine of St. Thomas Cantilupe in the north-west transept.

The world-famous Mappa Mundi of 1298 had never found a settled home, whilst the cathedral's chained library of some 1,500 books, dating from the 8th to the 19th centuries and the largest in existence, had not been on display in its entirety since 1842. In that year the Lady Chapel, which had housed it since the early 17th century, was restored as a place of worship. After that, only part of the library was displayed in a chamber above the north transept aisle and only those prepared to mount a spiral staircase of 54 steps could see it (a scene of two fatalities in the last 15 years of use). When in 1988 the world's spotlight turned on Hereford at the proposed sale of the medieval map to help provide funds for repair

*The new library and exhibition centre that
houses the Mappa Mundi*

work to the cathedral, energetic protests led to its withdrawal from Sothebys and the building of a permanent home. This is now shared with the chained library and that of over 300 similarly chained volumes from All Saints Church (a bequest of Dr. William Brewster in 1715). The entire reference library of over 10,000 volumes is available for study in a first-floor reading room, whilst archives and other rare books are stored in a basement. The project was funded with the aid of grants from the National Heritage Memorial Fund and a donation worth £1.75m from John Paul Getty Junior (who was later to be made an honorary freeman of the city and given a knighthood). The new building, designed by Sir William Whitfield and Partners and built by the 250 year-old Ludlow firm of Treasure and Son, is entered through an introductory exhibition in the south cloister and the existing Dean Leigh building. Termed a 'high-tech. medieval building', the stonework, although not local being from Derbyshire, is of a similar colour and grain to the existing cathedral sandstone. The opening ceremony was performed by Queen Elizabeth II on 9 May, 1996.

Parishes and churches

Served by a secular body of priests, the cathedral was equipped as a church, dedicated to St. John Baptist, and undertook functions like those of the other five parishes in the city (hence the occasional use of the Romanesque font on the south side of the nave). There was an altar of St. John Baptist against the west face of the stone choir screen on the south side of the choir doorway, but after complaints of disturbance during cathedral services the parishioners used the altar in the choir. The collapse of the west tower precipitated arrangements for a more suitable place for parish services, leading to the use of the north transept. Restoration of the tower from 1840 created further problems for St. John's and these continued until 1855 when the Lady Chapel became available following the transfer of the library. Upon the death of the last vicar of St. John's in 1919, most parts of the scattered parish were joined with surrounding parishes, the dean became the titular vicar and later priest-in-charge and the parish services were merged into those of the cathedral church.

St. Peter's is the oldest church in the city, standing to the east of fitzOsbern's market place on the north side of St. Peter's Square. It was founded in 1085 by Walter de Lacy, one of William the Conqueror's chief lieutenants, who was accidentally killed by falling from the battlements whilst on a round of inspection. No part of his church has survived and most of the building in its present form was erected around 1300. After many changes down the centuries, the church was partly rebuilt in 1718, restored in 1793 and in 1862 George Gilbert Scott rebuilt 30ft. of the 14th-century spire, when a cock replaced the previous key. Further drastic restoration followed between 1874 and 1885, under the direction of Thomas Nicholson, and in 1905 more work to the south chapel and the tower was undertaken. St. Peter's serves as the civic church, with a special service on the first Sunday of each year. (The mayor is then able to check the time on the church clock—to the cost of which the council lavishly splashed out £30 in 1905, in order, it was said, to save the expense of a clock planned for the apex of their new Town Hall!).

One of the final ambitions of John Venn (for whom also see p.180), vicar of St. Peter's and St. Owen between 1833 and 1870 was to establish a church at Bartonsham where many new homes were being built. It was first suggested that the old parish and church of St. Owen should be revived (the church had been built outside the Norman defences by Walter de Lacy soon after 1075, but was destroyed by the Scots army in 1645 during the Civil War siege). Eventually a building on a smaller scale was agreed and the foundation stone of St. James' was laid in 1868 though, as one of a number of tributes to him, the church was first known as the Venn Memorial Church. In 1901 a fire all but destroyed the church at a time when the insurance cover had expired. To its credit, the Ecclesiastical Insurance office accepted that the premiums were about to

be posted and promptly paid up in full and the church was fully restored and reopened in 1903. The parishes were later combined, to become St. Peter and St. Owen with St. James.

The present church of All Saints, High Street, is at least the second to have been built upon this site at the west end of the Norman market place. In the side walls of the chancel there are the remains of an early 13th-century church, evidently of considerable size. The interior of the present church is mainly late 13th and 14th centuries. The tower and spire at the north-west corner, belonging to the same period, were unfortunately built on 12th-century rubbish pits, causing the foundation to give. Tower and spire gradually tipped to the north and in the 1780s buttresses were added to support them. These did not prevent service by the city surveyor of a 'dangerous building order' a century later, and when the 225ft. (68.5m.) high spire was restored in 1885 the top section was rebuilt, vertically, producing a noticeable kink. Further extensive work was carried out throughout the church just before the end of the century and the tower and spire continued to need attention. By 1990 another dangerous building order was looming and the church came near to closure. The spire and west gable of the nave were a public danger, the roofs leaked and the interior, it was said, 'smelt of damp, jumble sales and drains'! A new priest-in-charge, the Reverend Andrew Mottram, quickly brought about a change. From 1992 a vigorous three-phase programme of works dealt with essential structural repairs and rebuilding, costing almost £1 million. During 1996-97 a third stage produced a new gallery and free-standing 'pods' containing an oval vestry, office, kitchen, servery and other features of the new 'Café @ All Saints'. As one enters through the main south door leading from the High Street, the view to the right is of an 'Anglo Catholic' place of worship, where regular Sunday and weekday services continue and where the Lady Chapel is always available for prayer and quiet. To the left there is the new café and south gallery, 'skilfully fitted into the medieval fabric to serve the human need for physical as well as spiritual refreshment', as the church guidebook puts it.

In the 20th century the need arose for a place of worship nearer to the new residential areas in the north-eastern parts of the parish of All Saints and in 1912 St. Barnabas, a chapel-of-ease constructed of corrugated iron, was erected in Barrs Court Road near the Garden City. It remained in use until a more permanent church was built in Venn's Lane towards the end of the century.

Land to the west of All Saints, beyond the walls, had developed rapidly during the second half of the 19th century and the parish of Holy Trinity was created from portions of All Saints, St. John Baptist, St. Nicholas and St. Bartholomew, Holmer in 1902. A new church, subordinate to All Saints, was earlier erected in 1885 in Whitecross Road to the design of F.R. Kempson (without however his proposed tower and spire) and this was followed in 1907 by a chancel by Nicholson and Hartree.

F.R. Kempson's drawing of 'Whitecross Church' (Holy Trinity) with its intended tower and spire

Prebendary Leland Blashford-Snell, MBE, vicar between 1936 and 1959, started the 'Animal Services' at Holy Trinity held each St. Francis of Assisi Day and, with his wife, the RSPCA Animal Shelter. He joined the city council after wartime service and became Mayor of Hereford in 1950. Born in nearby Bodenham, his son, Colonel John Blashford Snell, OBE, has become a renowned explorer and was made an honorary freeman of the City of Hereford in 1984.

All Saints maintained a long relationship with St. Martin's, another parish in existence before the Norman Conquest and one of the most ancient in the city. Sometimes regarded as equals, and then as chapels of the other, their relationship was not clear until the late 19th century, when St. Martin's recovered its earlier independent status. The former church, standing at the corner of Wye Street, was consecrated in 1325, well before the existence of the masonry Wye Bridge. Complete with tower and steeple, depicted by John Speede in 1610, it survived until 1645 when it was damaged and eventually pulled down as a measure to prevent its use by the Parliamentary forces during the siege of the city. As the population on the south side of the river was not large it was not replaced, but after 200 years parishioners presented a petition to Parliament for a special grant to build a new church, on the grounds that the old church had been sacrificed in protection of the Loyalist army in 1645. They were not successful, but instead Queen Victoria granted a sum of £1,000 from a special fund towards the cost of £5,000 and the present church was opened in 1845. To a design by J.W. Jearrad, it was extended in 1895, the year when a part of the spire was blown down, wrecking the west gallery. The population of the parish increased steadily during the 20th century, especially after the Second World War, and following the building of high density housing in the parish the church of St. Francis of Assisi was built at Goodrich Grove.

At Bullingham Lane an area of more than 50 acres was acquired in 1938 for a hutted camp to house the first militia soldiers called up at the time

The church of St. Nicholas in c.1816, drawn from Bridge Street

of the Munich Crisis. After other uses—as a receiving centre for Dunkirk evacuees, ATS driving school, dispersal centre after the war, a home for the Army Technical School, Royal Army Service Corps and as a convalescence depot—it was occupied in 1960 by the 22nd Special Air Service Regiment and 264 (SAS) Signal Squadron. Some 50 members of the regiment are buried, and those who died in the Falklands War commemorated, in a regimental plot in St. Martin's churchyard and in May, 1983, a window of the church was dedicated to the Regiment.

St. Nicholas at the north end of Bridge Street, first mentioned in 1155 and the only parish church built within the Saxon defences, was damaged during the Civil War and restored in 1718. It was taken down in 1841 and a year later a new church was erected outside the walls. Designed by Thomas Ducham, a local architect, it was not the choice of the rector and others. Architecturally they would have preferred an alternative submission by George Gilbert Scott, and if contemporary illustrations are a true portrayal of the former

church, the chosen replacement certainly looks to be a poor exchange.

Other churches and denominations

Growth of the city also led to the building in 1865 of St. Paul's, Tupsley. Designed by F.R. Kempson, with an added choir vestry dating from 1914, it is one of the few churches within the city with an attached churchyard still in use for burials. The Church of St. Bartholomew, Holmer, stands just outside the city boundary. Started in the late 12th and early 13th centuries, it was heavily restored in the 1860s, as part of a widespread Victorian desire to 'smarten up' the buildings. It lost a great amount of its historic character, not helped when a vestry was added without foundations at the west end in 1860. This became a long source of trouble until, with an added new meeting room, it was skilfully replaced in 1997.

Detached from the church (but spared the depredations of the Victorians) is a 13th-century bell tower, with a black and white belfry dating from the reign of Elizabeth I, one of seven detached towers in Herefordshire. Congregations in the north of the city are also served by the small St. Mary Magdalene Church at Huntington, built in 1850 in the style of a Norman memorial chapel, also with its own churchyard, and by St. Mary's, Grandstand Road, founded in 1911.

The first Roman Catholic Church in the city was the church of St. Ethelbert, the cathedral, but it was disestablished and disendowed in the reigns of Henry VIII and Elizabeth I, when the Protestant church took its place. The parish of St. Francis Xavier was established in 1684 and the present church in Broad Street erected in 1838-9 to the design of Charles Day, county surveyor of Worcestershire. A specimen of the Doric order of Grecian architecture, its giant portico consists of two 13ft. diameter fluted columns and other features which Pevsner found 'bewildering', feeling that they 'would have driven Pugin frantic had he known it'! The church required restoration in 1889 and, as a listed building needed considerable attention and expenditure at the end of the 20th century.

The Church of Our Lady Queen of the Universe in Belmont Road was erected during the 1970s and its fabric received considerable further attention some 20 years later. The Jewish community meets in the church hall.

The Roman Catholic community is also served at Belmont, not far from the city, by the Abbey Church of St. Michael and All Angels. Built mainly of locally quarried stone in the Victorian Gothic style it opened in 1859, the architects being the firm founded by Augustus Welby Pugin. The handsome 112ft. (34m.) high tower and the north transept were added in the 1880s and the fine sacristies, built as a memorial to the then prior, Dom Wilfrid Raynal, came after his death in 1904. Extensive alterations were started in 1967 to meet the needs of the growing Belmont Abbey School and of the new liturgical movement and in 1979 a careful restoration of the interior was carried out under the direction of Hardmans of Birmingham. The most important changes included the building of a new high altar and sanctuary beneath the central crossing and the conversion of the east end into a Blessed Sacrament chapel. Belmont has a community approaching 50 Benedictine monks and serves parishes in Herefordshire, South Wales and Whitehaven, Cumbria, and, during the past 20

Belmont Abbey

Salvation Army Citadel, Canonmoor Street

years, it has also been instrumental in founding Tambogrande Monastery in northern Peru. Hedley Lodge, its guest house, acts as a special place of hospitality.

The Congregational Church in Hereford was founded in 1662 and met in a private house in Bridge Street until 1707 when members moved to Eignbrook. The first chapel was erected in 1720, replaced in 1829 and again in 1872. Now the United Reformed Church, it has a second church at Hampton Dene, Tupsley.

The Religious Society of Friends, the Quakers, met in a house in Hereford as far back as 1656, suffering some harassment and arrest in 1660 by the mayor, aldermen and other officers. In no way put off, they erected a meeting-house in Quakers Lane (now Friars Street) in 1689 following the Act of Toleration of that year until they moved in 1826 to their present building, tucked away on the north side of King Street. The Hereford Buddhist group now also meets there.

It is said that the Hereford Baptists first met for worship towards the end of the 18th century in a cottage at the rear of the Merton Hotel in Commercial Road. A chapel was erected nearer the city centre on the opposite side of the road in 1832 and the present church was opened nearer still in 1880, the earlier building being used as a Sunday School. Another later church was built at Web Tree Avenue, Putson. In 1796 John Price described 'a very neat Chapel in Berrington Street', built for the Methodists, according to Duncumb in 1804 'erected by the late Countess of Huntington ... fitted up with some elegance within, but unfinished on the outside' — although thought to have been established in 1787. The building was sold in 1887, to become a 'picture house' and eventually a bingo hall. Instead an iron structure was opened for worship at Crozens in Eign Road, later to be occupied by the First Church of Christ, Scientist.

The Wesleyan Methodists opened their church in Bridge Street in 1829, which was enlarged in 1868 and further improved in 1882. Its pulpit was occupied by many of the greatest preachers of the day and it was sad for Hereford Methodists when, on grounds of cost, the church had to close in the 1970s, first put to commercial uses but eventually left derelict, masked by a modern 'Home/Small Business Centre'. The Wesleyan Church in Holmer Road, erected in 1879 and enlarged in 1900, has also changed hands, more happily remaining as a place of worship for the Christadelphians, a body originating in the USA in the 18th century which holds that Jesus will return to establish His kingdom on Earth. Methodism meanwhile has flourished at St. John's in St. Owen Street, erected in 1880 with a Sunday School at the rear, and at Chandos Street in 1903. Until it settled in Maylord Street, the Salvation Army operated from various premises and, due to development of the Maylord Orchards shopping precinct was again on the move in the 1980s. Initially there were proposals for a new citadel to be built on the site of the former Trinity Almshouses, fronting Commercial Street, but this became a Pizza Parlour instead. In September, 1986, the Army, assisted by compulsory purchase proceeds from the commercial developers, occupied a prize-winning new building on a plot of former railway land at the junction of Edgar Street and Canonmoor Street. Designed by Kevin Jefferson, in collaboration with Major David Blackwell, their chief architect, this provided greatly improved facilities and opportunities.

From the mid-19th century there was a large influx of people from far beyond Herefordshire, changing not only the appearance but also the social character of the city. This showed in the appearance of new denominations and creeds. The Christian (Plymouth) Brethren occupied a building in Barton Road in 1859 and their Barton Hall now houses the Barton Christian Fellowship. The Church of Jesus Christ and Latter Day Saints—the Mormons—have a far more modern building in King's Acre Road. Also present are: Hereford Apostolic Church, Belmont; Elim Pentecostal Church, Clive Street; Christian Life Centre, Edgar Street; the House of the Good Shepherd Christian Spiritualist Church, Hollybush Walk; Circle of Light World Spiritualist Association, Highmore Street; the Seventh Day Adventist Church, St. Guthlac Street; and the Baha'i Faith—registered at Penn Grove Road.

However, the increase in the number of places of worship and creeds has not, for the most part, been matched by increased attendances, espe-cially towards the end of the 20th century. Where once Herefordians, indeed most Britons, went regularly to church or chapel every Sunday, rapid social change by the year 2000 finds their descendants treading very different aisles—furnished not with pews but with the shelves of consumerism. When all shops can by law open for business on every weekday and Sunday of the year, except Easter Day, it is not too fanciful to count shopping as an important new religion, and supermarkets, DIY stores and retail warehouses its churches and cathedrals!

Schools and colleges

The churches and charities were the main providers of education until after the 18th century and cathedral schools can claim to be the oldest in the land. It is quite possible that there was a school of a kind at Hereford well before 1179 when an edict of the Lateran Council in Rome directed that there should be a school in every cathedral town. However, the earliest acknowledged date for the existence of a grammar school in the city is 1384, when Bishop Gilbert appointed a headmaster to govern the boys 'with birch and rod'. There was an *Oldescholstrete* by then and it is thought quite possible that the recently exposed timbered hall at the Harley Court house of the present headmaster of Hereford Cathedral School was a part of that early school. During the Civil War an Old Herefordian, Colonel Fitzwilliam Coningsby, commanded the front line of defenders during the siege of 1645 and 'employed our boys by day and night to steal out and fire' the works of the Scottish army. From 1762 there was a brick-built school room on the western walk of the bishop's cloisters which was also used for Three Choirs Festival concerts, and hence known as the Music Room. It was taken down in 1836 and the school made a final move to the site of the former canons' bakehouse at the junction of Castle Street and Quay Street. From 1876 the present 'Big School' and three form rooms were erected, then extended with the Gilbert Library and two more form rooms in 1881, and again in 1884-5 with more additions to School House. No. 1 Castle

Hereford Cathedral School seen from the cathedral tower

Street was acquired as the Headmaster's house in 1912 and a pavilion, combined with a gymnasium, was erected at Wyeside in 1923 and replaced in 1968. A new block of science laboratories was opened in 1935 and greatly extended in 1974. The Old Deanery was taken over as a second Boarding House in 1945 and New Block built in 1950. The former College of the Vicars Choral was acquired in 1977 and became part of the administrative centre of the school, linking with No.29 Castle Street, purchased in 1979. A continuing increase in pupils, not least through a crucial move into co-education in the 1970s (there were almost as many girls as boys soon afterwards), created the need for even further property purchases in and around Castle Street, St. John's Street and Church Street. Then in the 1990s the striking new Viscount Portman Centre for Art and Technology and the Zimmerman Building and Powell Theatre, converted from the former telephone exchange and named after two 'Old Herefordian' benefactors, were added to the school.

No longer a boarding school, the composition of pupils has changed with a falling away of children of service personnel, those from South Wales and abroad. Despite the ending of assisted places, at around 900 pupils the school roll is larger in 2000 than it has ever been, extended by the junior school as a feeder. Founded as an independent preparatory school for boys in 1897, this also became part of the cathedral foundation in 1987, admitting girls in 1990.

The only other remaining private school in Hereford at the end of the 20th century was founded by Margaret Allen as a preparatory school for girls in 1923. Famously run as joint Principals by Marjorie Gibbs and Doris Barnes between 1938 and 1976 and popularly known as The Redcap School, it takes $2\frac{1}{2}$ to 11 year-olds.

There had once been many fee-paying private schools, providing either for older chil-

Advert for the Broomy Hill Academy

Advert for Hereford High School for Girls

dren, or 'dame schools' for younger ones. Anyone could open one without any check on their suitability, buildings or equipment. *Lascelles Directory* of 1851 listed 13 boarding schools for 'gents' and 'ladies' and seven day schools, mostly within or near the city centre. Typically, Hereford High School for Girls was opened at 117 St. Owen Street in 1885 to 'offer a sound and practical education in accordance with the requirements of the day', its affairs administered by a council elected by shareholders. Chandos School, established by the Rev. W. Bowell in 1865, prepared boarders and day boys for agricultural and commercial pursuits, the learned professions, civil service and 'First Grade Public Schools'.

The English Benedictines have an educational tradition extending back for more than a thousand years and in 1926 the Belmont Community established Belmont Abbey School, a relatively small boarding public school for about 290 boys just outside the city. There were five houses, four boarding and one day, and, following an extensive building programme in the 1960s, it developed a strong reputation in academic prowess and sport, notably rugby football and rowing, with its aim 'to provide a lasting Christian influence for tackling problems of life in a rapidly changing world'. But numbers of pupils fell and even after a short trial admission of sixth form girls the school faced a financial crisis and sudden closure before the end of the century. Much of the school land has since been used for new housing and residential accommodation which includes Hedley Lodge, designed as a modern guest house and restaurant.

The Blue Coat School, once called simply the Blue, was a charity foundation for the education of Hereford's poor children 'in the knowledge and practice of the Christian religion and for teaching them such other things as are most suitable to their condition', dating from 1710. It provided clothing for its pupils consisting of one shift, one white apron, two caps and two tippets for the girls, and two shirts, one pair of leather breeches, one pair of blue hose and a suit for the boys—later called the Blue Bugs. The site of the present building, formerly that of a workhouse, was conveyed to the trustees in 1752, but the new schools and houses of the Master and Mistress were not built until 1827. Soon afterwards, in 1839, there was a financial calamity when the treasurer, Dr. John Bleeck Lye, was 'found to be in default to the extent of £1,644. 1s. 11d.' Little was recovered and the issue of free clothing to children was stopped, capital assets were sold and the school was in some difficulty.

In 1841 Miss Emma Yapp was appointed as Mistress of the Girls' School 'upon condition that she obtains instruction in the meantime, the most proper to qualify her as an instructress'! She was also expected to recruit monitors from among the girls, whose duty it was to be 'crammed' with the information for each lesson in order to act as assistant teachers, a standard cost-saving arrangement of that time. In 1851 Henry Henwood was appointed as Pupil Teacher for 'not more than 7d. per week' and soon afterwards Margaret Ward was appointed as a teacher in the Girls' School with a salary of 1s. per week—provided she remained unmarried. When in 1897 another teacher, Miss Norman, asked for approval to wed, it was resolved 'that it would not be to the interest of the school to grant permission'.

Means tested fees were introduced between 1863 and 1918 and in 1903 the schools became the responsibility of the city council, as the local education authority.

In 1921 the boys were transferred to St. Owen's School and Blue Coat School became a school for girls only—and in 1932 a Senior Girls School, when girls were transferred from St. Peter's and Lord Scudamore Schools. In 1944 it was reorganised as a Secondary School and by 1958 had a roll of 830 girls. In that year the High School for Girls moved to new premises at Broadlands, on Aylestone Hill, and the council placed their buildings at Coningsby Street at the disposal of the Blue Coat School. Further reorganisation led to a merger with the Bishop's School at Hampton Dene Road in 1972, creating the Bishop of Hereford's Bluecoat C of E School. This resulted in debilitating daily shuttling between the two establishments during the early 1970s. Meanwhile, the redundant school buildings in Blue School Street were first adapted for the sale and manufacture of windows and afterwards became a food, drink and entertainment centre (mis-spelt Bushwackers—suggesting, according to one definition, a rendezvous for unsophisticated persons, boors or guerillas!).

In 1827, the girls and boys of the Blue were settling in to their new schools at the present site at a time when many of the 'superior classes' were not convinced that it was at all a good idea to educate the children of the poor and lower middle classes—for fear that they would develop revolutionary ideas and create trouble (thus on 3 December 1827, the Blue Schools' managers solemnly met to consider 'the propriety of teaching the girls to write'!). In the early 1800s, no government would touch the subject, all believing that they had enough on their hands without embarking upon something so potentially controversial and troublesome (this not long after the French Revolution), and until 1833 they were content to leave the churches and charities to provide a basic education for the poor. Only then was £20,000 grudgingly paid as a grant towards the upkeep of all church schools. In addition there had been Sunday Schools, free and normally aimed at teaching children of the poor, sometimes even their elders, to read the Bible and to spell.

Voluntary schools were founded in 1811 by 'The National Society for Promoting the Education of the Poor in the Principles of the

Established Church' to provide education founded on the national religion. By 1814 there was a National School for girls and boys in Eign Street, but Hereford had no 'British Schools' which provided for children of any religious persuasion and run by 'The British and Foreign Schools Society'. Subsequent voluntary parish and charity schools were: St. Francis Xavier's, 1835; St. Peter's, 1837; St. Owen's, 1838; St. Nicholas', 1844; Lord Scudamore, 1852; Holmer, 1857, St. Martin's, 1859; St. Paul's, Tupsley, 1867; St. John's, 1868 and All Saints', founded in 1870.

As to the 'superior classes', Hereford Ladies College opened in 1860 'to provide the middle classes of Hereford and the district with a superior education for their daughters, at a very moderate cost', and Broomy Hill Academy, Breinton Road, a 'Commercial, Boarding and Day School', taught many subjects in a school room noteworthy as 'Lofty and Well Ventilated'.

Built in 1880 in College Road, the Hereford County College provided for 90 boarders and many day boys (with reduction of fees for brothers). In addition to a full academic curriculum taught by the Rev. C.F. Muller and five assistant masters it provided parade ground drill from Sergeant-Major Halford. Its later history as the Royal National College for the Blind is recounted on pp.163-4.

The Working Boys Home started at a small cottage in Workhouse Lane (now Union Walk) in 1874 as a home for two destitute boys. The conditions of the time soon led to its expansion and by 1877 a much larger building had been opened in Bath Street for 35 grey-uniformed boys, aged between 9 and 14. By the turn of the century there were places for 125, many of them sent there from the courts after relatively minor crimes. Registered from 1877 as an Industrial School, institutions created by an Act of 1857 for the education of juvenile offenders and street children, the curriculum of gardening, farming, shoemaking and basketry prepared 'the fine, healthy, robust lad with a well knit frame; a bright eye; a smart appearance; and an intelligent face ... to

take his place, either at home or in one of the colonies, among the battalions of this world's busy toilers', as the author William Collins put it with such fervour at the time. The school continued until 1934 when it ran into financial problems and was bought by Herefordshire County Council for use as offices. Inherited in 1998 by the new Herefordshire Council, the buildings house Environmental Health and Trading Standards, Social Care and other services, as well as the Registry of Births, Deaths and Marriages. For poor and destitute girls of the Victorian era there was the Hereford Orphanage and Industrial School at Ivy House in Tupsley. Girls under 12 were transferred from the workhouse, clothed, maintained and instructed in washing, ironing, sewing, cooking and other branches of domestic service, as well as in the Three Rs and were in due course 'placed out to service'. Later the building was used as a hostel run by Social Services for people with learning disabilities, and in the early 1990s was rebuilt as a cul-de-sac of houses to provide more independent living arrangements.

As the 19th century progressed, education increasingly became a public matter, and as more children were sent to schools of various kinds, the widespread illiteracy of its earliest years was virtually wiped out. But there was very little good teaching: in 1902, 36% of all teachers had never passed the examination for a teachers' certificate and 55% had not attended a training college of any kind. A state system of education slowly evolved, notably through legislation such as the Act of 1870 which sought to ensure that there would be school accommodation in the city to meet all needs and, if necessary, to establish directly elected School Boards in places where existing schools were inadequate. Hereford preferred to retain the existing mixture of church and private schools. A school-leaving age of 13 was introduced under Acts of 1876 and 1880 (to be raised to 14 after the First World War and 15 after the Second). However the earlier reluctance of governments to enter the minefield of education proved to be well-justified by the state of confusion reached in the whole system at the turn of the century.

In 1902, legislation was passed which abolished much of what then existed and created a framework which subsequent legislation has built upon. Local education authorities (LEAs) were formed from county councils, whilst larger boroughs were granted powers to provide elementary, as distinguished from secondary or higher, education if they so wished. The resulting division of authority was not necessarily the best arrangement, but city councillors quite naturally considered that they were well equipped to deal with the education needs of their area. As a larger borough Hereford became an LEA for elementary education on 26 March, 1903, and formed an education committee numbering 16, made up of eight members of the council, including the mayor, representatives from two Church of England, one Roman Catholic and one non-denominational school together with four co-opted members, two of whom were to be women. It was decided that two of the co-opted members should represent secondary education, but suggestions to co-opt head teachers were vehemently opposed.

Lord Scudamore's, one of the oldest voluntary elementary schools, quickly reached a crisis. Early in the century one large room had to serve as the Boys' School, a relic of the days when the head teacher supervised a number of classes conducted by pupil staff, monitors and other ill-qualified teachers. Conditions in the girls' and infants' schools were hardly any better. The school's managers were unable to find the funds to meet Board of Education requirements as to sufficiency of accommodation and the school was condemned in 1910. In February, 1911, the establishment was handed over to the city council, which accepted responsibility for 240 boys, 170 girls and 197 infants in badly ventilated, lit, heated and overcrowded classrooms and with defective sanitary conveniences. There had been similar problems at St. Peter's Boys and Girls School in Union Street and these were duly handed over to the new LEA and re-opened for

girls in 1905 after extensive alterations. The first new school to be erected by the city council as LEA was St. Owen's, just off Bath Street, which was founded in 1905 and took over the boys of St. Peter's with the Head Teacher and his staff. The only other was Holmer Infants School which was opened in 1906 to the design of John Parker, city surveyor, following an adverse report by the Inspector of Schools about serious overcrowding of the Holmer and Huntington National School. Built of local bricks and sited next to the old mixed school it cost £2,000 and by 1910 catered for an average attendance of 179. The population of the schools' catchment area to the north of the city continued to grow and the Holmer C of E Voluntary Controlled School gained an additional block during the 1990s.

Herefordshire County Council became the LEA for secondary education and in 1912 opened the High School for Boys in Widemarsh Street. Built of local Hampton Park bricks by E.W. Wilks of Hereford at a cost of £10,000, it provided accommodation for 150 pupils. Their school fee was £6 per annum, plus 5s. towards the sports fund. It closed in 1973 and after use by the Manpower Services Commission as a centre for the Technical and Vocational Initiative in Secondary Schools (and advertised for sale with planning permission for light industrial use during the 1980s), by the end of the century the buildings had been taken over as the Hereford Education and Conference Centre of Herefordshire Council. They were used as an administrative centre, a venue for training and for child-care services. The architect of the school buildings, G.H. Jack, the county surveyor, went on to design the High School for Girls across the road in Coningsby Street which opened in 1914. As with all schools, there were many memories: 'old girls' still recall the days of the fearsome Miss Medwin, strict but fair, who insisted on school uniform, with felt or straw hats, being worn to and from school. She did not permit sweets or crisps to be devoured in the streets. King's tuck shop on the corner was out of bounds (some hope!) and the girls were released at different times from the all-too-close boys' school across the road. Miss Attenborough ('Atty'), head-mistress from the mid-1930s, was quite different in her approach, even holding inter-school parties and dances, and after retirement kept lively contact with pupils to the end of the century, when she died aged 99.

During the 1939-1945 war, both schools were shared for a term with St. Philip's Grammar School for Boys and St. Paul's Grammar School for Girls from Birmingham. The Hereford schools attended 5 days a week from 9a.m. to 1p.m., and those from Birmingham from 1.30p.m. to 4.30p.m. In 1982/83 the Girls High School building was sold to the diocese for the setting up of the combined St. Thomas Cantilupe C of E Primary School.

From 1 April 1945 the Education Act passed the previous year placed all public education under the direction of Herefordshire County Council, giving it control of all maintained elementary and secondary schools, the Teachers' Training College and the School of Arts and Crafts. Duties included making provision for school dinners, milk and general health care by six doctors, three school dentists and a number of school nurses and health visitors. The County Education Plan was approved in 1946, when secondary education was divided into three types: Grammar, offering an education leading to a university or profession (an estimated 11% of county children were expected to benefit from this type of education); Technical, offering a more practical and scientific training for an esti-mated 23% of children, leading to posts of responsibility in industry, trade and commerce; and Modern, offering a good general education with an appreciable amount of practical instruc-tion for the remaining 66%.

Post-war expansion meant that there were soon 14 primary schools within the city. South of the Wye provision for 360 infants and 480 juniors was made at Hunderton County Primary Schools and St. Martin's School, Ross Road; Our Lady's R.C. School, Boycott Road and Marlbrook School, Redhill were also built. Alongside the city wall near the city centre, St. Francis Xavier R.C. School moved from old cramped quarters adjoining the home of the teaching Sisters of Charity of the Order of St. Vincent de Paul in Berrington Street, to a new rural setting close to the College for the Blind in Venn's Lane. Broadlands School, also built on the fringe of the city, overlooked the Lugg Meadows and was adjacent to the Whitehouse/Prospect Farms housing estate. Proposals were in hand in the late 1960s for the building of Hampton Dene County Primary School and additions to St. Paul's Church of England primary school.

For children of primary school age with learning difficulties education was provided at the Uplands Residential Special School and, for day pupils, at Barrs Court Road and Blackmarston.

At secondary level, Bluecoat School provided GCE and vocational courses, notably pre-nursing training for up to 700 girls and Whitecross School had a similar number of boys — whose curriculum could include pre-engineering instruction. R.C. boys and girls were eligible for entry to St. Mary's School, Lugwardine. By 1959 these resources were no longer sufficient and two further schools were provided by the county council at Tupsley and Redhill. As local educa-tion authority it was forming proposals to convert its secondary modern schools to comprehensive schools when national restructuring of local government took place in 1972, making Hereford and Worcester County Council the new local education authority.

The new authority decided to proceed with comprehensive education in any event. It provided separate schools for infants between the ages of 5 and 7 years and juniors between 7 and 11 years in some areas, whilst in others a child could attend the one school from the age of 5 to 11 years. Secondary education was organised on a comprehensive basis for all children between 11 and 16 years at Aylestone, Haywood, Whitecross, Bishop of Hereford's Bluecoat and St. Mary's R.C. High Schools and, for those wishing to continue their education on academic lines, a transfer could be made to the Sixth Form College.

In 1998 Herefordshire Council became the LEA for the city and county, employing 3,500 teachers and other staff at its 103 schools.

All state schools received periodic visits from feared government-appointed inspectors (HMIs) for many years and under the 1988 Education Act, this function was passed to the Office for Standards in Education (OFSTED), headed by the Chief HMI. Their inspection report has to be followed by the school governors with a plan of action, revealed to every parent and made public on the internet. From 1997 inspections are intended to occur once every six years, unless special circumstances call for a greater frequency. As a result of an inspection by OFSTED at Haywood High School in 1999, castigation and adverse conclusions led to it being placed in 'special measures' control, involving imposition on the school of a task force, and to considerable changes in management and staffing. Both head and deputy-head teachers along with the board of governors had been suspended and a temporary headmaster was brought in from another local school. By summer 2000, GCSE results showed distinct improvements on previous years and within just four terms the school had pulled itself out of its demoralising status. Whitecross High School also received a visit from the inspectors, following which the local press quoted reports of 'weak-

nesses in leadership/management at all levels and a failure to provide consistently high quality teaching'. On the positive side, the inspectors regarded the school 'as having the capacity to instigate necessary improvements'. An Action Plan was prepared by staff and governors, endorsed by the LEA and a restructuring of management processes was introduced. There were soon encouraging national assessment results in the important core subjects from the school's 14-year olds—a good indication of their future GCSE prospects.

Post-16 Education

Provisions of the Education Act of 1944 to compel local authorities to secure an education for people over compulsory school age had been anticipated by 60 years in Hereford, with the opening of the country's first ladies training college for elementary school teachers in College Road. The Hereford College of Education quickly expanded to admit men and women over the age of 18 years, a high proportion from outside the county (as forecast by objectors to the original proposals). A new library block was completed in 1973 and a sports hall and Students' Union building followed shortly afterwards, but in 1977 the college was closed, in an exercise which retained only one teachers' training college in the then county of Hereford and Worcester. In

The Royal National College for the Blind in Venn's Lane, previously the Hereford College of Education

1978 the buildings were taken over by the Royal National College for the Blind, whose students are prepared for entry into universities and higher education generally, or train directly for open employment in commerce. The college was also established as an Academy of Music and many students train as pianists, piano tuners, organists and other professions in music; there is also a course in braille music for qualified teachers. A department of living skills pioneered a course in which blind or partially sighted students learn to move and travel safely, to shop and cook, to manage a home and a family and generally to learn the techniques and conventions of the sighted world. This has enabled students from all over Britain and abroad to live entirely independent lives, and to hold down employment in open competition with sighted people. By 1980 the number of students had reached 160, the majority boarding in halls of residence in Venn's Lane which were modernised in the late 1990s.

In 1945 the county director of education had proposed that community centres for youth and adults should be provided on the same sites as secondary schools. The new duty of providing facilities for further education in such a manner 'would be more economical than their provision independently and at a later date. In this way much of the accommodation would be available for the dual purpose of secondary and further education, having the additional advantage of avoiding the duplication of halls and cinema and of gymnasia'.

Technical education was initially provided to a limited extent by the schools. During 1941-2, St. Owen's Evening Institute averaged just under 500 students and the School of Arts and Crafts and the Evening Technical School brought the total attendance to 929. In 1950 the Herefordshire Technical College was founded and moved in 1954 into the first phase of purpose-built new premises at Folly Lane. It quickly expanded until in 1993 it became independent of local authority control, becoming one of the top six employers in Hereford, with a staff of over 700 and an annual budget in excess of £6 million. Of these, around 150 were full-time and nearly 400 part time teachers, supported by over 70 non-teaching staff. Full-time courses are designed to equip students with a degree, HNC, HND, professional qualifications or skills for a future in business, industry, or higher education. Vocational courses include business and finance, education, health and social care, computing, construction, electronics, engineering, furniture design and crafts, hairdressing and beauty, the hospitality industry and secretarial administration. AS (Advanced Subsidiary) and A-level courses are available in the day or evening for 15 subjects and GCSE tuition is provided for English, mathematics, human physiology and health. Amid thoughts in 2000 that the college could have grown 'too far, too fast', it was obliged to consider ways of reducing expenditure and income losses in a 'recovery plan'.

Herefordshire College of Art and Design developed from early beginnings in 1852 and in 1969 the Hereford School of Arts and Crafts at Castle Green moved to purpose built accommodation next to the Technical College at Folly Lane. The only college of its kind specialising in art, design, media and performing arts in the West Midlands, it offers a wide range of vocational courses for entrance to the professional world of designer/maker, artist and craftsperson. Subjects are as diverse as ceramics, jewellery and silversmithing, blacksmithing, fashion and textiles, printmaking, photography, graphics and illustration, theatre studies, computer-aided design and general drawing and painting.

In 1973 the campus at Aylestone Hill was further extended with the opening of the Sixth Form College with about 250 students. They were taught in cramped conditions in Broadlands, formerly a private house, and in terrapin huts, but in 1974 it moved to purpose-built buildings in Folly Lane. It took over post-16 education from the secondary schools in the city and some adjacent areas and by 2000 had more than 1,000 students. This healthy expansion has enabled a wide range of subjects to be offered to prepare students for entry to university and other further education institutions, as well as posts in commerce and industry. The standards achieved have placed the college nationally in third place in an A-level Performance System (ALPS), which compares students' performance at GCSE with how they fare at A-level, and also identifies it as a top Department of Education 'Beacon' college. Modern buildings include a science block, lecture theatre, sports hall, a library and resources centre and facilities for arts, music, languages, computing and other specialist accommodation. Beyond the examination subjects, students also work at ways of extending their development, interests and skills and all are required to join in a recreational programme.

The demand for courses and places at the campus quickly meant that the buildings, and staff, student and visitors' car parks, were not adequate and colleges soon had to improvise and spread. Several 'temporary' mobile structures and large houses were put to use in Folly Lane and Aylestone Hill, causing the planning authority concern about a long-term loss of amenity and housing stock. Local residents and the highway authority also reacted badly to the day-long term-time invasion of kerbsides by staff and students' cars.

Space is not such a problem at the county's College of Agriculture at Holme Lacy, about five miles to the south-east of the city. This was a help when the technical college needed a new home for the blacksmithing and farriery centre, previously at the Burcott Road annexe, for there had been fears that, after 40 years, this renowned facility would be lost to the county. In the late 1990s the National Centre for Blacksmithing, Farriery and Rural Crafts was installed at Holme Lacy, where it is operated in collaboration with the College of Art and Design. It had long been appreciated that tuition in agriculture and horticulture would be most necessary in a county such as Herefordshire and during the 1940s expert tuition was provided at some of the larger schools. Young Farmers' Clubs also played their part but much more was needed and in the late 1960s the county council purchased much of the Bower Farm near its teaching farm at Holme Lacy and opened the new

College of Agriculture. With a declared purpose 'to maintain and enhance the rural economy', the college offers courses covering agriculture, animal care and veterinary nursing; countryside, forestry, environmental management and game-keeping; equine studies and horse care; floristry, horticulture and garden design; leisure, tourism and outdoor recreation.

Adult Education

From the 1950s, the many new schools, colleges and other educational establishments in the city increasingly provided part-time and evening classes for adults of all ages. This followed a 200 year-old tradition of encouraging people to learn to read and write—the chapel and church Sunday Schools were part of this effort, but their help was limited to half-a-day once a week. Another venture was undertaken by Benjamin Followes in 1815 when he set up the Hereford Permanent Library in St. John Street. When the Reverend John Venn became vicar of St. Peter's the first of his many enterprises for the improvement of life in the city was to establish the St. Peter's Literary Institution in a room over the vestry in 1836. Happily an Act of that year reduced the newspaper tax from 4d. to 1d. a copy, a valuable help in equipping the reading room with the daily London and provincial papers and magazines which would normally be beyond the means of poorer citizens. By the time the Institution moved to Bye Street (Commercial Street) in 1851 the reading room, lending library and popular lectures had become a much valued service and had been joined by similar ventures. Subscription reading rooms were opened close to the public baths at Castle Green and the Athenaeum and Mechanics' Institution was established in 1840 near the Cathedral Close. It was open from 7 a.m. till 10 p.m. for subscribers paying 5s. per year for use of the small library and reading room. Some time afterwards a reading room, furnished with arm-rest seats, was set up at the nearby 17th-century Grapes Inn for the benefit of leading tradesman to hear the *London Letter*, delivered weekly by stage-coach, read to them by an annu-

The room at The Grapes Inn where leading tradesman heard the weekly London Letter *read to them by an annually appointed chairman. Other inns had similar arrangements*

ally appointed chairman. Each seat was solemnly assigned, and described by one observer as 'sacred as the front seats in Parliament'. Other inns had similar facilities—until the arrival of the railways.

Innumerable clubs and societies formed from early in the 19th century, most notably the Woolhope Naturalists' Field Club, first limited to 40 members, which was founded in 1851 to hear and discuss papers and organise field meetings. In the 1870s the universities embarked on a movement to take themselves close to those who could not attend and in 1884 Oxford started classes in Hereford. Then in 1903 the Workers' Educational Association (WEA) was formed to unite existing adult education organisations and provided advanced classes for adult working class students. A branch was formed in Herefordshire, said to have been very weak up to the outbreak of the Second World War. The

appointment of a resident tutor soon produced a marked improvement and during five years from 1939 the number of classes increased from 13 to 44, and student enrolments from 202 to 760. By 1943-4 these classes were being held not only in Hereford and the five other market towns but also in many villages. The WEA has since flourished and expanded and, to the benefit of students throughout the county, has more recently established a good working relationship with the University of Birmingham Extramural Department.

Despite some representations, Hereford could never qualify for a university of its own but has shared in the success of the Open University, based locally at Birmingham. Since 1969 tuition by correspondence, linked with special radio and television programmes, residential schools and a locally-based tutorial and counselling service, has produced many Hereford graduates.

Library Services

The presence of a cathedral, as well as St. Guthlac's monastery, made Hereford a place of learning from its earliest days but, as with the school, it is not possible to say when the first library existed. One possible clue is provided by the oldest book in the present chained library, the *Anglo-Saxon Gospels*, which was written some 100 years before the death of Alfred the Great in 899. It was given to the cathedral before the Norman Conquest and is the only volume in the library which survived the Battle of Hereford of 1055. It would have had a liturgical use in the Saxon cathedral; a millennium later, as a ceremonial oath book at services for the enthronement or installation of bishops and deans, it is still in use. The origin of the library can more clearly be traced to the beginning of the 12th century: there is one volume of the 9th or 10th century, four of the 11th century, 92 of the 12th and 52 of the 13th century, including the *Hereford Breviary* of 1270, which is the only known copy with music (lost to the library for 300 years until 1834). There are 49 books of the 14th century and 28 of the 15th century, including the Wyecliffe ('cider') Bible, famous because of its alternative translation for 'strong drink' as used in the Authorised version. Some 227 items in the collection are manuscript volumes, but many of the remainder originate from the earliest days of printing, including about 70 'incunabula' (books printed before 1500), two of which are Caxton's of 1483. From 1590 the books were kept in secure chests in the Lady Chapel, but after the appointment of Thomas Thornton as precentor and master of the library, and not before time, extensive reorganisation and development occurred. As one measure, Richard Rogers, a Hereford carpenter, was employed in 1611 to make shelves, desks and seats, modelled on those which Thornton must have seen at Sir Thomas Bodley's library when he was a canon at Oxford. The brass clips and chains for securing the books by their covers were regularly bought and fitted from then until as late as 1910, although 'the cumbrous bookcases' so disliked by Dean Merewether had been moved from the Lady Chapel in 1841, prior to the major restoration of the cathedral. There have been many priceless acquisitions covering theology, law, medicine, botany, philosophy and a wealth of other subjects over the years, including books from the dissolved Jesuit College at Cwm (on the border with Monmouth), the 600 volume library of the vicars choral (some of it also chained) and, not least, from the libraries of F.C. Morgan and his daughter, Penelope. As former librarians they will always be associated with the collection and, thanks in no small way to their work, the modern library now contains about 9,000 volumes.

All Saints Church possessed the third chained library in Hereford, dating mostly from the 17th century, though some of its 326 books are older (for example a treatise of 1429 on the seven deadly sins, in Latin, by Alexander Carpenter of Balliol College, Oxford). The majority, consisting of books of divinity, morality and history, were bequeathed in 1715 by Dr. William Brewster, a parishioner, for the further education of the vicar! In the mid-1850s the entire collection narrowly escaped being removed to America, after a zealous churchwarden sold everything for £100. Books and chains were taken to London, but came to the notice of the Dean of Windsor, a patron of All Saints. His consent was needed for the sale, which he withheld, and all were safely returned to 'The Chapel of the Books' at All Saints. There they remained until 1992, when further financial problems led to their purchase by the Mappa Mundi Trust for safekeeping at the other end of Broad Street, in the cloister approach to the new cathedral library building.

By the middle of the 19th century the small reading rooms, libraries, clubs and Mechanics' Institute bookshelves were no longer sufficient to satisfy the increasing hunger for books and papers. Many were no better stocked than charity shop shelves of a later era and a national campaign led to new legislation. The Public Libraries Act of 1850 authorised towns such as Hereford to use the product of a half-penny rate to provide libraries. In 1855 this was increased to one penny, hardly enough to produce anything adequate. The city fathers did not rush to secure the necessary powers: as it was they were preoccupied with the urgent need to improve the sanitation and physical health of their citizens. Indeed, a passionate dislike for spending money caused some members to question the need for such profligacy. The chances for a free library seemed bleak, but interest in all forms of literature nevertheless continued to grow. In no way was this more proven than in attendances at popular Penny Readings of the day. A typical event advertised in a handbill advised of:

Hereford Penny Readings
The First Reading of the Session
will be given at the
Corn Exchange
on
Friday Evening, Nov. 9th, 1866
The Worshipful the Mayor in the chair
(F.G. Symonds, Esq.)
Readers and Reciters:- Messrs. Flavel Edmonds,
Owen Fowler
W.A. Hill, Bellamy, Greenhow, Humfrys and
Shellard.
Admission One Penny
Jos. Carless, Junr., Hon. Sec.

The audience comprised 378 people, many paying 6d. for reserved seats, and humorous and serious readings given by the intellectuals of the city were clearly appreciated by all.

But, as in many towns, it fell to philanthropy to provide the necessary means for new public libraries. The greatest benefactor was Andrew Carnegie who, from 1882, paid for buildings in 380 towns during his lifetime. Hereford did not need his generosity, for in 1871, when a penny rate produced only £325, James Rankin of Bryngwyn House, offered to help. Through the Woolhope Club he was prepared to provide capital to purchase a site and erect suitable buildings for a combined library and museum. The council had to adopt the Act of 1855, which this time it did with alacrity, and also agree to a separate room for the Woolhope Club. Designed by the local architect, F.R. Kempson, the tall building has been described as 'Anglicised

Venetian Gothic'. Featuring an intricate coloured stone facade of animal, foliage and zodiac carvings, it has at different times been described as 'a thing of beauty, which time seems to increase' as well as 'high beyond its station and pretentious in its architecture'. It eventually cost £7,600 of which Sir James paid £6,115 and the council covered the balance. The foundation stone was laid in 1873 and the library was opened on 8 October, 1874. It was an immediate success and the initial ground floor shops and later committee room were soon converted to library use, and as a reading room for women. By the end of the century, as the population reached 21,000, over 60,000 book issues a year were being made. Thanks to a bequest from Sir Joseph Pulley and a gift from his nephew Charles Pulley, extensions at the back to Aubrey Street enabled a new lending library, reference library and art gallery to be opened in 1912. From then on, borrowers had free access to the shelves and a growing number of acquisitions was enhanced by valuable collections willed by Walter Pilley, Alfred Watkins and others.

By the late 1950s space was obviously at a premium and to the accompaniment of official assurances that plans were 'in hand' for a new library for Hereford, a mezzanine floor was added above the old lending library in 1963. Another mezzanine floor was built in the reference library in 1974 and a lift was introduced, but these were about the last improvements by the city council before local government reorganisation placed its function in the hands of Hereford and Worcester County Council. This body also inherited the library of Herefordshire County Council in the former Garrick Theatre, where it had moved in 1946. Originally in Bath Street, the county library service had commenced in the late 1930s, operating six district branches. These corresponded to the six market towns and functioned through sub-branches and some 230 other issuing centres, often found in village shops. The old theatre building was demolished to make way with its neighbours for the Garrick House multi-storey car park and from 1974 the two library services were concentrated at Broad Street. The

A detail of the carving on one of the pillars at the library

college libraries were also made accessible to the public by the education authority, those of the technical and art colleges being amalgamated in 1988 to form a new Herefordshire Campus Library.

The new county council quickly committed itself to the building of a new library for Hereford, its space problems compounded by the continuing dual use of the building. The new city council had retained the museum and art gallery functions, and for the next 24 years there was continual wrangling between the two authorities as to the ownership of the whole property. The dispute was only settled for good when the Herefordshire Council came into being in 1998 and took on all the functions.

Almost a quarter of a century after the previous pledge, and 40 years after the first, the next new authority also undertook to provide a new public library in Hereford. After considering factors for and against sitings at the council-owned town hall, butter market or Gaol Street car park, Herefordshire Council announced at the end of 2000 that its preferred choice, funding permitting, was for conversion of the privately owned, and unlovely, 30 year-old Kemble House in Broad Street. Negotiations commenced with owners Sterling House Estates of Ross-on-Wye for use of the site to provide 38,000 sq. ft. of 'open plan'

floor space, accommodated on three levels at an estimated construction cost of £3.4 million.

Museums

The Woolhope Naturalists' Field Club (named after the Woolhope Dome, a famous haunt for geologists and naturalists, to the east of the city) was formed in 1851 to study local natural history and archaeology. It first lodged at the Castle Green premises of the Hereford Literary, Philosophical and Natural History Society, but when James Rankin became President in 1869, he indicated that he would like to provide the club with its own museum and in 1871 the club and Hereford City Council agreed upon the scheme for Broad Street. A large room of 44 ft. by 20 ft., with a balcony, was dedicated to the use of the club and also used as a reference library. The museum room was on the next floor. Collections of natural history, zoology, botany, geology and Roman remains were exhibited, many donated by Woolhope Club members. One special contribution came from the collection of coleoptera, lepidoptera and hymenoptera orders of insect of Dr. T.A. Chapman, whilst practical help came from the Hereford Society for Aiding the Industrious with a loan of £300 to help with more furniture. But even by the early 1900s the city council could lawfully only spend up to the product of a halfpenny rate (about £270 a year) to cover mainte-nance and other museum purposes. It is not known in 1907 how Sir James Rankin, Bart. (as he had become), viewed museum attendance figures of over 6,000 during his second Presidency of the Woolhope Club, but he might well have been disenchanted by the use made of the Woolhope Room at the time, for it was 'not patronised to the extent one might desire', according to William Collins. Nearly a hundred years later, keys to the room and its well ordered reference library are still available to the 700 or so Woolhope Club members, and books, although not manuscripts, may be borrowed for up to 12 months of study. Otherwise, because of fire regu-lations, the room is limited to no more than 40 people during library opening hours.

In 1912 a new Art Gallery was opened above the extended lending library and in 1925 Mr. Frederick C. Morgan (1878-1978) was appointed librarian and curator, a position he held for the ensuing 20 years. Doubtless he had a part in the formation of the Friends of Hereford Museum and Art Gallery in 1928 through which the permanent collection of the gallery and the range of museum exhibits was considerably boosted

with funds. Many donations of domestic, agricul-tural, industrial and archaeological items were also received, to the stage when there was great pressure on space, not always in the interests of the articles. Lack of adequate museum space severely limited the variety and frequency of displays, and much of the collection has remained in perpetual storage. Since the retirement of Mr. Morgan, successive curators have hoped that, one day, the library service will move to new quarters and give them the room and opportunity to provide the museum service at Broad Street which Hereford has long deserved.

One opportunity did occur in 1965 when the house and grounds of Dr. Wood Power at 3 Venn's Lane was purchased by the city council to provide a memorial to Sir Winston Churchill, who had died that year. Churchill Gardens Museum was opened in 1966 and, set in a large park overlooking the city, it houses an extensive costume collection, including smocks, and fine 18th- and 19th-century furniture, watercolours, glass and porcelain. On the first floor there is a furnished Victorian nursery, butler's pantry, kitchen and parlour. The Sandford collection of straw work and corn dollies and displays of local

The Churchill Gardens Museum

Inside the Old House

and left in 1837, almost by chance, as the only relic of Butchers' Row, it had a variety of commercial uses. In 1877 it was occupied by Matthew Oldfield, an ironmonger, and Henry Fletcher, a fishmonger, and eventually was bought by the Worcester City and County Banking Company, later incorporated into Lloyds Bank. In 1928, when the bank moved to its new building next to the Buttermarket, it presented the building to the city. The Old House was turned into a museum, furnished on three floors in the Jacobean period and later relieved from the harmful effects of 20th century traffic flows and enhanced in 1989 with a final phase of 'pedestrianisation'.

The gathering, treatment and piping of pure clean water from the mid-1850s was as important an advance in the shaping of Hereford as any, and the early pumps, steam, diesel and gas engines, boilers and other plant are as much a part of the heritage of the city as the polluted wells and watersellers' buckets which they replaced. The first waterworks building was

clocks, dolls, barometers also delights visitors prepared to make their way up Aylestone Hill. Adjoining the main building, the Hatton Gallery was erected in 1973 in memory of Hereford artist Brian Hatton, who was killed in 1916 during World War One. Described as 'a genius unique in the history of British art' and compared with Lawrence, Landseer and Millais, his work in the gallery includes drawings, water-colours and pastels depicting Edwardian Herefordshire. Larger items, including the judge's coach and a painted gypsy caravan, are stored in an outbuilding. Although within enticing sight of the city centre, the museum and gallery are beyond the acceptable range of too many people, and low attendances and revenues have resulted in a sorry state of neglect and deterioration by the end of the 1990s, despite local protests.

The Old House, St. Peter's Street does not suffer from such 'remoteness'. Dating from 1621

Fire engine c.1805 pumped by 13 men, at the Waterworks Museum

begun in 1856 and when, just over a hundred years later, the chairman of the newly formed Water Board first entered the Broomy Hill buildings and saw the 'wonder and majesty' of the old pumping engines, he recalled 'they took my breath away'. The experience was not forgotten and in 1974 the Waterworks Museum was officially opened by the first chairman of Welsh Water, Lord Brecon. The museum's main aim is 'to tell the story of drinking water supplies and distribution in Wales and the Marches from pre-industrial revolution to the present day'. In achieving this, many skilled and devoted volunteers have, with the curator, produced a nationally acclaimed live working museum and striking tribute to Victorian engineering; some machines are the last examples of their type working anywhere in the world.

When the water was unfit to drink it was, within limits, always much safer in Herefordshire to drink home-produced or farm cider. Many farmworkers were partly paid in cider and some were said to manage two gallons a day. Percy Bulmer made his first cider with apples from the garden of his father's rectory at Credenhill and in 1887 founded in Ryelands Street what was to become the largest cidermaking company in the world. Esmond, his grandson, became chairman in 1982 and at around the same time, Bertram Bulmer a previous chairman and son of Fred, one of the two founders, was the chief inspiration for the Cider Museum and King Offa Distillery. At Pomona Place, off Whitecross Road, close to where the two brothers started the family business (apart from a very modest first step in a Maylord Street warehouse), it contains an enormous 17th-century French beam crushing press, a cooper's shop, an old farm cider house, travelling cider-maker's tack, champagne cider cellars, pressing house and a 1920s bottling line. After challenges by French producers and debate over EU rules concerning use of marketing names such as 'Apple Brandy' and 'Calvados', one of the galleries finally houses the first cider brandy distillery to be licenced in Britain for over 200 years. In a less fruitful dispute Bulmers was

forced to abandon the description of 'Champagne Cider' for its annual 600,000 case output of Pomagne, making do with 'sparkling cider' instead.

For a period from 1968 the cider makers opened the Bulmer Railway Centre, a standard gauge steam railway museum. Its attractions included the famous 1927 GWR locomotive King George V, which was restored for main line duty by H.P. Bulmer and used with five Pullman coaches to form an exhibition train and reception centre at Hereford and other towns. Eventually the long Pullman coaches became unsuitable for the company's level of business and were sold to become part of an 'Orient Express' holiday-train enterprise, whilst the King George V was returned to the railway museum at Swindon. The sale proceeds went towards conversion of redundant cellars at Ryland Street for use by the museum.

The St. John Medieval Museum at Coningsby Hospital, Widemarsh Street dates from the 13th century and includes the chapel and hall of the Knights Hospitaller of St. John of Jerusalem. The chapel has some Jacobean heraldic glass and furniture and contains a museum showing fine armour, blazons, documents, medals and models connected with the Order of St. John during the 300 years of the Crusades. Upstairs the Infirmary has a window into the Chapel from which the sick could follow the services and has been arranged with life size models in period dress showing how the sick pensioners of the hospital were cared for.

The Herefordshire Regimental Museum, Harold Street at the Territorial Army Centre houses a collection of uniforms, colours, weapons and documents from much later Actions. Exhibits also include medals and regimental silver and visitors may be surprised to see, at an army museum, the pennants of Grand Admiral Karl Doenitz, commander-in-chief of the German navy from 1943 - 1945. He became the last Führer of the Third Reich after the death of Adolf Hitler and was captured in 'Operation Blackout' by the 1st Battalion Herefordshire Regiment on 23 May, 1945 at Flensburg with Dr.

Doenitz Pennant

Speer, Col-General Jodl and other top Nazis. His pennants were removed for safe keeping and brought to Hereford: he was responsible for the final surrender to the Allies and in 1946 sentenced to 10 years imprisonment for war crimes. (The regiment, in which many citizens have served, received the Freedom of the city on 25 September, 1945).

Herefordshire Record Office is also in Harold Street, at the Old Barracks, and stores written records of very many aspects of Herefordshire life, from the 11th century to modern times. It is extensively used by authors and other researchers in local or family history: among the large number of documents placed in the archive are most of the county parish registers, and census returns for the half century from 1841.

Other Public Edifices and Establishments

Duncumb in his *Collections towards the History and Antiquities of the County of Hereford* refers to a conveyance in 1763 of the late Dr. Brewster's house of 1698 in Widemarsh Street for 'the accommodation of the judges on their circuits, and to the public uses of the mayor for the time being'. It was thus called the Mansion House, but it suffered from neglect and was sold in 1795 to John Sherburn. The judges were afterwards lodged at Bodenham Road (Judges Close), 5 Commercial Street (from 1937 the site of the Odeon cinema) and then Carfax, in Aylestone Hill.

By the 1900s, new mandatory and discretionary functions placed on the council concerning provision of gas, water, electricity, roads, sewers, estates, health, housing, markets, libraries, museums and accountancy services, increased the need for office space. Responsibility for education was to follow in 1902, by which time the search for extra room became increasingly urgent. Options at the Mansion House and in Commercial Street were considered, and John Parker, the city surveyor, produced a striking design for the junction of Widemarsh Street and Maylord Street (the later Elts/public conveniences/electricity showrooms corner). It might well have been adopted, but out of the blue came a gift to the council of Nos. 140, 139 and 139a St. Owen Street from the son and daughters of the late town clerk. After purchasing adjoining YWCA and other land, it advertised for designs in an open competition, which produced several proposals. The recommendation of an appointed assessor was not adopted by the council who instead chose the design of Mr. H.A. Cheers of

The Town Hall

Twickenham. A foundation stone was laid on 13 May 1902, by Queen Victoria's youngest daughter, Beatrice, Princess Henry of Battenberg, and on 9 June 1904, Hereford's new town hall was formally opened by Mayor Beddoe. Congratulatory speeches were dampened only by accounts of overspending, the final cost of building, furniture, fees, heating and lighting amounting to well above expected costs. Externally the new town hall was described at the time as 'massive, commanding and artistic, probably a little out of harmony with its surroundings'. Internally it was well adapted to the business of the city, containing an impressive entrance hall, offices of the town clerk, medical officer of health, sanitary inspector, school attendance officer, collector of rates, chief accountant and numerous clerks. The ground floor committee room was lined throughout with solid oak taken from the house bought from the YWCA. There were four rooms off the half landing for the city surveyor and his clerks and further stately stairs led to the main landing. This served the large assembly room and a stairway to its gallery, the mayor's parlour and reception room, a waiting room and a further flight of steps to the council chamber and a committee room. There were apartments for the caretaker off the third landing, whilst the basement housed the gas fitting and lamp lighting department.

The county council had been created under the Local Government Act, 1888, with powers similar to those of the city, and operated from the Shirehall in St. Peter's Square which had opened in 1817. Erected from the designs of Sir Robert Smirke, its portico is supported by eight giant columns of the Grecian-Doric order. An entrance hall leads to courts of law, jury and committee rooms and a library, terminating with a flight of steps leading to the assembly and concert hall — to which a stage for orchestras and choirs was added in 1863. The buildings contained offices for the county clerk, chief constable, director of education and other officials and in course of time other accommodation was acquired at Bath Street, at Daws Road for the county surveyor and Chandos House, St. Owen Street for the county planning officer.

In 1894, Hereford Rural District Council was created to take its share of growing local government functions affecting the villages and parishes around Hereford and initially shared 8 St. John Street with the Hereford Board of Guardians (which continued to function until it was replaced by the county council in 1929). Subsequently the district council moved its headquarters to 1 Ledbury Road and remained there until the early 1970s when local government reorganisation produced South Herefordshire District Council. When the police moved from Brockington, in Hafod Road, to De Lacy Street, the district council took over, adding extensions for its council chamber and further offices.

After considerable argument against the use of gas during the early 1820s, the first works was situated near Herrons Works on Commercial Road (near the modern Safeway supermarket site) and operated by the Hereford Gas-Light and Coke Company. It was eventually purchased by the council in 1872 but was soon found to be too small to meet the growing demand and a new works was built eight years later at Perseverance Road in Holmer. By the turn of the century some 4,500 houses were connected to the supply, their standard of lighting greatly enhanced by newly introduced incandescent mantles. (Hereford's gas supply is now tapped off the national pipe network at Ross and brought by high pressure main via Lugg Bridge into the city.)

Britain's first power station became operational in 1882, from when many applications were made to the council for permission to establish works in the city. All were refused and it took until 1897 for the city fathers to apply to the Local Government Board and the Board of Trade for the necessary powers to establish a power plant. As in the case of gas at the start of the century, there was opposition: in 1899, when the Electricity Supply Works at Widemarsh Street, near the market, were about to start production, Alderman Bosley issued a circular to city ratepayers advising them, on grounds of cost, to keep to gas. Yet, the town hall was among the first buildings to be lit, at least in part, by electricity, and the alderman's fears soon turned out to be ill-founded. The production cost fell from 2.81d. per unit in 1902 to 1.2d. by 1911 and the selling price reduced in proportion—the whole enterprise placing no burden on the rates. Much of the credit was due to the design of the installation and it attracted increasing numbers of consumers. Its capacity was often increased, notably to cater for the special demands of the ordnance factory at Rotherwas during the First World War. The introduction of the National Grid greatly increased the areas of the county that could be served by electricity and production came to be concentrated from 1929 in the hands of the Shropshire, Worcestershire and Staffordshire Electric Power Co. Gradually much of the gloom and drudgery of the ubiquitous paraffin lamp and open range were removed from rural areas, whilst a large part of the city converted from direct to alternating current.

In 1978 Hereford became a focus of attention with the announcement that the Midlands Electricity Board (then responsible for electricity supply to Herefordshire) was to build a Combined Heat and Power Station at Moorfields. In addition to supplying electricity to Hereford it provided hot water and steam to two major companies—H.P. Bulmer and Sun Valley—and some smaller concerns. The thermal efficiency of the station was 76%, more than double that of a conventional power station, where much heat is dispersed and wasted. The oil used to drive the engines and fire the four boilers was a cheap, low grade residue which could be delivered by rail, using Bulmers' private siding rather than adding heavy fuel tankers to the roads of Hereford. However, the privatised Midlands Electricity, created in 1989, found the unit commercially uneconomical as a source of energy when compared with that of its much larger generating stations. But the local factories still require their steam supply and as the oil-driven engines were not free from troubles, the station was converted to gas (but not before a tragic explosion of one of the oil tanks killed a repair worker). Meanwhile the private siding is likely to be employed as part of a new initiative for greater use of rail transport by Bulmers.

Hereford had a postmaster in 1672 and its first official Post Office in 1682. It was situated at the Sun Tavern, High Town in the 1730s and by 1783 the London post went out first thing every Sunday, Tuesday and Thursday morning via Gloucester and Monday, Wednesday and Friday through Worcester—returning every Sunday, Tuesday, Thursday, Friday and Saturday at 7p.m. By 1805 the Post Office had moved to the City Arms, Broad Street, letters being put in a letter-box, through a window, before transferring to King Street in the 1830s. The present main office in Broad Street was opened in 1882 and has changed very little in appearance for well over a century. There were proposals in 1981 to replace it and the St. Peter's Street Post office with a new one on the north side of Maylord Street, with offices extending over adjoining unit shops and with an area for GPO vans at the rear. Despite several meetings with Norwich Union, developers of Maylord Orchards, terms could not be agreed. A new post office was opened at 14/15 St. Peters Street in June 2002, replacing those across the road and at Broad Street and Eign Street.

Although the telephone had been patented by Alexander Graham Bell in 1876, the service spread rather slowly, partly due to objections to the wires and poles. It was initially operated by private companies and some local authorities, but in Hereford the council did not become involved and the National Telegraph Company set up a Telephone Exchange and Public Call Office at 107 East Street, near its junction with Church Street, and awarded itself the number: Hereford 1. The Post Office became responsible in 1912 for the telephone system, by when there were nine public call offices and almost 350 subscribers to the Hereford Exchange. There were also exchanges at Bartestree (with 16 subscribers), and Burghill (with six, including the asylum: Burghill 4). The Hereford Post Office became included in a Wales and Marches Telecommunication Region and the city and its immediate neighbours were served by a local telephone exchange at Cathedral Close and the national and international exchange centred at Breinton Road. It had also been in the forefront of global satellite communications and in 1978 a new earth station was brought into service at nearby Madley. As technical advances and miniaturisation reduced the space requirements for telephone equipment, the modern exchange at the opposite end of Church Street from the first exchange was sold to Hereford Cathedral School, restoring an educational use to land once performed at Nos. 24 and 25 by St. John Baptist School.

During the 20th century, as more and more duties were placed upon the city council, extra office space was built or adapted at the rear of the town hall to accommodate additional legal, financial, housing, town planning, building control and architectural staff. Extra land was purchased at 24 East Street (the stable building for the carriage horse which Dr. Cyril Francis eventually had stuffed for display at his surgery in St. Ethelbert Street) and, on either side in St. Owen Street, as tourism, town planning and treasurer's offices. A former Widemarsh Street drill hall was adapted for the housing department, but eventually even all this was not enough and in 1986 Garrick House in Widemarsh Street was added to the council's office accommodation. The 'spending' departments had also operated through works depots originating at the road depot in Stonebow Road, next to the corporation slaughterhouses, Waterfield & Sons (gut cleaners) and a more recent hospital mortuary. Many of the buildings were formerly used in connection with the 17 horses stabled for drawing the vehicles required for waste collection and the various maintenance departments. These had become totally unsuitable with the arrival of motor transport and equipment, but it took until 1981 before a modern depot was provided at Grimmer Road for the housing, highways, sewerage, refuse collection and other technical works services. By 2000 discussions were taking place between Herefordshire Council and Sainsburys envisaging disposal of the depot property to make way for a larger supermarket on the former GWR sidings and engine sheds land.

Law and Order

Hereford's position at the heart of a large rural hinterland made it a main centre for the dispensation of law and justice. The 13th-century castle acted as the administrative base for the shire, containing a hall for the county courts and a prison. Castle Cliffe afterwards served the county as a house of correction or bridewell for many years until 1800. The city also boasted a range of other gaols for wrongdoers and the bishop operated his own prison at the palace, much in use during his 'scrape-prolific' nine days' fair. Under licence from Richard II, the Boothall (between High Town and East Street) was used from 1393 as the city courthouse, with an adjoining special prison for freemen guilty of minor offences. For other miscreants there was the city prison at Byestreet Gate, with 'a rude representation, in stone, of two human figures chained and placed over the entrance' to imply its original purpose, as it seemed to John Duncumb in 1800. The county gaol stood at St. Peter's Square until 1793, when a modern replacement for prisoners committed

The county gaol designed by John Nash,
now the site of the bus station

from the city, county and Radnorshire was built in Commercial Road on the site of St. Guthlac's Priory. It was designed by the renowned architect John Nash, according to the 'solitary confinement' principles of John Howard, prison reformer, and was enlarged and improved to provide cells for 105 prisoners in 1902. Used as a military detention centre during the Great War, it remained until 1929, when male prisoners were sent to Gloucester and females to Birmingham. All but the governor's house and some of the high boundary walls were demolished, to provide space for a cinema, bus station and offices.

A new Shire Hall was built on the former county gaol site in 1817 to house the assizes, quarter sessions, petty sessions and county courts. Twenty-five years later a new city gaol was built in nearby Gaol Street and equipped for weaving and the manufacture of mats and hearthrugs from cocoa-nut fibre. Part was adapted in the late 1870s as the city police station, drill ground and car park, and later also a magistrates' court and offices. The remainder was converted into a fire station, fronting De Lacy Street, and has since been demolished.

The city held a commission of the peace distinct from that of the county, entitling it to have its own court of quarter sessions taken by a recorder appointed by the Lord Chancellor, until the Courts Act of 1971 came into effect. The last

city recorder (Mr. Gordon Slynn, Q.C., later Baron Slynn of Hadley, a Law Lord) presided over the final city quarter sessions in December, 1971, and became the first honorary recorder. City and county magistrates' courts were combined in petty sessional divisions, and assizes and quarter sessions gave way to the crown and county court systems, normally presided over by a circuit judge, very occasionally by a High Court 'red judge'. In 2000, the poor facilities at Gaol Street were replaced in Bath Street by four magistrates' court rooms under a privately financed deal between the county council and a consortium called H. and W. Courts Ltd.

Through the centuries, responses to crime and measures of punishment varied greatly according to prevailing social attitudes and conditions. Malefactors were once gibbeted at Gallows Tump (on the Abergavenny road near the later Pembridge Close and Newport to Hereford Railway bridge) and at one time there were 223 crimes in the penal code punishable by death, ranging from the trivial to murder. Between 1770 and 1832 Hereford saw 57 executions of 'felons', and only 13 for murder. In St. Peter's Square in 1786 a pickpocket, witnessing the hanging of a girl of 17 condemned for setting fire to her master's barn, was arrested, taken before a magistrate and committed to the same assize. Arraigned, tried and convicted, he ended up on the gallows soon after her. In 1790, William Jones and Susannah Rugg, partners in crime in a love-triangle affair, were hanged in the square in full public view. Until 1868 hangings regularly took place in public; the last at Hereford was in 1864 above the entrance to the Commercial Road Gaol. The last ever execution at Hereford occurred in 1903 and by the time Major Herbert Rowse Armstrong, a prominent Hay-on-Wye solicitor, came to be convicted of murder at the Shire Hall in 1922, he was to face his executioner at Gloucester Gaol. Not so final, and valued as a way of relieving prison overcrowding, transportation was also used for dealing with many offences such as poaching and rioting until 1852, when it ceased following protests from the Australian colonies.

Under local control, the prisons had a largely unsegregated population of all ages, ranging from those awaiting trial, debtors and minor offenders to murderers, rapists and confirmed blackguards. Disease was rife, particularly typhus (also known as gaol fever), erysipelas and other contagions. John Howard had concluded that filth, a close atmosphere and poor sanitation were largely responsible and he incorporated moderate hygiene measures into his plan for the Commercial Road gaol. However 60 years later the prison medical officer, Dr. Henry Bull, was to report to the Rammell Inquiry about the unhealthy effects of blockages of the Stonebowbrook upon the ventilation and heating at the gaol. The flooding of boilers was caused by accumulations of refuse and sewage of the kind noted in 1853 by the Board of Health Inspector at the city prison in Gaol-lane, where, in the absence of cesspools, all waste from nearly 30 inmates drained directly into the nearby brook.

For the punishment of lesser crimes there were the stocks at St. Peter's Square, which held the ankles, or the more painful pillory which stood near the High Cross at the west end of High Town. Held by the neck and wrists for exposure to public vilification and various missiles, 'scolding women' in earlier times did long penance there and many other miscreants experienced great ignominy until its removal in 1816. One woman suffered for an hour as late as 1812 and another received a public whipping in 1816. This form of market-day 'entertainment' did not end before 1830, although disorderly women were 'drummed' out of the city until 1835. Another common punishment was the ducking stool (an example is still to be seen at Leominster Priory) on which immoral, nagging or scolding women were plunged into a suitable pond.

During Saxon times, law enforcement was under the control of the Shire Reef, or Sheriff, who may be regarded as a forerunner of the modern JP. The Hereford Watch, the forerunner of the police, was instituted in about the 13th century under the principles of 'Watch-by-night' and 'Ward-by-day'. Constables were elected annually and they appointed and controlled watchmen, who were penalised if they refused to carry out their duties. During the Tudor period, policing was carried out by parish or petty constables under the control of the Vestry. From the days of Charles I the prevention of crime and the pursuit of offenders has been in the charge of local magistrates, assisted by elected parish constables, the watchmen (often known as 'Charlies'), private citizens and, as a last resort, the military. 'Watch and Ward' commenced in 1814, when watchmen patrolled the city and called the half-hours at night. Calls for a regular police force were resisted well into the 19th century, on grounds of cost to the rates, loss of traditional freedoms and civil liberties and unease about the military associations of a uniformed force. Finally, the 1835 Municipal Corporations Act gave voluntary powers to boroughs to establish police forces, paid through the rates. In Hereford a watch committee was immediately established and this led to the formation of the 17 men strong Hereford City Police Force on 1 February, 1836. Three years later, further legislation permitted counties to raise and equip their own paid police forces, but it required a mandatory Police Act of 1856 before Herefordshire, and many other counties, took action. In 1888 the county constabulary quickly came under the newly constituted Herefordshire County Council, whilst the city force retained its independence at Gaol Street. The county police station for Hereford and Abbeydore division was based at the Commercial Road gaol before moving to 35 Union Street, following erection in 1899 of a new headquarters building adjacent to the Shire Hall.

In 1912, the city force consisted of three inspectors, five sergeants and 25 constables under a chief constable, but from 1929 this post was combined with that of the county force under Mr. Freeman Newton. In 1947 the two forces amalgamated, to form the central division of Herefordshire County Constabulary, operating from Gaol Street. A police authority comprising councillors and magistrates was established from 1964, and three years later chief constable Robert

McCartney saw his Herefordshire force merge with those of Shropshire, Worcestershire and Worcester City to form West Mercia Police Constabulary. The city formed part of 'E' division, which included Leominster and Ross-on-Wye. Hereford's police station remained at Gaol Street until 1976, when a new divisional headquarters was built alongside the city wall facing Bath Street. For the year 2000 the authority, officially classified as 'the most economical Force in the country per capita', employed 2,007 police officers and 1,053 civilian support staff, and provided policing services expected to cost £125.7 million, or £110.65 for every person in its area.

Fire and Rescue

One of the earliest actions of the city council created under the Municipal Corporations Act of 1835 was the voting of a sum towards the purchase of a city fire engine in 1837. This was probably intended to replace an earlier model, one of the first to be used in England, presented by Paul Foley, M.P. in the late 17th century. Additional finance was soon made available by fire insurance companies and in 1846 a mobile fire escape was also provided and £25 was spent to provide it with shelter at the city prison. A fire brigade was established by the council in 1849 and 'twelve mechanics accustomed to the construction of buildings' were appointed at a retainer of £2 per annum and attendance fees from the owners of burning property. They were called The Hereford Brigade, placed under the command of the superintendent of police, annually sworn as constables and provided with an axe and a badge. An electric bell was connected with the homes of all the firemen and two ladders were kept in readiness under the old market-hall in High Town. An early scheme of 'performance related pay' allowed 10s. to those who arrived first at the fire with the longer of the ladders, and 5s. to those who brought the other within ten minutes from the commencement of the ringing of the first fire bell.

The fire engine house had started as a shed but it was gradually enlarged between 1875 and 1888 and a drying-house tower was erected for preserving the hose and other appliances. The need for protection had been increased from 1880 when the steam fire engine *Nell Gwynne* (originally built for the monarch's use at Sandringham) was purchased to reinforce the manual engines. Lessons from a severe fire at Greenlands' store in High Town in 1885 produced a telescopic fire escape and 300 yards of canvas hose, couplings and stand pipes. One of the main drawbacks was the delay in bringing horses from Merton Meadow for the steam engine, especially for country fires. A Dennis patent fire engine was therefore bought in 1908 and soon after the Great War, Hereford Rural District Council purchased a Merryweather motor engine, with a pumping capacity of 350 gallons a minute and road speed of 35 m.p.h. Staffed by the city brigade, it was intended primarily for country fires but otherwise became available for the city. By the 1920s the equipment at Gaol Street consisted of the steam fire engine, the motor pump, tender and new motor engine, a portable fire escape and patent 'escalades'. An equipment store was set up at Bath Street, but the fire station remained next to the police station and under the direction of the chief constable until a new fire brigade headquarters was built at 109-113 St. Owen Street. The service came to be operated by successive county councils until 1998, when further local government reorganisation placed it under a joint authority based at Worcester. Over the years, the 'bread and butter' roles of fire fighting, fire protection and rescue have been greatly extended by regulatory duties, complications of modern building practices and toxic materials, and by constant calls for emergency rescue service on roads and in other hazardous situations.

The Workhouse and Philanthropy

Problems of poverty were nowhere more acute than in England's rural areas and what Duncumb in 1804 described as 'the multiplicity of the poor' had been a problem in Herefordshire throughout the medieval period. The Poor Law Act of 1601 established a pattern of relief for the following two centuries, placing the responsibilities on parishes, supervised by the local justices. By the end of the 17th century changing social and economic conditions were placing a great strain on these arrangements and in 1834 new poor law provisions were enacted. Parishes joined together to form unions and shared one central workhouse, governed by a Board of Guardians. The Hereford Poor Law Union was formed with offices at 8 St. John Street (now a car park), employing a salaried clerk, treasurer, a staff of relieving officers and district medical officers, and served 49 parishes with an initial population of some 25,000. It had almost 80 elected and ex-officio Guardians.

The Union Workhouse was opened in 1838 near the County Gaol in what came to be named Union Walk. It had room for up to 300 inmates and was ruled by a master and matron appointed by the governors, assisted by a superintendent of industrial labour, a schoolmaster, schoolmistress and a chaplain. At all workhouses, rigid rules, discipline and uniforms were designed to be humiliating, conditions for destitute able-bodied men meant to be less comfortable than those of the lowest paid labourers at work. However, in order to reduce injuries from flying debris from stone-breaking, special cells were provided in 1896 and the 'very awkward' siting of the mortuary near to the dining room was considerately placed on the agenda of the Board of Guardians for attention. Any man was obliged to take his family with him once admitted and he and his wife were separated, their children over 7 years old permitted to see the mother for short periods only. Other inmates included unmarried mothers and illegitimate children, widows with children and apart from the youngest, oldest and obviously infirm all were made to work very hard.

The stigma and harsh conditions associated with the workhouse led some people to prefer starvation, or even crime when they might be better treated and fed. Some of the winters of the late 1830s and 1840s were very harsh, and matters were made worse by bad harvests and the failure of potato crops. One of the worst was 1841 and despite a distribution of coal and bread to the poor and destitute, by early February admissions to the workhouse had mounted to 207. Their situation prompted a public meeting at the guildhall at the end of the month, led by the mayor, bishop and dean and all listened to a forceful address by the vicar of the central parish of St. Peter and St. Owen, the Reverend John Venn. Reckoned to be one of Hereford's greatest philanthropists and social reformers of the second half of the 19th century, John Venn devoted himself to a combination of Christian idealism and a zeal for the improvement of life for the industrious poor. His pleas led to the creation of the Hereford Society for Aiding the Industrious, and by March the organisation had secured an office at the dispensary at 49 Bye Street (next to the much later McDonalds across Union Passage). The society had two main principles:

John Venn

The Masonic Hall, which was the building that held the public baths

1) That the truest charity is that which enables the working man to maintain himself and his family in comfort and independence by his own prudence and industry.

2) That the upper classes are bound by all considerations of benevolence, of morality, and, above all, of religion, to try to place every working man in a situation which will enable him to do this.

Through the guiding force of John Venn the society embarked upon many enterprises. By June, 1841, a loan system had been started to help in the setting up of small businesses, and later that year 28 acres of land were obtained at Portfields and Clehonger to be let in allotments of one eighth of an acre each to allow people to grow their own food on manured land for an all-in rent of 15s. a year. The city plots were oversubscribed and soon taken up by 172 tenants. Another enterprise was the purchase of coal at cheaper summer prices for sale in the winter. At between 6d. and

11d. a hundredweight, delivered to the door, this also was very popular; during the severe and long winter of 1846 the tonnage rose to 1,047.

Also during that harsh winter 33,239 quarts of 'good, wholesome and nutritious soup' were distributed from a room behind the Bye Street office. A Mrs. Phillips had been engaged for 2s. 6d. a day in 1844 to make batches of 80 gallons, with 80 pounds of gravy beef, a beast's head and other meat, vegetables, herbs and spices mostly contributed in kind or money and sold at 1d. a quart between December and March each year. Again many people had to be turned away as the demand exceeded supply. For a time the soup was produced at St. Peter's church house, and eventually at a new building next to the later society offices on De Lacy Street (both being demolished in 1966 as part of the Bath Street relief road scheme and to make way for the new divisional police headquarters).

The most ambitious and profitable enterprise of all commenced in 1847 with the purchase of land at Portfields for a corn mill project. Wheat or meal could be bought by 'the working classes' at cost price and ground for 8d. a bushel—the general public paying market prices. Waste steam was used to heat the water at adjoining public baths (now part of the Masonic Hall) and at a time when water was still being sold by the bucketful or drawn from polluted wells this was a great factor in the early fight against ailments caused by uncleanliness. Swimming baths were erected next to the bath house, eventually being taken over by the city council and only closed when new baths was completed at Edgar Street in 1930. The mill was in continuous use; within ten years debts had been paid off and by 1876 it was producing an annual profit of £1,000. This helped to subsidise the other ventures, extending to ten model cottages and a waste recycling establishment in Venn Road (now Kyrle Street), an experimental trial garden, a hire service for invalid chairs (forerunner of today's 'shopmobility' scheme), a service for savers and a tea and coffee shop. By 1871, after its first 30 years, the society had property worth £20,000 and a disposable annual income of about £700 for the welfare of the working classes. Land was sold at Portfields in 1874 to enable the Working Boys' Home to be built, whilst the mill continued in use long after Venn's death in 1890, creating many jobs in the area. During the Second World War, with the bombing of flour mills at Avonmouth and elsewhere, it operated at full stretch for long periods in order to meet the needs of much of Herefordshire. It was then sold to become a printworks for *The Hereford Times* and, when the paper moved to Holmer Road, the building was sub-divided into units as Berrows Business Centre—an initiative which might well have gladdened the heart of the enterprising John Venn.

Chapter VIII
Leisure and Recreation

St. Ethelbert's or the Nine Days Fair had been the social and entertainment highlight of the year for many people, but as with all fairs throughout history, it had a sleazy side and was not all just good clean fun. It could attract criminals and lead to drunkenness and debauchery and, believing that many citizens could pinpoint former nine-day visits which marked the abandonment of their virtue, the council reverted to the three days' limit decided by Henry I. The city fathers expected that this curtailment 'would greatly tend to the advantage of the city and to the improvement of the morals of the inhabitants thereof'. Passed in the first year of the reign of Queen Victoria, an Act of 1838 provided that the fair would normally be held on the Tuesday after the first Monday in May and on the next two days (so excluding the modern May Day bank holiday). Victorians flocked to the attractions—the switchback railway, swing boats, large steam horses, boxing booths, coconut shies in addition to many wonders of humanity, including the 'transparent ossified man', a 38 stone fat lady and long-bearded man, 'Ida the sharpshooter' and 'Captain Lawrence and his trained lion'.

But not everyone was fond of the fair, and Victorian concern for propriety added to the annual disruption of local trade and chaos in the streets, produced regular pressures to have the fair stopped, or at least removed elsewhere. In 1911 even the normally respectful, sometimes rather unctuous, William Collins wrote: 'May Fair is still held in the High Town and Broad Street, and has degenerated into a three days' revelry which the authorities are not strong enough to remove, because the interests of the brewers and publicans are supreme, or thought to be supreme, in the Council Chamber. All candidates for a seat in the Common Council who were supposed to be in favour of its abolition, or removal to another site, have ignominiously failed at the polls'. Sitting and aspiring members of all subsequent councils have clearly taken this message to heart, in spite of regular objections from some voters. The street fair lives on into the 21st century, and not only because, as in 1911 'the citizens appear to be resigned to this old custom, mainly because it provides a fund of amusement for country folk and children', but it is no longer more than a shadow of the great event it was. The early 19th century tradition of the bushels of best wheat is still, however, meticulously performed at the ceremonial opening, despite being formally commuted in 1971, and whilst not yet publicly indulging in candyfloss or hamburgers, recent bishops have been seen to augment their bounty of cereal with reckless free rides on the dodgems and helter-skelter. In practice the Showmen's Guild of Great Britain (South Wales Branch) now runs the fair, negotiating terms with the council which greatly exceed the value of the bishop's load of best wheat. Each

Bishop John Eastaugh hurrying to join the
official opening of the May Fair in 1988

King Street and the May Fair
at the end of the 20th century

showman's pitch is scrupulously marked out by officials, and payments include the cost of clearing up the streets. It has always seemed a miracle that, as the city shops open on the following Friday morning, everything has been spirited away during the night, the fair still the ephemeral thing as ever it was.

Theatres and Cinemas

Wherever there was business and commerce there were always people turning up to offer entertainment for some reward, and those who 'followed the fair' included musicians, dancers, strolling players, and a whole range of performers who set up their boards to introduce variety shows and serious plays to the *hoi polloi*. There was no actual theatre in Hereford until the second half of the 18th century, and no cinema until

much later: the travelling fair first introduced 'the moving image' to Hereford from the late 1890s by means of bioscope shows. These were powered by majestic, smoky steam traction engines which, starting from around 1865, had worked all the spectacular new merry-go-rounds, carousels and rides and generated the electricity to flood the fair with multi-coloured light.

Hereford's lowly first actual theatre was erected half way down the west side of Broad Street, and in Duncumb's words was 'dedicated to the tragic and comic muses'. It opened every third year for 60 days with the permission of the mayor and aldermen and quite soon became regarded as a nursery where leading actors of the day learned the rudiments of their theatrical education. Sarah Siddons, affectionately known locally as Sally Kemble—daughter of the famed

Kemble family and destined to be described as 'the greatest English tragic actress of all time', spent her girlhood at Leicester Place, off Church Street. Early in her career, during the 1760s and 70s, she acted at the theatre with her parents. Said to be 'very much frequented', and regarded in 1806 as a 'neat modern building', it boasted a pediment adorned with busts intended to represent Shakespeare and Hereford-born Powell and Garrick. However, before long it had come to be regarded by many as a 'barn of a place', far too small and ill supported, despite the fame and quality of its performers. By 1858 it had been removed to make way for a corn exchange, but not in every-day use, and so for some 50 years until 1911 this became a makeshift theatre. Then modernisation and enlargement by Hereford

The Corn Exchange in Broad Street, also used for performances. It was demolished in 1963

builders, Beavan and Hodges, to the design of local architects, Groome and Bettington, created The Kemble Theatre. It was intended for stage plays, picture shows, concerts and variety entertainment, with its front portion used as a corn exchange on regular Wednesday market days. Broad Street resounded to the sounds of music direct from the shows, such as 'The Country Girl', 'The Chocolate Soldier', 'The Merry Widow' and 'The Arcadians', but by the 1930s the Kemble had inevitably joined the other entertainment houses in presenting 'film programmes of the most modern character'. Herefordians were queueing to see Greta Garbo, Jack Hulbert, Ralph Lynn and Tom Walls and the 'musicals' were left to later amateur societies. The theatre finally became 'dark' from 1961 and was demolished in 1963 to make way for Kemble House.

The Garrick Theatre, 29 Widemarsh Street, was built as a Forester's Hall in 1882, not far from the birthplace of the great actor/manager David Garrick. (Garrick, who was born at the Angel Inn, 22 Widemarsh Street, and baptised at All Saints Church in 1717, brought about the revival of interest in Shakespeare.). First renamed The Athenæum, then The Theatre Royal, and owned by a local branch of the Oddfellows, it proved very popular for its burlesques, reviews and melodramas, becoming known by some as the 'Blood Tub' due to the many gruesome murders staged there. However, it was long remembered for a real life horror, when eight small girls were burnt to death in 1916 whilst performing in a charity concert for the troops. Amidst great sorrow the theatre was rebuilt and subsequently had a variety of uses, including cinema and wartime ARP headquarters, finally housing the county library following its move from Bath Street in 1946. It closed in 1974 and the auditorium was demolished in 1978, its highly decorative front and ornate balcony columns living on for a time in the Nell Gwynne Theatre in Edgar Street. Eventually the whole building disappeared, along with its immediate neighbours, to clear the way for the new Garrick House and multi-storey car park.

The Countess of Huntingdon's Chapel in 2001

For the first hundred years of its life from 1789, the Palladium building in Berrington Street was a Countess of Huntingdon's Chapel, built for the evangelist George Whitfield. From 1885 it served as the Beethoven Hall, a piano and organ showroom of the House of Heins. Despite the chapel's former rules against 'a vain conformity to the world in card-playing, dancing, frequenting playhouses and places of carnal amusement', it thereafter indulged in all these offences — commencing in about 1912 as a cinema. After major extensions, it reopened from June 1939 as a theatre with 600 seats for live shows every two or three weeks. A well known Midlands producer, Derek Salberg, entered into a contract with the manager, Montague Franklin, and was instrumental in providing a wealth of repertory entertainment until 1942 when lack of support and wartime difficulties brought 'Rep' to an end with a production of Clemence Dane's 'Bill of Divorcement'. After the war Mr. Salberg acquired the theatre outright, renamed it The County Theatre and relaunched it in 1947 with a performance of J.B. Priestley's 'How are they at home?'. His company was reinforced by actors who included Arthur Lowe (then at the Manchester Rep., a regular broadcaster on BBC Northern Childrens' Hour, and later to play Captain Mainwaring in 'Dads' Army'), Donald Finlay, Beryl Johnstone and Nancy Roberts (of the TV Grove Family), and for his producer he engaged the prominent West End film actor, Martin Benson. By the end of 1950 audience support was again flagging and in 1957 it closed as a theatre and showed widescreen, 3D and Cinema-scope films. After that it was used for roller-skating and as a restaurant cabaret. It became the Regal Cinema in the 1960s and by the end of the century was a bingo and concert hall, (which doubtless kept the pious countess of 200 years ago spinning in her grave).

Rather tucked away and approached by a narrow passage from Gwynne Street (opposite the supposed cottage birthplace of the favourite mistress of King Charles II, and grandmother of Bishop James Beauclerk of Hereford), the Alhambra was constructed in 1830, with galleries on three sides supported by round wood pillars and with ornamental palisaded balustrades. It was popular as a music hall, but also showed plays and even held penny readings and spelling bees. Built on part of the land of the then Royal Oak Inn, by 1892 it became a seed and grain warehouse for Messrs Rogers and Co. (later Franklin Barnes) and was demolished in 1936. Much of the property is now occupied by the Crystal Rooms night club in Bridge Street (which stands not far from a magnificent five storey grain store of 1890 in Gwynne Street, a rare gem of commercial architecture which has happily survived all redevelopment pressures).

Because of its size, the Drill Hall in Friars Street could take companies which would not pay in the smaller theatres. Opening in the 1890s, remembered entertainments included Savoy Operas and, on at least one special occasion, a performance by the Carl Rosa Opera Company. Apart from an initial lack of heating, except by one open stove, it was well suited for musical comedies of the time, including 'The Geisha', 'Floradora' and 'The Stage Girl', and everyone warmed to music hall performers like the celebrated Albert Chevalier, and his cockney songs 'My Old Dutch' and 'Knock 'em in the Old Kent Road'.

St. George's Hall, St. George's Square, was built opposite the Maidenhead Inn, Eign Street (later the Eigne Gate Hotel and Jessons Stores) and used as a roller skating rink and theatre, and for special events such as a 1911 fancy dress carnival. Sadly it turned out to be structurally unsound for public entertainment purposes, but had a variety of other uses, briefly even as winter quarters for a circus, and also organ building by Ingram and Company (said to have sent the world's biggest organ to Melbourne in around 1910), before becoming Hereford Motor Company's St. Georges's Garage and dramatically ending its variable history in a blaze in 1942.

The earliest true cinema in Hereford opened soon after the First World War at 74 St. Owen Street. Built in 1838, it was formerly a chapel and then a Salvation Army barracks. From 1919 until 1923 it was called The Kinema and seated 368 people, at a time when an estimated half of the British population attended the silent films once a week, and Charlie Chaplin had become the first real film star. Renamed The Pavilion in 1924, it offered 'The Pick of the World's Pictures' twice nightly and at Saturday matinees, but closed in 1926, never to show a 'talking movie'. The premises became one of nine shops of the Hereford Co-operative and Industrial Society, before ending the century as a coin-operated launderette and dry-cleaners.

The Odeon, the city's second cinema, opened in 1937 with a gala performance starring Will Hay in 'Good Morning Boys'. Built by W.H. Peake of Hereford on the site of the former Judges' Lodging at 5 Commercial Street, it was designed in the art deco style universally adopted by Oscar Deutsch and was the epitome of 1930s modernist architecture, as interpreted by the architect, Roland Satchwell. It seated 788 in the stalls and 345 in the circle, and at one time employed some 40 full and part-time staff in burgundy uniforms with gold braid. Patrons were able to enjoy 'star performances', (augmented in the double-seated back rows), from 1 p.m. to 10.30 p.m. each week, and take refreshment in the restaurant next to the circle foyer to the accompaniment of a piano and string trio. But cinema audiences declined in the 1960s, and in 1975 the lease was taken over by the Brent Walker Group, which introduced the Focus and Cherry's Disco, Hereford's first nightclub, replacing the restaurant. Finally the cinema became the Classic before all was demolished in 1985, to be replaced by the Commercial Street portion of the Maylord Orchards redevelopment. Although not listed (as probably it would have been had it survived) some Herefordians feel that it should have been designed into the scheme.

The old County Gaol in Commercial Road was demolished in 1930 and the Associated British Cinemas' Ritz was opened in January 1938, complete with a two-manual 400 pipe Compton organ—which rose with the organist from the orchestra well with coloured lights flashing to entertain the audience during interludes. As with the films, this also lost its appeal during the 1960s, so the instrument was sold in 1967 and, because by 1972 some 87% of the 1000 seats were regularly unsold, the building was divided into a 250 seat 'bijou' cinema in the circle area, and a bingo club was opened in the stalls. By the end of the 1990s, however, there was a revived interest in cinema and queues were once more forming outside the, by then, antiquated and ill-equipped ABC cinema, next to the 'bouncer'-controlled Lovejoy's, subsequently Marilyn's and Eros night clubs. Disgruntlement was finding its way into *The Hereford Times*, one young student contrasting the 10-screen cinema complex near her small-town university with the 'smelly, stuffy auditorium, poor film quality ... no air conditioning ... poor leg room and general unpleasantness' at the 'mediocre' Hereford ABC.

By 1998 there was a modern alternative at the new Courtyard theatre, although picture and sound qualities were below the expectation of some cinemagoers. There were newspaper reports about a planned multiplex cinema as part of redevelopment around Edgar Street, but no-one was holding their breath.

After the loss of the Kemble, Hereford and the county were for many years without a public theatre, or any purpose-built facility for the arts, but playgoers could travel for entertainment to Malvern, Worcester, Cheltenham and larger cities in the region. The amateur drama and operatic societies and flourishing drama groups also maintained a high standard of enthusiasm. The Wye Players won national acclaim in the British Drama League finals, whilst annually the 'Drama Festival of One-Act Plays' played an important part in raising the standard of both performance and appreciation. Amateur choral, orchestral and operatic societies performed at a range of venues, such as the hall of Belmont Abbey School, Greenland Hall, the Art and Blind colleges and the Garrison Theatre at Bradbury Lines. The 'Wiggin Panto' started in the early 1960s at the Holmer Road factory soon after the loss of the Kemble, and went from strength to strength, productions generally being sold out weeks before first performances.

Thoughts about building another theatre developed in 1963 when the newly formed Herefordshire Arts Association raised the question of a site with the city council. Proposals started to take shape in 1968 and two years later they appeared in the form of an arts centre, 250 seat theatre and a theatre club to be built at 25 and 27 St. Owen Street and an adjacent vacant plot. Even the lowest of the builders' bids came in at close to three times the estimated cost, which was attributed to 'technical difficulties' and building costs inflation—then running at 28% a year. In the end the project was abandoned during the flurry of local government reorganisation in 1974.

Not long after the dust from this upheaval had settled, and with co-operation from the newly formed city council, a small group of local stage enthusiasts embarked on a scheme for converting the redundant swimming baths in Edgar Street into a theatre. A charitable trust was set up, a £100,000 building fund quickly launched and in March, 1979, the old baths re-opened as the 350 seat Nell Gwynne Theatre and Arts Centre. Largely built by volunteers, it had a raked auditorium, a stage 24ft. deep from the 30ft. wide proscenium and with 4ft. of fore-stage, that could be extended by a further 6ft. when the orchestra pit was not in use. Backstage amenities included a large 30ft. high workshop area, dressing rooms, rehearsal and meeting rooms, and the front of house foyer contained a licenced bar, lounge and

The entrance to the former baths and Nell Gwynne Theatre, later renamed the New Hereford Theatre

The Courtyard Centre for the Arts

restaurant area, with adjoining kitchens. The theatre was run by a large team of enthusiasts and it quickly became established as a centre of entertainment for professional and local amateur companies. In 1984 negotiations were conducted with an organisation led by Stan Stennett, a familiar TV personality with wide experience in the theatre and entertainment world. Subsidised by up to £60,000 p.a. by the city council, the New Hereford Theatre, Arts Centre and Cinema took the place of the Nell Gwynne and provided for local groups, visiting companies and films. A studio theatre was added in 1989, intended for 'workshop' and smaller productions and especially directed towards the encouragement of youth theatre. However, after eight years differences in approach and style, especially in attitudes towards local amateur productions, led to management being taken over directly by the council in the early 1990s. The deteriorating condition of the electrical installation and the prohibitive renewal costs to meet public entertainment licence standards, estimated at over £15,000, could not be justified, for there was the prospect of demolition within a very short while because a new theatre was already being proposed. The building was closed, leaving the city once again without a theatre.

In 1995 applications were made to the National Lottery for a grant towards the estimated £1.7 million cost of totally refurbishing and redeveloping the property as a focus for the arts—but without success, in view of the poor long term prospects for the building. Instead, a grant of £3 million was offered by the Arts Council for an entirely new centre and a competition was mounted to produce the best design, a shortlist being drawn up by the Royal Institute of British Architects. The winner was Glenn Howells, a Birmingham architect, his design then being within the budget allowed by the lottery grant and contained in the available ground area of the old theatre without any sacrifice of its car-parking space.

The design provided for a 400 seat multi-purpose theatre and 140 seat studio theatre, both with flexible seats and cinema projection equipment and screens, art gallery, artists' studios; bar and restaurant, rehearsal-room and dance studio; meeting and conference rooms; dressing rooms for up to 100 people; a large public area; and, most discussed of many other features, a vast glass-fronted front elevation bordered by gardens and trees. Building tenders came in at more than had been estimated and there was a delay whilst they were evaluated. In the process an additional lottery grant of £750,000 was awarded which, with a city council contribution, met the anticipated construction costs of approximately £4.2 million. Equipped with one of the largest of provincial stages, the Courtyard Centre for the Arts duly opened with gala performances of 'Cabaret' in September, 1998 and has since lived up to most expectations. The source of some of its problems has been water. It has leaked in from above, in the tradition of many flat-roofed buildings, and rises into the austere orchestra pit in line with the water table. And, as rain it upsets walkers along the lengthy pathway between the car-park and main theatre entrance, and has weathered special American oak-wood facing disappointingly on the opposite side. Conversely, water would be welcomed by aggrieved performers, inconvenienced by the absence of toilet facilities in their ground-floor dressing rooms and the backstage areas, and by some parched audiences in hot upper levels of the auditorium. Lack of a fly tower is disappointing, but this has not prevented the production of more than 20 highly applauded in-house productions since the opening, all of them financially successful and critically acclaimed. During its first two years the Courtyard has overcome much early scepticism, attracting more than 500,000 visitors, and in so doing earning a growing regional reputation in bringing the arts to rural areas. This has been acknowledged by a major grant from the Arts Council, worth nearly £750,000 over five years from 2003, 'in recognition of the talent, energy and vision of the Courtyard and its plans to extend the venue's capacity'. In the words of Jonathan Stone, the centre's artistic director and main inspiration, it 'also takes into account the work of staff, friends, performances, volunteers and the support of incredibly diverse audiences'. Subsidised annually by Herefordshire Council and with an active Friends group, it has achieved much of its success through an ambitious programme catering for virtually all tastes and ages, presenting theatre, music, opera, comedy, dance, film, talks, visual arts, craft fairs, exhibitions and much else. Its

repertoire usefully complements that at the Hereford Leisure Centre in Holmer Road, which can be adapted for a wide range of popular concerts by top international artists, exhibitions and other big events catering for attendances of up to 2,400 people.

Festivals and other entertainment

The 273rd Annual Meeting of the Three Choirs of Gloucester, Hereford and Worcester was held at Hereford in August, 2000, and it was a good first opportunity for The Courtyard to prove its worth as a suitable venue for classical music events. The Main House was in daily use for instrumental and vocal concerts and recitals, and the Studio Theatre and Garrick Room resounded with Fringe Festival events originating from all over the world. It was all far removed from the days of the early 18th century when a small band of singers from the three cathedral choirs met socially once a year and, through their vocal efforts, contributed also towards a charity for clergy orphans. The music was confined to the normal cathedral repertoire, but at Hereford a great step was taken in 1759, when Handel's 'Messiah' was performed for the first time in an English cathedral. Another Hereford innovation occurred at Samuel Sebastian Wesley's first Three Choirs Festival in 1834, when the cathedral nave was used by the chorus. There were times when the event came close to abandonment through lack of support, but 'the vulgarising influence of the railway', as someone put it, transformed the festival, as well as the city. In 1855, soon after the arrival of the first passenger trains, special excursions brought people pouring into the city at festival time. The reporter of *The Morning Post* found the old city in holiday attire: 'The sun shone upon her mirth, her streets were thronged with visitors, and she looked bright, joyous and animated as though new youth had come upon her'. *The Times* noted a vast number of visitors pouring down the line from Wales, 'even the aborigines of which hilly principality are relaxing their antipathy to the "Saxon" music, and beginning to admit that there may possibly be even better vocal melody than the improvised "Penillion", and greater harmony than can be swept from the strings of an antique Bardic harp'. The cathedral and festival also brought grand people, including the future Queen Mary, and many celebrities who would not otherwise have been seen in Hereford. Jenny Lind, 'The Swedish Nightingale', gave some of her numerous 'Final' performances at the festival and many great composers—Delius, Vaughan Williams, Britten, Howells among them—came to conduct or listen to their works. Elgar composed a special Civic Fanfare for the mayoral procession at the opening service in 1927. He kept up a regular contact with the Three Choirs Festival which, according to his biographer, became 'the focal point of his year'.

Until recently, people did not require anything very elaborate for their amusement, and with little ready-made entertainment they devised their own. No Hereford home was far from open countryside or the common fields—Widemarsh Port Field to the north and Prior's Port Field to the east. There were many convenient and popular walks, especially Castle Green, originally the city cemetery around St. Guthlac's monastery and later the bailey of the royal castle. This was first used as a public park in 1753 and by the end of the century the terrace overlooking the river was thought by John Price, author of *The Historic Account of the City of Hereford* in 1796, as 'supe-

The Wye Walk in front of the General Hospital

Bowling on Castle Green in the 1960s, with the Nelson memorial in the background

rior to any other walk of the kind in the Kingdom'. Castle Green is said to have been first formed under the patronage of Bishop James Beauclerk and was rented to The Society of Tempers by the county justices in 1752. As in many country places, May Day was always a big social occasion and when the maypole was moved from the city centre it became the hub of great jollification in Castle Green. The park passed to a committee of citizens in 1824 and in 1873 was leased by the council from the justices at an annual rent of one guinea for 200 years, provided that at least £20 each year was spent on upkeep. Baths were built, reputedly supplied with water from the nearby St. Ethelbert's Spring, and in 1893, to mark the wedding of the future King George V and Queen Mary, a garden was added at the south-eastern corner and a public path was extended below the Infirmary's boundary wall towards Bartonsham Meadows. In 1910 this made a convenient route to the new river bathing station, providing depths of down to 7ft., a diving board, changing rooms and an attendant, opened at the Bartonsham, or Bassom, meadows that year.

To meet a long-felt need, a two-passenger ferry, the *Princess Mary*, was also introduced near the site of the former castle ford in 1893. She was superceded after five years by the Victoria

The Princess Mary *passenger ferry, which operated before the Victoria Suspension Bridge was opened, just visible on the edge of the shadows on the water*

Suspension Footbridge, financed by public subscription and some 'creative accountancy' involving The High Town Improvement Fund, to mark the royal diamond jubilee of 1897. Judged near the time to be 'artistic in design, elegant in form, light in construction and beautiful in effect', it survived everything that the Wye, the weather and vandalism could hurl at it until the winter of 1967/68, when £12,000 (ten times the stipulated cost in 1897) was spent on complete reconditioning and refurbishment.

The bowling green was opened for public use in 1908 and an 18-hole putting green laid out on the filled-in castle moat and mill-pond alongside Mill Street at the approach to Cantilupe Gardens. Not for the first time, Castle Cliffe was eroding badly during winter floods in the 1970s at great risk to the stability of the terrace walk, and so its 'bosky' character was temporarily sacrificed, upsetting some local naturalists. Before any further trees, wildlife, habitat and more could be washed downstream, however, the river bank was reinforced with a masonry-faced wall and concealed concrete work and provided with a footpath and seats. It was then fittingly resown

and replanted, thereafter looking far boskier and 'natural'—and more stable—than it had been for a long time. After use as council nurseries, the area of the castle keep was laid out in the 1970s to become the Redcliffe Gardens. A bandstand and water features were installed, but later removed because of vandalism, under-use of the bandstand, and a lack of resources.

Shortly after the little ferry entered service, a new walk was built on the south side of the river between Wye Bridge and paths leading to Putson and Hinton. In 1914, use of the 11 acres of land opposite the cathedral and Castle Green was granted in perpetuity by Bishop John Percival to the city council as a public place and playing field. The leasehold of Bishops Meadow was converted to a freehold by Bishop Lisle Carr in 1937 and a new riverside walk was planted with a row of trees and named Queen Elizabeth Avenue on Coronation Day in May that year. The adjoining 36 acres King George's Field was also acquired as a recreation ground and Queen Mary unveiled memorial stones there two months later. With cinders from their grates, residents of Hinton Road near the wartime British Restaurant on the

The Grandstand at Hereford Races in the early 19th century

Races in 1997, with All Saints, the cathedral, Dinedor Hill and the old grandstand in the background

193

site of the present Welsh Club car park, gradually laid down the present Ash Path leading to St. Martin's Street. Alongside St. Martin's Avenue the Home Guard was seen training in trenches, which were not wasted by the children at other times. Other than for grazing, little use was made of the fields until after the war, but in 1946 invitations went out for ideas as to the best leisure facilities for the two sites. During the following years many of these were implemented.

By the early 1970s increasing concern about the condition and inadequacy of the Edgar Street Baths led to the preparation of draft proposals for a £400,000 complex at St. Martin's Avenue, and the new Hereford Leisure Pool opened in 1976. The main hall provided main, diving and learner pools and accommodation for 168 spectators. There were two squash courts, a cafeteria for 100 people, club rooms, an extensive sauna and a pleasant patio area for sunbathing and lounging. Fifteen years later, at a cost of £1.5 million, extensions opened for the 1991 school summer holidays, providing a 'free-form' leisure pool and wave machine with four preset wave patterns, a 37m. 'Twister' slide (used 205,000 times in its first three months), a children's bubble bath, water cannon, cascade, geyser, beach jets and a grotto waterfall. All could be operated manually or by programmed automatic computerised sequencing and everything was designed to be fully accessible to disabled users. The combined facilities are wide ranging, providing 'fun' to serious swimming.

Out of doors, increasing leisure time called for additional new parks, playing fields and open spaces, and by 2000 these totalled some 600 acres, or nearly 12% of the area of Hereford, as well as the prominent 20 acre Dinedor Camp, acquired for the city many years before, Newton Coppice and three local nature reserves.

From the late 18th century it was possible to enjoy a day at the races and, with the Hereford and Ross Jockey Clubs inviting entries for events like the City Stakes and Gold Cup of Widemarsh, also there was provision for a variety of entertaining side shows. In 1819, Tom Spring, destined four years later to be Champion Boxer of All England, and afterwards a well respected landlord of the Booth Hall Inn, gave a display of his art, and other attractions could include 'natural curiosities (such as a black-bearded rhinoceros from Goodrich, "Annie Jones the Bearded Lady" and "Tomaso the Human Pin-Cushion"), gymnastics, pugilism, music, arts and sciences, sleight of hand and transformation'. The first racecourse was larger and nearer to the centre of the city than the present one and embraced parts of the present Grandstand Road, Millbrook Street, Newtown Road and Burcott Road. The modern 1.5 mile track adjacent to the A49 road at Holmer (which it crossed over until 1950) has been operated by the Hereford Racecourse Company on lease from the council since 1945. The entire course and jumps are clearly seen from rising south-facing ground overlooking the track, where a modern grandstand, catering and corporate facilities have produced vital support from the Horse Racing Betting Levy Board. The course attracts good entries and attendances for some 15 National Hunt meetings a year, and on non-race days the company provides pitches and the use of its facilities for touring caravanners.

In 1946 the council agreed to lease one acre to a company which was planning a flying club and air-taxi service at the racecourse and the following year the mayor opened a new airfield. However, apart from helicopter landings on race-days, aviation was not to flourish closer than Shobdon, the nearest approach being intermittent military use of land within the course for captive-balloon parachute training.

The Wye has provided a source of leisure and sport for many years. From the 18th century, elaborate river tours were made in pleasure boats rowed by between two and six men. Embarking at Hereford, Ross or Monmouth, passengers took a day for each stage of the journey to Chepstow. Although the new railways of the Wye valley largely displaced such leisure traffic at the end of the 19th century, the GWR actually provided an alternative for a while by operating special river

Skating on the Wye in December 1892

excursions from Paddington. For 27s. a third-class ticket covered the rail journey to Hereford and a boat trip down the Wye to any favoured landing place and then onward passage to Chepstow and the return train to London.

Above the Wye Bridge at Hereford, Jordans Boat Yard hired out pleasure boats for nearly 80 years until the 1950s. In 1861 Mr. Wegg-Prosser took delivery (by Gloucester-Hereford Canal barge) of a paddle-steamer for his own pleasure purposes. An annual regatta was held in July, later moved to the Spring Bank Holiday, which still continues.

Severe winters sometimes converted the river into a vast skating rink as in 1881 when Hereford experienced 28 degrees of frost. In December 1892 and in 1895 as many as 600 skaters were on the ice at once, and in 1917 the Wye was again thronged with hundreds of people. The Lugg Meadows were equally popular, whilst the cleaned-up Castle Pool became the scene of moonlit ice carnivals.

During the 1980s, Frank Barton towed a converted and 'stretched' Dutch barge up the Wye after passage from Holland. Rechristened

Wye Invader, it was intended for fitting out as a floating restaurant, but was greeted in some quarters of Hereford with the level of welcome which it would have received in a former intended role as part of the Germans' invasion fleet of the 1940s! Landing facilities were also part of a problem for local Dutch developers, Dr. and Mrs. Albert Heijn, in connection with their Left Bank Village development. This included a restaurant, brasserie, banqueting suite and cocktail bar on a site adjoining the Wye Bridge, much of which had been blighted since the 1920s by unsightly motor show-room buildings. English Heritage raised an objection to steps and a landing stage for small boats, but appreciating the heritage of the location, once part of the former North Wharf quay and site of the Bell Inn ('headquarters' of the Wye bargees for many years), the local planning authority gave its consent and the development opened in Spring 2000. Not long before, consent had also been given for the operation of the pleasure boats *Wye Queen* and *Wye Princess* from the frontage of the Saracen's Head Inn.

Despite earlier gross pollution, the Wye could be an angler's paradise. In addition to its renown as a premier game fish river, it has supported pike, chub, perch, dace, roach, gudgeon, grayling, twaite shad and countless eels, but not since 1864 has anyone matched James Posten's exceptional catch of an 8ft. long 'Royal' sturgeon at the Weir, near Hereford. The all-time Wye salmon weight record is held by Doreen Davey, of Kinnersley Castle, for her 59.5lb. fish caught in the Cowpond at Winforton in 1923. It was sold to Messrs Nurse and Co. of Broad Street for 2s. 6d. a pound and a donation of £7 10s. went to the General Hospital. In 1967 a record 7,864 salmon were landed, averaging 15.85 lb., but despite a 'catch and release' policy the total barely reached 500 fish in 1999.

Sport for All

Not everyone regards fishing as a sport and many people are even more strongly against hunting with hounds. Fox hunting in Herefordshire started from kennels off Kings Acre Road in 1829 and in 1869 the county was divided into North and South, when the South Herefordshire Hunt moved to Wormelow. The traditional Boxing Day meet once occurred in the city centre, but now usually takes place just outside.

Bowling can claim to be the longest established sport in Hereford. The Green at the rear of the Bowling Green Inn is reputed to have been laid in 1484, before the famous game played by Drake on Plymouth Hoe, and to be the oldest in the world. Such was the awe of speculative commercial developers in 1974 that they were prepared to incorporate the precious turf at an upper level of their proposed shopping development (see illustration on p.29). It was not to be, and the Green remains in play where it was shown in 1757 on Taylor's map. Ancient records of Hereford Bowling Club reveal other activities there, including the annual distribution of charity to the poor of the city, the holding of the Hunt breakfast each year and a mustering point for defenders of the city to receive their orders before taking up positions around the city walls and gates. The Liberal Club had a Green nearby, but from its condition it would appear that members lost their appetite for the game long before it closed. A bowling green at the former Henry Wiggin's sports ground at Grandstand Road has been passed to the council, which also owns the green leased to the Castle Green Bowling Club. Former private greens at the rear of the Greyhound Dog at St. Martin's, and off King's Acre Road have been superceded by redevelopment schemes.

Hereford Cricket Club was first established at Widemarsh Common in 1836 and in 1850, in the presence of 3,000 spectators, entered a team of 22 of its best county players against an All-England XI. Thanks partly to the lively support, Herefordshire triumphed, beating the England team by 14 wickets. In 1866 the immortal 'W.G.' brought a team which included E.M. and G.F. Grace, and he is said to have had a high opinion of the pitches and frequently returned until the 1890s. In 1909 the club left Widemarsh and its half-timbered pavilion which remains there, and moved to a new ground at the edge of the racecourse in Grandstand Road. Since then the Hereford City Sports Club has developed excellent facilities at the ground and has hosted Sunday League matches for Worcestershire and has won in the Three Counties League many times. There was a great boost for the game when Herefordshire was admitted to the Minor Counties Championship in 1992 (following the promotion of Durham).

Some of the earliest football matches took place annually between the cathedral school and the city in the 1860s. Affiliated to the Herefordshire Football Association, the Herefordshire Football League, which organises amateur football in Hereford, was formed in 1889 and by the early 1920s comprised 46 clubs. When the professional game hit the heights the number had risen to over 70.

Hereford United was formed in 1924 and played in the Birmingham Combination and the Birmingham League before they were elected to the Southern League in 1939. They performed well during the post-war years and in the 1970s captured national attention in the role of 'giant-killers', with successful progress as a non-league

The old stand at Hereford United's ground, replaced with finance generated by the road widening scheme in Edgar Street

club in the F.A. Cup in 1971-72 and 1972-73, the first for 58 years to beat a 1st division club, Newcastle United, a victory which came after a replay, followed by election to Football League status and within four years promotion to Division II. During this period United benefitted greatly from improvements to its accommodation at Edgar Street. The old stand had to be demolished due to the needs of the new inner relief road and was replaced by the slim-line Len Weston

Goal of Ron Radford's epic 30 yard drive, to be followed by an extra-time winner by Ricky George, producing a 2:1 victory for the non-league 'Bulls' against First Division (now Premier) side Newcastle United in 1972

stand, there were extensions to the Merton Stand, new offices and supporters' social club. With a capacity of about 12,000, gates of over 10,000 were attracted for home matches, but later, beset by a litany of financial problems, after 25 seasons in the competition, The Bulls were relegated from the Football League in 1997 and entered the Nationwide Conference competition.

Founded in 1870, Hereford Rugby Football Club is one of the oldest in England. It had many homes in its formative years, initially at the Castle Green, then Edgar Street, Three Elms, Hafod Road, the racecourse, the Barrack Ground and Rockfield Road, before settling by the river, at Wyeside, in the 1980s to become one of the most powerful clubs in the Midlands. By then it had produced six international players, commencing in 1881 when J.A. Bevan captained the first ever Welsh XV, to be followed by A.T. Voyce, brothers Jack and Deneys Swayne and Len Saxby in the 1930s and Alan Brinn in the early 1970s. Progress in the field has been matched at the club's base. Floodlights were installed for the 1979 season and two pitches are served by an all-seater grandstand, a modern clubhouse and bar.

The Hereford Rowing Club was first established at Jordan's boathouse in 1872 but some years later moved upstream to the opposite bank of the Wye, to the end of a stretch of water extending over one and a half miles. Often regarded as second only to that at Henley-on-Thames, the course is renowned for its depth and straightness, crossed only by the Hunderton railway bridge. The first boathouse was built in 1888 and steps to the river were constructed by club members, using sand and gravel brought laboriously downstream in old punts in around 1894 — as their successors have been reminded by photographs in the clubhouse. Crews or scullers have competed at Henley Royal Regatta and most of the regattas on the Thames and in the provinces, and many 'pots' and other trophies have been brought home to adorn the clubhouse, rebuilt in 1955. Training facilities include an indoor training 'tank' which allows coaching and preparation to continue during all states of the river. The club's regatta, formerly held in July or on the Saturday before Whit-Sunday, is now held on Spring Bank Holiday Monday, when a non-stop 10-hours programme of racing brings over 250 crews from all parts of the country to one of the highlights of the city's sporting calendar. It is also a major social event, attracting to the river-side some 10,000 visitors to a whole day of enter-tainment, in the main fête ring, funfair and numerous stalls. (It was one of the casualties of the foot and mouth epidemic of 2001.)

The Wye and other local rivers offer good scope for canoeists, and the Hereford County Canoe Club and the Hereford Kayak Club have provided family and leisure cruising for consider-able distances up and down-stream, between Hay-on-Wye and Chepstow. In May each year they need to keep a sharp look-out for very strange craft (and crews!) which have appeared on the Wye since the 1970s. Rafting began from very modest beginnings of planks, barrels and rope, but the craft have since become more sophisticated and take many days to build. The annual 100-mile men's race takes three days, attracts thousands of spectators along the banks and has raised many thousands of pounds for charity. Not to be outdone, a women's race over 40-miles later on in the year produces rivalry and dedication which is equally intense.

In 1879 the Wyeside Tennis Club laid down its first three courts near the boating stations and boasted turf which, regularly inundated by the river and its nutrients, was of exceptional quality. By the early 1930s there were five grass courts and one hard court and these were the scene of an annual tournament each July. There were 11 courts at The County Tennis Club, near the County Cricket Ground at the racecourse, and in 1922 a pavilion was built and six courts were laid down at Bishops Meadow. The Southbank Club at Aylestone Hill had six courts and the Whitecross Club, Sollars Close was well equipped with three red shale and four grass courts, as well as two indoor squash courts. It was in many respects regarded as a pioneer club of the city, having men and women players of a high standard; its open meeting always attracted leading players from city and county clubs, usually on August Bank Holiday. Public courts were available during the summer at the Edgar Street sports ground and private clubs played at the Three Counties Hotel and 'En Tout Cas' courts at Penn Grove Road. Because of the popu-larity of the game, some local firms later arranged block bookings for employees at set times at various courts in the city, and also provided facil-ities at their own sports grounds at Grandstand Road and Kings Acre. But by 2000 all that remained were seven hard courts at Whitecross and ten, six of them on grass, at Bishops Meadow.

By the end of the 19th century, golf was becoming popular in towns all around Hereford and on 27 August 1897, the Herefordshire Golf Club first played on a 9-hole course at Broomy Hill, just beyond the waterworks and above the rifle range. It suffered badly from winter flooding and was described as 'heavy walking but with good greens'. Membership was generally small, even after the formation of a ladies' club in 1897, although it managed to prosper when other clubs at Weobley and Ledbury failed. However, members' dissatisfaction about course conditions finally led to moves to find a more suitable site and play ended in August 1910. Overtures to the racecourse committee failed, and at the end of the year, with a balance in hand of £29 2s. 10d., the club optimistically rented 50 acres of land at Holmer House Farm. At the very centre of Herefordshire, high above the city and Wye Valley to the south, the view from its highest point at the 'punch bowl green' extended over six counties, from the Clee Hills, Malvern Hills, Skirrid Mountains, Black Mountains to the Brecon Beacons. Play commenced in early 1912 and a £400 club house, containing a dining hall, smoking room, ladies' and gentlemen's dressing rooms, kitchen and garage, was built under the 'off duty' supervision of Mr. G.A. Jack, the county surveyor. It was not long before some of the land was ploughed up as part of the war effort and this reduced the course from 18 to 7 holes, fortunately the most sporting ones. By 1930 'the very heavy soil and general unattractiveness' of the course created new doubts about the future of the club, and Holme Lacy and Wormsley were considered as alternative new venues. Raven's Causeway, part of the Foxley Estate at Wormsley and 700ft. above sea level, was owned by Capt. R.T. Hinckes, and after much dissension among members about the move, he built a golf course there at his own expense. The single storey Holmer clubhouse was transferred to its new location and the first Monthly Medal was played over 12 holes in April 1933. Steady progress followed, aided very much by Capt. Hinckes and the Davenport family, until Second World War measures reduced the course to 13 holes and introduced many hundreds of sheep (all of which nevertheless saved the course from being ploughed up and probably destroyed). The pre-war growth in popularity of the game quickly resumed after 1945, despite access problems due to petrol rationing. Not of billiard table flatness (the eighth hole is about a hundred feet above the level of the clubhouse), the course has been skil-fully designed to make the most of its contours. It has a reputation for some steep slopes (there is a

prominent cardiac defibrillator kit at the club-house entrance), but they have not deterred appli-cants. By 1995 the full playing membership had reached a stipulated maximum of 515 and the waiting list, introduced in 1971, had extended to more than six years. Despite an ever-growing interest in the game, this had reduced to two years by 2000, influenced by the opening of the Burghill Valley and Belmont clubs, a municipal 9-hole course at the racecourse, Leominster, Bodenham, Kington, Ross-on-Wye, Knighton, Madley, Upton Bishop, Clifford and Sapey clubs and a driving range at Lyde.

Archery flourished from the early 19th into the 20th century. The Herefordshire Bow Meeting Society was established for men and women in 1836, followed in 1844 by the Grand National Archery Society, which in 1868 held its 25th annual meeting at the racecourse. Early in the 20th century the county could boast at least eight societies and clubs, including the formi-dable Ladies Archery Round Society and, at Holme Lacy College grounds, the Hereford Company of Bowmen continues to operate.

There has been a keen interest in cycling and this was heightened during pre-war days by the spectacular successes of Herbert (Mickey) Minton, an amateur who achieved two world records and many championship wins. Events took place at the Canonmoor athletic ground at the rear of the old public baths and the Hereford Road Cycling Club was followed in 1928 by the Hereford and District Wheelers Club, who took pleasure in touring the countryside and meeting other cycling clubs. There was also a very active racing section from 1932 and a 25 mile time-trial on Easter Mondays regularly attracted a field of up to 120 riders. In addition, the club promoted an exciting Kermesse, or 'round the houses' event through closed city streets during carnival weeks and has organised grass track events at the race-course. The Gannet Cycling Club was formed in 1946 as a touring club, but branched out into all forms of racing, in 1979 celebrating its 25th anniversary with a special Dinedor Circuit Cyclo-cross event.

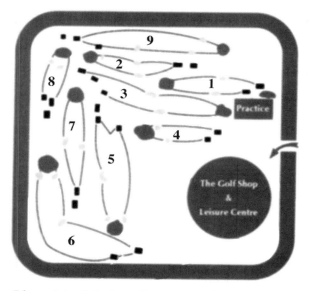

Plan of the 9-hole golf course within the ring of the racecourse at the Leisure Centre

Regular sightings of solitary joggers on the roads are a reminder of a continuing interest in running and the Hereford Couriers Running Club and the Hereford Marathon and Half-Marathon Committee attract many competitors each year. The Hereford County Amateur Athletic Association and its predecessors have also organised annual championships and sports days at a variety of venues, including Edgar Street and a temporary track at Grandstand Road, always hoping for better things to come.

For many years the 166 acres of city-owned racecourse lands were chiefly used for a few regular race meetings, the occasional Three Counties Show—before it moved to Malvern, cricket, hockey, tennis and squash organised by the Hereford City Sports Club, grazing sheep and sporadic parachute training. About half was capable of more effective use and in 1983, assisted by a golf-course architect, the city council constructed a 9-hole public course. The high standard of the greens was enhanced by a special 'pop-up' watering system, fed from a borehole shared with the racecourse. Golfers are served by the course professional and his shop at the Hereford Sports and Leisure Centre in Holmer Road. Opened in 1985, this was built on 'Design and Build' principles by the city council, in collaboration with the Sports Council, and provided a main hall with capacity for 12 badminton courts, but also available for basketball, tennis, trampolining, volleyball, gymnastics and other indoor sports. There were four squash courts—two glass-backed to tournament standard, and a well equipped 'Gym 'n Tonic' fitness room. Ancillary features included a bar and lounge, snack bar, and viewing areas at first floor level. Out of doors, a floodlit 8-lane artificial surfaced track, with allied facilities for field events, was constructed to international standards for athletics training and competition. The range of outdoor sports facilities was extended in 1990 with help from the Sports Council and Football Trust, by an 'all weather' sand-filled synthetic grass surface sports pitch. Enclosed by 3m. high fencing, this too was fully floodlit to allow high intensity use in both summer and winter. Five grass soccer pitches and the golf course complete the municipal leisure centre. In 1992, to provide much needed sports facilities for the south-west of the city, a new sports field was constructed at Newton Farm.

After ten years of use and changing requirements, features of the Leisure Centre were rearranged and refurbished. In order to improve arrangements for major concerts, the entrance doors were moved to face the car park and a large bar and reception area was created after transfer of the 'Gym n Tonic' room and offices upstairs. A new multi-purpose function room, catering for up to 400 people, was created from the former bar area and one of the squash courts, and another squash court was converted to form part of the LIFT (Lifestyle Improvements for Today) G.P. referral service, which had started in 1993. This service is also available at the Leisure Pool and was taken up by 4,700 people in its first four years. The service allows people regular exercise under the guidance of trained staff, who give particular attention to those who are overweight, arthritic or suffer heart problems or the aftermath of strokes.

Nearly two centuries ago, the city was said to have offered 'most amusements which can engage the attention of elegant society'. From each October, Assemblies were among the chief social pleasures. One of the earliest took place at a coffee house in Milk Lane (now St. John Street), providing for card playing and dancing. At that time, the minuet, cotillion, rondeau, hornpipe and reels featured among the most popular dances, and for those travelling some distance, dates were considerately arranged 'near to the Full Moon to accommodate the country Ladies and Gentlemen, wax candles substituted for oil lamps, and the half-year's subscription raised in consequence from 10s. 6d. to 15s. 6d.' From the 1803/4 season the assemblies moved to the City Arms Hotel, and thence in 1845 to a large assembly hall at the Green Dragon Hotel until they were wound up in the late 1850s. Grander and more exclusive Assize and Hunt Balls, with their valses, quadrilles, lancers and galops, continued well into the 20th century, until they too all but faded away, leaving Old Time Dancing clubs and Come Dancing TV contests as nostalgic reminders.

For 'other classes of society', many other amusements were to be found in the public houses, which by the end of the 19th century numbered one for every 145 inhabitants of the city. By then cockfighting, which had been a regular sport for the 'gentlemen of Herefordshire' and others at pubs such as the Redstreak in High Town and the Ship and Castle in Broad Street and the Coach and Horses in King's Acre Road, had been outlawed for a century—along with bull, bear and badger-baiting and other such 'sports and amusements'. But pub billiards, which had been an offence since 1662, was restored to favour and legality. There was a subscription billiard room in Milk Lane in 1837 and another in a Tudor building in Church Street (which in 1868 became St. John's school for girls). The Bowling Green Inn in Bewell Street, Nags Head in Broad Street, the David Garrick in High Town and the Mason's Arms in Barton were among a number of pubs equipped with tables, some such as the Maidenhead in Eign Street needing to add special extensions to cater for the ever-growing popularity of the game (a business factor not lost on Montague Burton, national gentlemen's outfitter, who made a point of installing billiard rooms as part of many of his shops, as was the case above High Street / Broad Street) into the 1960s.

Skittles originated in the 14th century, and the nine-pin version has become one of the most popular pub-games. There were alleys at the Thatched Tavern in Widemarsh, at the Mason's Arms and probably elsewhere in the 1820s and the game has been played as an indoor sport in Hereford regularly since 1902. By the 1980s it occupied 42 alleys in 39 pubs and clubs, in which 96 men's teams and 48 ladies' teams—some 3,000 players in all—competed in their respective leagues. Interest has not abated at the start of the 21st century, for comparable numbers of teams compete in six divisions of the Central Felt Roofing Hereford League, and three divisions in the Hereford City Ladies' League.

Many games supplied by the landlord, to help swell his patronage, are as old as the pubs themselves. Shove-halfpenny, dominoes, darts, quoits, quizzes, pool and card games such as phat and cribbage, are among well over 40, with many variations, which have been, and remain, as much of the pub's attraction as the beer—some pubs, such as the Half Moon in Broad Street, even once provided livelier customers with fives courts.

Many Victorian and Edwardian working-class men found that the pubs provided a warm, comfortable and companionable refuge from their often poor, overcrowded living conditions, when otherwise there was little else to do but hang around on street corners. It was taboo for a woman to go into a pub until well into the 20th century, but by the 1930s the motor car was beginning to enable some to enter pubs away from where they might be recognised, and then gradually they felt confident to move nearer home. The change brought new requirements and publicans gradually responded with higher standards of comfort, cleanliness and decor. Bars were refurbished, many assuming an Olde Worlde character which sprouted dark oak beams, panels and undulating floors where none had existed, horse brasses, copper warming pans and open log fires. Where food was served, the menus changed from those described as 'Dainty little suppers' of sausage and mashed potatoes, stewed tripe or roast hearts and bacon, as served at Ye Old Kings Head in Broad Street early in the 20th century, to bar meals and pub lunches later venturing into ambitious country and continental dishes, Thai, Balti, Tandoori and bistro-style dishes. Such has been the change that some bars now serve as little more than ante-rooms to carveries and cosy candle-lit restaurants.

Tourism

Without the support of custom from beyond its boundaries, it is likely that some of Hereford's leisure and recreational amenities, like a number of its shops and other businesses, would not be economically sustainable. As it is, the city regularly serves the population in the rest of Herefordshire, as well as parts of the adjoining counties of England and Wales, amounting to almost three times the number of its own 53,000 residents. In addition the scenery and heritage appeal of the area draw many other seasonal holiday, 'short break' and day visitors. In 1998/99 it was calculated that 6.5 million people came to Herefordshire, stayed a total of 2.4 million nights and spent £158 million in the county during the year. The main direct beneficiaries were those providing accommodation and in the catering and retail trades, but £22 million was also spent on entertainment, leisure and other attractions. Approximately 5,570 jobs are thought to be supported by tourism, helping to make it the fourth largest 'industry' in the county. The three principal local attractions prove to be Hereford Cathedral, the Mappa Mundi and Symond's Yat, and work is underway through tourist information centres, and the industry generally, to increase awareness of other places worth a visit.

Chapter IX
New Horizons

A 'shotgun marriage' between the poorly matched counties of Hereford and Worcester was a major blow for many public spirited individuals in the early 1970s with increasing control from beyond the Malverns and via Whitehall rapidly causing interest and enthusiasm in local politics to wane. Although the subsequent divorce of 1998 seemed like an answered prayer, to many the settlement outcome has been disappointing and tangible benefits for Hereford slow in coming. With only 17 seats out of the total 60 on the new council this presents a strong challenge for city ward members, for whilst they can now join in addressing Herefordshire needs as a whole, they must also work at restoring a diminished sense of local civic pride and interest at its heart, supported by only trifling parish powers.

The new council has responsibility for planning for the future, with much to consider. The population of the county is expected to grow by about 10,000 over the next decade and apart from indicating where more housing should be provided, provision for further shopping/retail space is also regarded as a 'key concern' of the Herefordshire Unitary Development Plan (UDP), being prepared by Herefordshire Council to guide the use of land and buildings until 2011. The draft plan proposes a new 'City Development Boundary' to define the general limits of new building so as to avoid sprawl into open countryside. The UDP will also pay attention to the protection of air, land and water quality, conservation of landscape and natural habitats, reduction of energy consumption and waste and the encouragement of less polluting means of travel. The process of following on from the previous Hereford City and South Herefordshire Local Plans will involve consultations with the public, local authorities and service companies. A significant early event occurred in August 2001 when the council's planning committee approved the 'First Deposit Draft UDP'. But reportedly considered as 'unimaginative' and 'in need of a rethink', this came under fire from cabinet councillors. The re-thought proposals were in turn referred back by the next full council and eventually approved for public response in the early summer of 2002. Six weeks between 31 October and 12 December 2002 were allowed for comments, after which a second Deposit UDP Plan will be open to further reaction. Then an independent inspector will hold a public inquiry. Depending on the scale of objections and the inspector's recommendations, the council hopes that a second inquiry will not be necessary and that the Plan will become operative during 2004.

Commerce

The conduct of most aspects of life in Hereford had been undertaken by local people well into the 20th century, but by the end this completely changed—nowhere more so than in the business of shopping. When in 1905 the writer A.G.

Bradley saw High Town as the place 'where the pulse of commerce beats fastest', the only 'foreigner' was Boots the Chemist, who joined with the familiar Greenland, Gurney, Edwards, King and other big business names in creating the beat. Many of these local shops were still present until early in the second half of the century—but most have since vanished. The business rhythm is now controlled from distant chain-store boardrooms having little local loyalty.

In the 1970s a tight grip was kept to avoid overprovision of new shop floor space, for there were fears that any excess might 'suck in too great a proportion of trade from the existing city centre'. An inquiry inspector and shopping assessor urged a maximum addition of 150,000 sq. ft. before 1986, fearing that any more would reduce the viability of existing shops and leave owners with less to spend on the upkeep of their buildings, many of which were listed, 'to the detriment of the quality of the historic environment [and] putting at risk the unique quality of the centre'. But since then different criteria have applied and retailing practices have undergone massive change. The amount of extra shopping

floor space has risen far beyond anything previously contemplated, much of it placed well away from the city centre in the form of supermarkets, DIY stores and other retail warehouses. It has been estimated that these have contributed to an increase of about 1 million square feet of gross (with storage) retail floorspace between the late 1970s and the end of the 1990s. Despite this, a need was seen to identify further land for shops in the first decade of the new century 'to ensure the continued viability and vitality of the city centre as a sub regional shopping destination'.

In order to attract modern multiple retailers, shopping consultants have recommended 'retail requirements of 14-16,000 sq. m.(net) more selling space. Applying the Maylord Orchards ratios of the 1980s, which produced about 13,000 sq. m. lettable floorspace (including storage), this is broadly equivalent to about 23-26,000 sq. m. If applied, adopted standards of one car space per 25 sq. m. (gross) and a requirement for over 30 lorry spaces could double the area of land needed. The area behind the Green Dragon, off Berrington Street and Aubrey Street, is seen as the 'primary focus' for such retail development (plus 25

A 1995 view of the city centre which might change again at the Livestock Market and football ground by 2011

The plan drawn up by HGP Architects for the proposed ASDA site south of the river. A is the site for ASDA itself, B is the proposed community facility with first floor health centre, with four-storey flats and three-storey town-houses roughly where the boarded up Greyhound Dog public house stands

dwellings), although it seems likely that additional land will be necessary and that some of the 'requirements' will have to be met by further smaller scale city centre schemes. In addition, 11-15,000 sq. m. (net) of new retail warehouse floorspace is planned for Holmer Road, Blackfriars Street and other places. Further attention is being concentrated on the 3.60 hectare council-owned livestock market land, and after planners considered 46 alternative sites they proposed a disputed two to the north-west of the city for a new livestock market—before ending just with a 'criteria-based' policy with no specified site. Immediately to the north of the market, in what has become labelled the 'Edgar Street Grid', Hereford United FC has to repay loans and interest to sub-lessees Chelverton of £1.3 million by May 2003. This ground is also owned by Herefordshire Council

and, with the market site, is seen as crucial to a long-heralded multi-million pound development scheme. A report in September 2002 described a proposed 'social, leisure and cultural centre' for which there would be displays in early 2003. It was expected to include new council and police headquarters, a conference centre, arts academy, multiplex cinema, multi-sport/leisure centre and possible other features which could include a new Hereford library. All this would be linked with other land 'ripe for redevelopment' towards Barrs Court Station.

South of the Wye, at Causeway Farm, there are plans for an ASDA supermarket, 'community facility', health centre, nursery/creche and play area, bowling club, four-storey apartments and three-storey town-houses and 530 car spaces. Special flood prevention measures are being

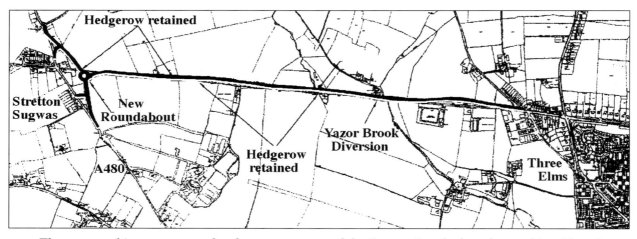

The proposed improvements for the western part of the Roman Road when the road is widened

proposed and an involved trunk road connection has been under discussion with the Highways Agency. At Belmont, Tesco is expanding its 1989 store and so, at the former Barton railway land and council depot, is Sainsbury.

Transport

After many bewildering changes of plan by successive Administrations since 1985 it has been made clear by the Blair Government that local solutions will first need to be applied to road traffic problems in and through the city before ministers can reconsider the case for an A49/A465 Hereford Bypass (a message driven home in July 2001 by a decision scrapping a comparable scheme at Hastings.)

Accepting this, Herefordshire Council has prepared a Local Transport Plan (LTP) as a blue-print for the five years from 2001 to 2006. This was put to the Government for funding approval in July 2000, resulting in a grant of about £30 million towards the costs of a five-year programme of work. In Hereford it will for example provide for the long overdue widening of a further length of Roman Road along the northern edge of the city. Subject to the necessary land being acquired and the gaining of planning permission it is hoped that work can start during 2004 on the section between the already widened portion at Tillington Road (just east of the once intended crossing place with the 'Green Route' of the now defunct by-pass (see plan on p.89) and the Travellers' Rest at Stretton

Sugwas. The road will be built to a standard single 7.3m. carriageway with a 3m. wide footway/cycleway leading to a new roundabout at the A480 Credenhill and Kington road. The UDP safeguards the required land, and also that for an extension to the A438 Hay road at Swainshill—as well as a small section of the A4103 on either side of the railway bridge at the opposite end of Roman Road.

City residents south of the Wye are beset by two busy trunk roads and the South Wye Regeneration Partnership has secured funds for a catalogue of practical remedies. These include 'safer routes to school' projects and measures to reduce the impact of traffic on residential areas along the B4399 Holme Lacy Road near the Rotherwas Industrial Estate. Results of the Rotherwas Integrated Access Study have persuaded Herefordshire Council to provide for a new road linking Ross Road and the estate. Subject to the outcome of many processes, work could start on the 7.3m. wide road by 2005. So far the council has safeguarded land forming part of the line of a potential Hereford by-pass through Rotherwas between the A465 Abergavenny and A438 Ledbury roads at least until the UDP is adopted. A transportation study by consultants has examined the likely effects of this link, taking on board all possible housing, employment, retail and other UDP proposals, and has concluded that it would produce little benefit for general traffic relief through the city. To the contrary the study predicted that chronic effects would be felt in several residential areas to the east, notably Hafod Road, Ledbury Road, Folly Lane and Whittern Way. It warns that the amount of traffic passing as a result through the Hampton Park Conservation Area along the B4224 Fownhope road could well double.

Allowing for all expected developments, the transportation study forecasts that traffic volumes in Hereford will have increased a further 20% by 2011. It concludes that, even with limited redevelopment of brownfield sites, at peak times the main road system is either already operating at capacity or will be doing so within three years. This is presented as an argument for a 'full Outer Relief Road' and all aspects of this are likely to be included in a further study to consider all options for dealing with the transport problems of the future. Vital to these will be solutions which produce a reduction in car based trips. Special emphasis is being placed on the role of public transport and the great need for a central integrated bus station when, for the present bus passenger, the primary terminus is that behind the Bewell Street supermarket. Signposted from High Town as the 'City Bus Station' it was in no way designed or intended as such when Tesco was built, nearly 20 years ago. Its very circumscribed area was also meant to cater for the store's own supply lorries, as an exit to the Edgar Street roundabout for vans and lorries serving Bewell Street and for taxis departing the adjoining rank. All these vehicles now mingle dangerously with

Two buses trying to enter the Edgar Street roundabout from Fryzer's Court (Tesco) bus station

people and manoeuvring buses, which during their busiest 12 hour period each day are catering for over 5,500 passengers. For some services there are other smaller, unconnected stations at the Shirehall, Maylord Orchards and Broad Street, but despite persistent pleas over many years, little has been done to provide convenient 'cross-town' services linking, say, Belmont and Tupsley. There is no integration between the termini and, except for the Union Walk country bus station all lie about two thirds of a mile from the railway station. Had the Victorians of the 1850s not wished to have the noisy trains kept that far away from their city centre homes it might now be possible to form a combined road/rail transport hub in a convenient central location. As it is, the draft UDP suggests that, as part of a 'package', an integrated bus station for all city and out of town services might be considered. The LTP encourages greater integration between rail and local bus services and, on a smaller scale, seeks to provide for lifts to serve all the Barrs Court platforms. The chances of improving the quality of service on the Hereford to Oxford line, much of it now single track, to Birmingham and along the Marches are also under examination. Although previous closures limit the scope for greater use of trains by rural communities, positive benefit could arise from restoring the former stations at Pontrilas and Withington. A Herefordshire Rail Study has been weighing the freight transport potential of reopening dedicated sidings at Bulmers Cider, Sun Valley Poultry and Special Metals Wiggin, linked with a railhead at Barrs Court yard. A restoration of rail services to Rotherwas and Moreton-on-Lugg estates could also provide worthwhile returns and in addition the UDP aims to safeguard land for rail transport at Moorfields/Westfields, Holmer estate and Roman Road east.

The five-year LTP programme provided for a £250,000 refurbishment of the Union Walk country bus station, completed in July 2001, and there have been improvements at smaller stations. Dedicated bus priority lanes in Edgar Street, Victoria Street and Commercial Road, cycle and walking routes, a further 'Park and Ride' trial, 'traffic calming' and residents' parking schemes are being planned. And it is to be hoped that further 'safe routes to school' and other schemes will reduce the number of 'school runs', which are shown to have doubled for 5 to 10 year olds in 20 years. (In some areas at around 8.50 a.m. during term-time weekdays they now account for some 1 in 5 car trips at what is one of the busiest times of day).

For its size, although not everyone agrees, Hereford is reasonably well provided with central car parks. There are over 2,500 off-street 'pay and display' and 400 time-limited kerbside spaces, as well as provision for several hundred cars at five supermarkets and retail parks. There are also some 5,000 privately owned commuter spaces and added together they make up a high proportion of the central area. Discharging together at peak periods they can generate much traffic 'chaos' and the new study will be expected to produce ideas on this and other traffic conundrums in time for the second draft of the UDP. Meanwhile the feasibility of something rather different, an 'eco friendly' Hereford Metro, is being studied for the Great Western Way walkway/cycleway, subjected to guarantees that any vehicles in use would not compromise conditions for walkers and cyclists or disturb wildlife margins along this safe and quiet traffic-free artery.

Industry and skills

During the closing decades of the 20th century unemployment in Herefordshire fell from levels which, in some areas, had previously reached double figures. By June 2000 Herefordshire Council and the Chamber of Commerce found that the rate had reduced to 2.4%, which compared favourably with the national level of 3.7%. Their joint Herefordshire Economic Assessment for 2000-2002 examined 7,915 VAT-registered businesses and confirmed that the sectors with the greatest number of employees are in agriculture, wholesale and retail services, manufacturing, health and social work. It is not surprising that as the city acts as a major centre for a large area, many jobs are in services but manufacturing industry has been expanding. Its 'base' has become quite wide and reasonable diversification has reduced the impact of recessions or retrenchment when Hereford is compared with some other communities. Not for the first time Herefordshire suffers from an ailing agricultural industry but otherwise the general conclusion of the analysis is that 'the local economy is thriving and faces a prosperous future'. Regrettably this is not reflected in the 1999 level of average wages, for at £286.40 per week for a woman and £340 for a man they were

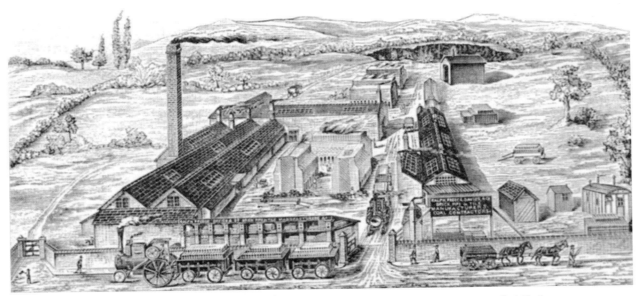

The Albert Brick and Tile Works, Holmer, in 1892 presently a 'greenfield' site which may revert once more to industrial use

the lowest of any county in the region—and well below the national average. Rotherwas Industrial Estate features strongly in proposals to provide for the increasing population. Over 56 hectares of land have been identified but not all are expected to be available by 2011 because of flooding, archaeology, contamination or nature conservation constraints and, not least, the transport problems which will only be solved by completion of the access road scheme included in the LTP. A wide range of opportunities exists over some 13 hectares and to complement these north of the city a greenfield allocation of 14.64 hectares of land is proposed at Roman Road, partly on the now 'green' former Albert Brick and Tile Works site. This move, and the building of any of the proposed new houses nearby will first require improvement to the A4103, realignment of the bridge across the railway (see above) and sensitive treatment of the proposed new settlement boundary.

Less than 2 miles north of Holmer, the vacant former military supplies depot at Moreton-on-Lugg does not fall within planners' ideas of an opportunity for 'balanced employment and housing communities' like the others but it is within the designated A49 'corridor'. Like Rotherwas it is a brownfield site and offers a considerable infrastructure and many usable buildings. The depot also has great potential for a reopening of the previous busy rail link to the Marches main line and through their company, Greatwest Investments, the new owners of Moreton Park, J & J (City) Ltd., have announced plans for a local rail freight depot. If brought to fruition this could be used for movement of some of the one million tons of sand and gravel which, with aggregate company Tarmac, they are reported as planning to extract from over 80 acres of land included in the county mineral deposits plan. Other parts of the site possess substantial scope for business and industrial enterprises which, if the reported proposals and forecasts are achieved, could provide work for about 500 people within 10 years.

Housing

Most new houses are being built to satisfy the need of the projected increase of *c*.10,000 in the county population over the next 10 years. Much of this will come from indigenous natural growth but it will also be fuelled by migrants attracted by the area—for retirement or as younger settlers prepared, if need be, to commute for some distance. Advances in healthcare enable 'third agers' to remain in their homes for longer than before whilst the overall number of households is also increasing as people of all ages either choose to live alone, or have to do so as a result of broken marriages and relationships. If no extra provision is made in the face of these factors, an unsatisfied demand for houses will soon create shortages, 'overheating' the market and producing increased prices of existing stock. Whilst this would benefit those owners looking to 'trade down', the majority, notably those on or below average earnings and first time buyers struggling to gain a foothold on the housing ladder, would face limited options. (Approval of a full home loan for a typical modern 3-bedroom Hereford house in mid-2001 would require annual earnings of about £30,000 and, even with mortgages at their cheapest in decades, monthly repayment of at least £600.)

The Government, through the Office of the West Midlands, has told Herefordshire Council of a need for 11,700 further homes in the county between 1996 and 2011. About 4,200 are meant for new local households and 7,500 for people migrating to Herefordshire. The city is expected to cater for 3,195 of the total number, and 1,185 dwellings had already been built or committed by 2001. Of the remainder, it is thought that sites for 763 will emerge as 'windfalls' and 1,247 either on previously used urban land or on 10 hectares of 'greenfield' between Attwood Lane and Munstone Road at Holmer. This will not be started until 60% of the brownfield land has been used. For each of the following 'land allocations', an 'affordable housing' target of 35% has been set. This category is defined as 'housing provided for rent or sale at a price level which can be sustained by local people in housing need'.

	Dwellings
Bradbury Estate	400
Belmont	35
General Hospital	70
Friars Street	80
Barrs Court Road	62
Walton Close	20
Holmer	300
Victoria Eye Hospital	15
Whitecross High School (built land only)	60
Berrington St./Aubrey St.	25
Livestock Market	80
Widemarsh Street	80
Causeway Farm	50
TOTAL	1,247

Two Plan phases would see an estimated 642 dwellings appear in 2001/6, and 605, including the 300 at Holmer, in 2006/2011.

Before the UDP Local Inquiry is held, demands for water, electricity, gas, telephones, drainage, school places, healthcare and most other necessities of 21st century life will have been gauged and costed by the various providers. Welsh Water Dwr Cymru has already announced plans for expanding the capacity of the Eign and Rotherwas sewage works at a cost of £1.2m. Three sets of new equipment, including high rate filters and associated humus tanks, will be divided between the two sites by the end of 2002 and will provide capacity to treat sewage from places beyond the city, including Burghill where the small treatment works will be closed. Bulmers Cider, which already discharges a great volume of industrial effluent, has been in discussions about the extra costs to the company of piping and treatment resulting from 4,500 acres of further apple orcharding in the county.

The housing scene for 6,000 Herefordshire Council tenants will change as they acquire a new landlord. Transfer of housing stock to a new independent housing organisation, Herefordshire Housing Limited, was supported in a secret ballot by a majority of 58% of tenants who voted. Equipped with greater financial powers than councils, the company will be better able to catch up with a backlog of repairs and improvements. A management board will include company and tenant representatives and independent members, whilst the council itself will retain a more strategic approach to social housing needs.

Healthcare

If predicting the future housing requirements and where to build appear fraught, with each suggestion causing knock-on ripples in transport, education, sewerage, health provision and other services, trying to plan the health service is complicated by seemingly continual reorganisation, countless directives and a great push for consultation at all levels. For example, Herefordshire Health Authority, Herefordshire Council, West Mercia Constabulary, the Chamber of Commerce, Advantage West Midlands and voluntary bodies have formed a partnership to produce The Herefordshire Plan with the purpose of improving the lives of people living and working in the county. Of ten ambitions listed in an attempt 'to address those things that are most important to Herefordshire', the first in order is: 'To improve the health and well being of Herefordshire people'.

In 1997, the new Labour government produced a national policy document: The New NHS: Modern and Dependable, quickly followed by further health strategies, action plans and targets, leading to the creation of the NHS Plan. Since 1999 Herefordshire Health Authority have had to produce an annual Health Improvement Programme (HImP) which sets out how national priorities will be delivered in the county. In developing the HImP, a Health and Care Partnership aims to involve, as 'stakeholders', Herefordshire's NHS organisations and social care and housing agencies, relevant members of the voluntary sector, users' and carers' representatives, the Community Health Council and key clinical staff.

The HImP for 2001-2004 contains 22 Strategies for Health Improvement. These deal with: heart disease and stroke; cancer; mental health; older people; children; smoking; sexual health (including teenage pregnancy); drug misuse; youth offending; inequalities; physical disabilities; learning disabilities; accidents; diabetes; oral health; osteoporosis; communicable disease control; alcohol misuse; palliative care; specialist services; housing and health; and transport. According to the then Herefordshire Director of Public Health, Dr. Mike Deakin, the main health problems tend to remain the same from year to year and include circulatory diseases (particularly heart disease and stroke), cancers, accidents and mental health. Coronary heart disease was the underlying cause of about 22% of all deaths in the county. Within a 'National Service Framework' the NHS Plan sets a target for 2010 to reduce the level, along with that for death through strokes, by at least 40% for people under 75 years of age. Locally, four 'major modifiable risk factors' have been listed in the HImP. Two of these are: smoking, said to create by far the greatest health problem in Herefordshire; and obesity—countrywide one in five women and one in seven men are said to be clinically obese, and children may soon catch up. Obesity, which adds to the risk of developing diabetes and other serious diseases, is probably caused by the other two factors: poor diet and insufficient physical exercise.

Mortality rates for cancers are generally lower in the county than nationally, but nevertheless account for about one quarter of all deaths. Again a reduction in smoking and an improved diet are seen as major factors in producing a better picture. Accidents are said to pose the greatest single involuntary threat to life, especially for children and young people, and fatalities are comparatively high in Herefordshire—particularly on the roads. A national and HImP priority, attention is being given through the LTP and safer routes to school projects have been introduced at Whitecross and Haywood High Schools and Trinity Primary School. These include improved lighting, better paths and parking arrangements and speed reduction controls. As an important source of illness, disability and distress, mental health disorder is also one of the four national priorities for relief. Although only one of many aspects of the burden, suicide rates in

Herefordshire have been a cause for concern when compared with the rest of England and Wales. In recent years there have typically been around 20 deaths per year, but 1999 figures suggest that a total of 30 residents may have died by their own hands or from 'undetermined deaths'. A Mental Health Strategy has been prepared and, as one practical measure, the Health Authority has contributed charitable funding towards the cost of erecting a barrier at the top roof level of the Garrick House multi-storey car park, 'the site of a small but significant number of suicides in recent years'.

The battered state and image of the NHS remains of huge concern to both patients and staff, as exemplified during the June 2001 general election campaign in the neighbouring Wyre Forest constituency, where retired consultant Dr. Richard Taylor converted the former Labour majority of 6,946 to one of 17,630 for the Kidderminster Hospital and Health Concern Party, dislodging a junior minister in the process.

The government was intent on another reform, decentralising power and control of 75% of funding to Primary Care Trusts, and so placing doctors and nurses 'in the driving seat'. This process lead to a reduction in the role and number of health authorities. After fighting for independence from Worcester as far as the floor of the House of Commons in 1995, Herefordshire Health Authority has been merged with more than one counterpart, gaining other functions devolved from the Birmingham Regional Office. Some reaction is cautiously favourable towards more influence being thus placed at the local level, not least because Herefordshire is well placed in having one Trust covering the whole county. But one GP, writing in the national press, feels she is not alone in being 'fed up with constant reorganisation', regarding yet another change as being a further blow and distraction for the people actually working with patients. However, if the manifesto pledges can be fulfilled during New Labour's second term, by 2005 she may be working in a service benefitting from a further 10,000 doctors and 20,000 nurses, somehow to be 'delivered' in a reformed NHS. The new 250 bed

County Hospital opened in 2002 amidst worries about its capacity to cope with patient numbers — to meet extra government targets since the 'Full Business Case' was approved in 1998. As a result the Hospital, Health and Primary Care bodies commissioned independent research by a University of Birmingham team to re-examine the planned number of beds. In August 2001, its report *Beds in Herefordshire* produced a forecast need for 14,700 extra bed-days upon the closure of the last hutted ward in 2006/7, and a possible further 3,500 bed-days by 2008 to meet July 2000 NHS Plan waiting list targets. It concluded that if the required intermediate care services could be provided in community hospitals and in the home, the hospital plan is likely to be a success. As part of this approach a measure to help reduce 'bed blocking', by patients whose treatment at the hospital has been completed, will entail conversion of Herefordshire Council's Hillside residential home into an intermediate care centre providing 22 beds and a rehabilitation service.

Meanwhile Parson Talbot's Grade I listed General Infirmary of 1783 is to be transformed by Laing Homes into 45 dwellings, together with 42 new flats, maisonettes and houses in the grounds and a converted lodge. After more than 100 years of service, the Victoria Eye Hospital is also to become a complex of houses and apartments within the old building and its acre of land.

Public institutions, leisure and regeneration

It is difficult to make out which of the public services has undergone the greatest number and variety of reforms in recent years. Healthcare is a leading contender — but so is education and both function under constant political and bureaucratic regulation and scrutiny. Education has been designated New Labour's 'number one priority', notably at the level of secondary education, but there are already problems, as seen in the review called for the only recently introduced AS level examination and its organisation.

Before planners' early housing proposals for the Whitecross area were withdrawn from the first draft UDP they had incorporated a 12 hectare replacement site for Whitecross High School, as well as land for a primary school. In August 2001

Holmer C of E Primary School which might require additional facilities or a new site if further housebuilding takes place off the Roman Road at Holmer

a suggested new 6¾ hectare site was substituted on land west of Three Elms Road, and subject to necessary approval should open in 2005. The arrival of possibly 300 extra families east of Roman Road by 2011 is likely to mean a further reassessment of need in the Holmer school's catchment.

Particular attention is being focussed on regeneration in large areas in the city south of the River Wye. The South Wye Regeneration Partnership has obtained £4.3 million from the government as part of a £13 million seven-year programme. The Partnership is working towards improving opportunities for people in South Wye and includes representatives from the community, voluntary, private and public sectors.

It has already funded almost 30 projects and approved several more for future support, ranging from refurbishing and equipping an adult learning centre at Haywood High School; redeveloping a new changing room complex at Hereford Leisure Pool; improving access to Rotherwas Industrial Estate; developing healthier lifestyles with the Health Authority; serving elderly and disabled residents of South Wye at St. Martin's Church Centre in a social/educational group aimed at stimulating and enhancing contact in a 'Silver Threads' project; assisting the Young Persons Drug Outreach project, designed to assist young people at risk from drug abuse; supporting a Newton Farm Community Association project to build a skatepark; aiding the council's Haywood High School safer routes to school project; providing improvements at Hinton Football Club Ground through the installation of floodlighting; and a survey to examine the condition of substandard private sector houses—covering unfitness, vacancy levels, socio-economic issues, energy efficiency and the state of occupants' health.

Some of the programmes involved in improving leisure and learning facilities are well in tune with further aims of the Herefordshire Plan to 'develop [the county] as an active, vibrant and enjoyable place to be, and to protect its distinctive environment'. If public consultations concur a 40-acre park will be added at Aylestone Hill. Preliminary plans contain senior and junior football pitches, a cricket ground, bowling green, children's play area, a pavilion with changing facilities and areas of natural grassland for informal recreation and habitats for wildlife. At Holmer, racegoers should soon benefit from better facilities and additional

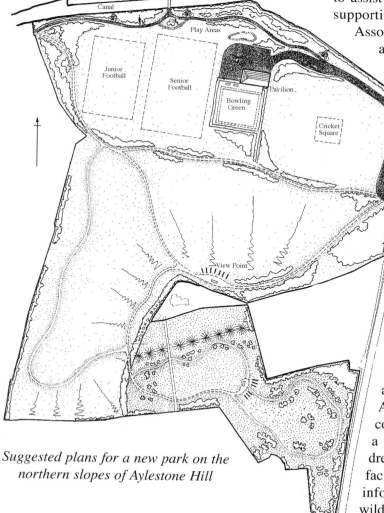

Suggested plans for a new park on the northern slopes of Aylestone Hill

Herefordshire Nature Trust's headquarters at Lower House Farm, Tupsley, drawn by Peter Manders

meetings at Hereford Racecourse following promised investment and resources there. These come from Northern Racing, who have purchased a stake of more than 90% in the remaining 28-year lease granted by Herefordshire Council. At the south-west fringe of the city, the Belmont/Haywood Management Plan contains proposals for countryside areas and recreational facilities at Haywood Country Park, the Belmont Meadow Local Nature Reserve and Newton Coppice, whilst creation of a potential Countryside Centre is also being widely encouraged. However, in Broad Street, late 1950s local authority promises of plans being 'in hand' for a much needed modern library for Hereford have still to be honoured—more than 40 years on.

There was farmland just a short walk from the city centre well into the 20th century, but as Hereford grew the fields disappeared under bricks and tarmac and by 2000 only Bartonsham Farm remained undeveloped, largely because much of its land often floods (not a drawback, however, to one former Medical Officer of Health, who in his Annual Report wrote of the great health benefits which would come from some form of riverside marina there). Of the 5,031 acres of land within the city boundary, public and private open space accounts for some

650 acres, not including the rivers Wye and Lugg. The banks of both are classified as Sites of Special Scientific Importance (SSSI) and therefore of national importance. This was stressed during the River Wye Navigation Order Inquiry in 1997 which in mid-2002 resulted in the Environment Agency being placed in control and management.

The last working farm to cease was at Tupsley, the former township whence Whitehouse and Prospect Farms had already disappeared since 1960. Town planning obstacles have prevented Lower House Farm land, overlooking the Upper Lugg Meadow SSSI, from being similarly used for housing. Its 41.57 acres of grassland, Baynton Wood (site of artist David Cox's cottage between 1815-17, which burnt down in 1923) and a Jacobean farmhouse were purchased in 1995 by Herefordshire Nature Trust for use as its headquarters. Through the medium of the Biodiversity Action Plan of 2000 the Trust has taken a leading role in identifying and recording species and habitats which are under the greatest threat—and establishing why. Candidates for local attention range from otters, water voles, barn owls, brown hares, great crested newts and even house sparrows, to elusive and irregular features of local flora and fauna for which identification requires a practised eye—such as the ghost orchid, and barred toothed-stripe, buttoned snout and common fanfoot—moth species which might already have become extinct.

Amidst everything that 21st-century Herefordians have to think about, concern for subjects such as these might appear unimportant and trivial to some. Yet, along with moves to ensure a prosperous, healthy and sustainable Herefordshire, any steps which can still be taken now to protect and improve the county's unique natural and historic heritage will surely earn the gratitude of all future generations as well as our own.

Appendix
Chronology of Notable Events

c.75	Romans established *Magnis,* occupied for *c*.300 years
760	Battle of Hereford. King Offa defeats the Welsh
778	Offa's Dyke built - 795
794	Murder of Ethelbert, King of the East Angles, at the Court of King Offa near Hereford. Canonised as a saint, becoming joint patron with St. Mary of Hereford Cathedral
1055	Gruffudd ap Llywelyn and Earl Aelfgar burnt down cathedral and the city
1069	William fitzOsbern appointed Earl of Hereford
1085	St. Peter's Church founded by Walter de Lacy
1086	Herefordshire Domesday Book
1154	Hereford ancient customs sanctioned by Henry II. Royal charter since lost
1189	Richard I granted citizens by charter the right to hold the town in perpetuity at an annual rent of £40
c.1290	Hereford Mappa Mundi made
1320	Bishop Cantilupe declared Saint Thomas of Hereford
1349	Black Death reached Hereford
1362	Second visit of Black Death; White Cross probably erected (base only remaining)
1384	Cathedral School in existence
1461	Battle of Mortimer's Cross; Owen Tudor, a grandfather of Henry VII, executed at Hereford
1484	Bowling Green, Bewell Street, reputedly laid
1490	Present masonry Wye Bridge built
1526	Corn and cloth mills on Wye destroyed by order of Henry VIII
1596	Earliest archive date for commencement of High Town market-hall and guild-hall
1597	Charter of Incorporation confirmed Hereford's previous privileges; additional privileges granted
1610	Last visitation of plague to Hereford; John Speede's map of Herefordshire and city
1614	Coningsby Hospital, Widemarsh Street founded; Lower House Farm, Tupsley, half-timbered farmhouse built, now headquarters for Herefordshire Nature Trust
1621	Completion of 'The Old House', St. Peter's Street; 'Pilgrim Fathers' arrival in New England
1645	Civil War Siege of city by Earl of Leven's army. Grant of augmented coat of arms and motto
1650	Castle keep razed; Nelle Gwynne reputedly born in Pipe Lane (Later Gwynne Street)
1679	Father Kemble hanged on Widemarsh Common
1710	Bluecoat School founded
1717	Three Choirs Festival under way; David Garrick born, the Angel Inn, Widemarsh Street
1730	Hereford Turnpike Act for road repairs and tolls
1753	Castle Green first used as a public park
1757	Isaac Taylor's map of Hereford; city population 5,592

George III

1761	Industrial Revolution under way; Bridgewater Canal opened, precursor of 1790s 'canal mania'
1774	Paving, Lighting and Licencing Act—Hereford's 'Lamp Act'
1776	High Cross, stocks, pillory ordered to be taken down
1782	First city gateways demolished, concluding with Widemarsh Gate and Byster's Gate in 1798
1783	Hereford General Infirmary opened
1786	West front, half the nave, aisles and roofing of cathedral collapsed
1789	French Revolution; Countess of Huntingdon's Chapel built, later Beethoven Hall and Regal Cinema
1791	Act for construction of Hereford and Gloucester Canal
1792	Market-house and guild-hall reduced to two storeys; coal gas first used for public lighting
1793	Outbreak of Napoleonic War; county gaol in St. Peter's Square closed
1796	Hereford County Gaol opened; vaccination against smallpox introduced
1799	Lunatic asylum opened at the infirmary
1800	County prison, Castle Green, relic of the castle, converted into a house
1802	Lord Nelson admitted to Freedom of the city; short peace with France until 1803; Trafalgar 1805
1809	Lord Nelson's monument erected in Castle Green; Rivers Wye and Lugg Navigation Act
1810	New butter and poultry market erected
1811	River Wye tow path opened; Guild hall, Widemarsh Street built
1814	Night watchmen to call the half-hours

1815	Shirehall erected; Permanent Library, St. John's Street founded; Battle of Waterloo
1817	First assize court; David Cox appointed art master of the Cathedral School until 1827
1818	Hereford Medical Library started by James Price, Surgeon
1819	Judges' Lodging, Bye Street (Commercial Street) purchased

George IV
1826	Wye Bridge widened, new footway added; Friends Meeting House, King Street, erected; first gas works, Commercial Road
1827	Blue Coat School, Town Ditch (later Blueschool Street) built
1829	Abergavenny to Hereford tramway completed
1830	Liverpool and Manchester Railway opened, 'Railway Age' dawns; visit of Princess Victoria Alexandrina - future Queen Victoria; Alhambra Theatre, Gwynne Street opened

William IV
1832	First Reform Act; *Hereford Times* founded by Charles Anthony
1833	Reverend John Venn became Vicar of St. Peter's
1834	Cathedral Music Room demolished, school and Three Choirs events relocated
1835	Municipal Corporations Act reduced aldermen and councillors to 24; St. Francis Xavier School opened; St. Peter's Literary Institution, Bye Street (Commercial Street) opened
1836	City lit by gas; charter confirms Hereford right to a court of quarter sessions; police force established; Hereford Dispensary established; Hereford Cricket Club formed
1837	The Old House became the only survivor of Butcher's Row; St. Peter's School founded; Hereford Choral Society founded

Victoria
1838	City purchased St. Ethelbert's Fair rights from Bishop of Hereford and fair reduced from 9 to 3 days; St. Francis Xavier's RC Church, Broad Street, built; Union Workhouse built
1841	Society for Aiding the Industrious founded
1842	St. Nicholas Church built, replacing former medieval church in King Street; city gaol built
1843	Cathedral closed (for 20 years) for restoration of tower and other fabric
1844	Old city prison, Commercial Street demolished, St. Nicholas' School established
1845	Gloucester and Ledbury Canal finally reached Hereford; St. Martin's Church built
1848	Public Health Act; fire brigade established; flour mill opened in Bath Street
1851	Post Office built in Broad Street; Woolhope Naturalists' Field Club founded; Abergavenny - Hereford Tramway closed; Scudamore Schools erected; Great Exhibition
1852	Arts College founded
1853	Hereford's first passenger trains: Shrewsbury, Ludlow (October), Newport, Abergavenny (December); first Hunderton iron bridge built; Hereford washing baths, Kyrle Street built; Report of Thomas Rammell, sanitary commissioner; appointment of Timothy Curley as council consulting engineer
1854	Hereford Improvement Act—basis of many city reforms; Crimean War (until 1856)
1855	Barr's Court station built; many Hereford streets renamed; Athenaeum and Mechanics' Institution, Church Street; Hereford; Ross and Gloucester Railway opened; commercial navigation of River Wye ended
1856	New cattlemarket opened; reservoir and water supply works
1857	Holmer School founded
1858	Corn Exchange opened; Herefordshire Medical Association formed (Herefordshire Medical Society in 1910); 'The Great Stink' of the River Thames alongside Parliament; Indian Mutiny
1859	St. Martin's School opened; Belmont Abbey Church built, additions in the 1880s and 1904
1860	Butter, meat and poultry market opened, High Town
1861	Guildhall, Widemarsh Street rebuilt; Worcester and Hereford Railway opened; death of Prince Albert
1862	Market-hall and guild-hall, High Town demolished
1863	Scott/Skidmore screen installed at the cathedral
1864	Hereford, Hay and Brecon Railway opened; Hereford Penny Readings started; last public execution at Commercial Road county gaol
1866	Railway bridge at Eign erected; public slaughterhouse opened, Stonebow Road
1868	Hereford county and city lunatic asylum commenced, completed 1872; St. Paul's Church, Tupsley opened; St. John's School. Church Street opened
1869	St. James' Church opened; Hereford - Gloucester line converted from broad to standard gauge

1870	City turnpike gates taken down; retirement of Reverend Venn; Hereford Rugby Club formed; All Saints School opened
1871	Hereford public swimming bath, Kyrle Street established
1872	Hereford Rowing Club established; county and city asylum, Burghill opened
1873	First (part time) medical officer of health appointed; Castle Green leased by city council from county justices for 200 years
1874	Museum and public library, Broad Street opened; Working Boys' Home founded, moved to Bath Street 1877
1876	Cathedral School moved to present 'Big School' site, former canons' bakehouse, Castle Street/Quay Street
1880	New gas works opened at Holmer; County College for boys erected, later teachers' training college and college for the blind; First Anglo-Boer War until 1881
1881	Hereford Dispensary building, Union Street erected; Land at Hampton Park purchased for new sewage works; present Post Office, Broad Street erected; old gas works closed
1882	Council offices moved to Mansion House, Widemarsh Street (until a new Town Hall is built); Victoria eye and ear hospital established, Commercial Street; death of Timothy Curley, civil engineer; Garrick Theatre built
1885	Holy Trinity Church opened; death of Dr. Henry Graves Bull, physician and naturalist
1886	Completion of water tower, Broomy Hill
1888	New Herefordshire County Council created; H.P. Bulmer works started in Maylord Street; Hereford Orchestral Society founded
1889	Hereford eye and ear hospital opened, Eign Street
1890	New sewage works opened
1892	Barton passenger station closed
1893	Tupsley isolation hospital opened; *Princess Mary* ferry introduced below infirmary
1894	Wholesale fruit market established
1896	Cattle Fair moved from streets to cattlemarket
1897	Herefordshire Golf Club founded at Broomy Hill
1898	Victoria suspension bridge opened, ferry moved upstream to Hunderton
1899	Electricity generating station, Widemarsh Street opened; Second Anglo-Boer War until 1902
1901	St. James' Church destroyed by fire

Edward VII

1902	Smallpox isolation hospital, Hollywell Gutter Lane, Tupsley opened
1903	Workers' Education Association founded; rebuilt St. James' Church opened
1904	Town Hall opened; Teachers' Training College opened; National Light Car Trials at Hereford; Edward Elgar moved to Plas Gwyn, Hampton Park until 1911
1905	St. Owen's School founded—the first council school under Act of 1902
1906	Holmer council school for infants
1907	New west front of cathedral consecrated
1908	First city bus service; public bowling allowed at Castle Green
1909	Westfaling Street municipal cemetery opened; Garden City opened
1910	River bathing station opened at the Bassom, Bartonsham

George V

1911	Corn Exchange enlarged, public hall and theatre added—The Kemble Theatre named in 1911; first Labour Exchange, Commercial Street/Gomond Street (Laura Ashley)
1912	St. Barnabas (iron) Church, Barrs Court Road, dedicated; Herefordshire Golf Club move to Holmer; Boys' High School opened; Public Library and Art Gallery extensions, Broad Street; Scudamore Schools redeveloped
1914	Worcester Sidings constructed by GWR at Edgar Street—later extended through market; Bishops Meadow land leased to city council—freehold in 1937; outbreak of First World War
1915	Girls' High School, Coningsby Street opened; Dean Leigh Temperance Canteen, Cattlemarket opened
1916	Garrick Theatre, Widemarsh Street, fire; Rotherwas Estate land acquired for a munitions factory
1919	First buses to market towns and villages; housing development at Portfields; The Kinema, 74 St. Owen Street opened
1922	Hereford War Memorial, St. Peter's Square unveiled; Butter Market fire (Reopened 1925)
1924	Hereford United football club formed
1926	Belmont Abbey School established
1929	Old House of 1621 opened as museum, a gift of former occupants, Lloyd's Bank
1930	Old County Gaol, Commercial Road, purchased by city council for a bus station; public baths, Edgar Street opened; Herefordshire Golf Club moved to Wormsley

1934	Working Boys Home, Bath Street closed
1935	Bus station built on former county gaol site
1937	Odeon cinema opened

George VI

1938	Wye Bridge traffic averaged 5,500 daily; 6,698 UK railway stations open; ABC Ritz Cinema opened; Bradbury Lines, Bullingham Lane acquired for army
1939	Government agreement for route of Hereford relief road and bridge; outbreak of Second World War
1940	County Hospital opened; 10 hutted wards added, intended to serve for 10 years
1941	Accidental explosion at Rotherwas, killed three workers and injured six
1942	Hereford's only air raid. Many killed and injured by two bombs at Rotherwas
1944	Accidental explosion at Rotherwas, killed two workers and injured 30
1950	Crossway Farm, Holmer, selected by government as a site for metal industry; Hereford Technical College founded

Elizabeth II

1953	Henry Wiggin & Co. Ltd. opened Hereford factory
1954	Hereford Technical College started move to Folly Lane
1956	Cattle market 'centenary' redevelopment scheme; Three Counties Show final staging at Hereford
1960	Maximum recorded Wye flood level of over 19ft. above summer level; 22nd SAS Regiment move to Hereford; first 'supermarket' in county (Maypole) opened, High Town
1962	Closure of Hereford-Hay-Brecon railway
1963	Kemble Theatre demolished; Beeching measures, Hereford-Ross-Gloucester line and stations, Barton engine shed closed in 1964
1964	Bath Street East works commenced east-west relief road scheme
1966	Greyfriars Bridge opened; Blueschool Street works commenced; Churchill Gardens Museum opened
1967	Bath Street West works commenced, cathedral's Scott/Skidmore screen removed to Coventry, later to Victoria and Albert Museum; West Mercia Constabulary formed; outbreak of Foot and Mouth disease
1968	Newmarket Street roadworks commenced; Merton Meadow car park and lorry wash built
1969	City walls inner relief road officially opened; Art College moved to Folly Lane
1970	Eign Gate (former Eign Street within the gate) pedestrianised
1972	Hereford United's famous FA cup run - elected to League status to 1981; outbreak of Dutch Elm disease
1973	High Town pedestrianised; Hatton Gallery opened; Sixth Form College opened
1974	Wye Valley Nuffield Hospital opened; Waterworks Museum opened
1976	Leisure Pool opened; distribution of the Royal Maundy by the queen
1977	Teachers' Training College closed
1978	Royal National College for the Blind moved to Hereford
1979	Nell Gwynne Theatre and Arts Centre opened
1983	Great Western Way walkway and cycle-path constructed; effects of fire at Goldings, ironmongers, prompted later pedestrianisation of Commercial Street; Tesco development, Bewell Street opened; 9 hole golf course at racecourse opened
1985	Sports and Leisure Centre opened; by-pass scheme for Hereford added to government's trunk road programme
1986	Garrick House multi storey car park and offices built
1987	Maylord Orchards shopping development opened
1988	Mappa Mundi proposed to be sold
1989	Commercial Street and St. Peter's Street pedestrianised
1991	New Leisure Pool opened; Hereford By-pass Inquiry opened - target construction completion 1995
1994	Belmont Abbey School closed
1995	First closed circuit television cameras, city centre
1996	Queen Elizabeth II officially opened the Mappa Mundi and chained library building
1997	All Saints Church reopened after extensive repairs and incorporation of a café
1998	The Herefordshire Council took over most functions of former Hereford City Council; the Courtyard Theatre and Arts Centre opened
1999	New District General Hospital building commenced as one of 13 Private Finance Initiative schemes—target completion April 2002, with Phases 3 and 4 to follow for completion by 2003
2000	Hereford City status and title reinstated by royal charter. New city council granted parish council powers

Bibliography

Abbreviations used:

TWNFC   Transactions of the Woolhope Naturalists' Field Club
HCC/800 cel.   Hereford City Council *800 years - a celebration*
HCC - OG   Hereford City Council Official Guide

Anon. *Hereford Turnpike Roads*, 1863
Attfield, C.E. 'Hereford in the 1850s', *TWNFC*, 1986
    The Environmental Health of Hereford, (HCC report), 1975
Austin, W.H. *The Proposed Waterworks at Broomy Hill, Hereford*, (report) 1970
Aylmer, G. & Tiller, T. (eds.) *Hereford Cathedral, A History*, 2000
Bannister, A.T. *The Cathedral Church of Hereford*, 1924
Beale, John *Herefordshire Orchards, A Pattern for all England*, 1724
Bettington, E.J. 'Some Old Hereford Customs', *TWNFC*, 1938
Bick, David and John Norris *The Hereford and Gloucester Canal*, 1979
Bluecoat School, The *Semper Christe Fidelis*, 1972
Booth, Gavin *The British Motor Bus*, 1977
Bradley, A.G. *In the March and Borderland of Wales*, 1905
British Railways Board *The Reshaping of British Railways*, 1963
Brown, Jonathan *The English Market Town,* 1986
Buchanan, Colin *Traffic in Towns*, 1963
    and partners *The Hereford Transportation Study - Final Report*, 1992
Cadbury, George *Hereford Walls*,1946
Cameron, David Keir *The English Fair*, 1988
Cement and Concrete Association *Greyfriars Bridge*, 1966
Chadwick, Edwin *Report on the Sanitary Condition of the Labouring Population of Great Britain*, 1842
Chamberlin, Russell *The English Country Town*, 1983
Cohen, I. 'The Non-Tidal Wye and its Navigation', *TWNFC*, 1955
    'The Herefordshire and Gloucestershire Canal', *TWNFC,* 1959
Collins, William *Modern Hereford Part II*, 1911
    A Short History of Hereford, 1912
    Historical Landmarks of Hereford, 1915
Cook, R. and C.R. Clinker *Early Railways between Abergavenny and Hereford*, 1984
Crippen, J. *Public Health in Hereford*, (HCC/800 cel.), 1989
Curley, T. *Hereford Sanitary Improvements Report*, 1854
Currie, Diana C.D. 'Improvements in Hereford', *TWNFC*, 1969
Davey, James, *Hereford. Visitors Guide*, 2000
Defoe, Daniel (ed. Rogers) *A Tour through the whole island of Great Britain*, 1971
Dunabin, J.E. *The Hereford Bus*, 1986
    Yeomans of Canon Pyon, 1978
    Hereford Transport, 1970
Duncumb, John *Collections towards the History and Antiquities of the County of Hereford*, 1804
Evans, Charles *Hereford's Ancient Booth Hall*, 1952/3
Fiennes, Celia (ed. Morris) *The Journeys*, 1947
Forrest, G.E. *800 years of Policing Hereford City* (HCC/800 cel.), 1989
Foxton, Derek *Hereford in Old Postcards*, 1983
    Hereford. Then and Now (3 volumes), 1988, 1991 and 1997
    and Betty Grist *Edwardian Hereford*, 1993
Gent, Stuart *A brief look at Social Housing*, (HCC/800 cel.), 1989
Girouard, Mark *The English Town*, 1990
Godwin and Toulson *The Drovers' Roads of Wales*, 1978
Gregg, Pauline *A Social and Economic History of Britain, 1760 - 1965*, 1969
Grundy, Joan. E. 'Population movements in 19th century Herefordshire', *TWNFC*, 1986
Halliday, Stephen *The Great Stink of London, 1858*, 1999
Hereford Times *The Cavalcade of a Century, 1832-1932*,1932

Herefordshire Federation of Womens Institutes *Herefordshire Within Living Memory*, 1993

Herefordshire MIND *Boots on! Out!*, 1995

Hibbs, John *The Country Bus*, 1986

Hill, C.P. *British Economic and Social History 1700-1982*, 1986

Hill, Lt. Col. T.J.B. *Manu Forti! A History of the Herefordshire Regiment*, 1996

Hillaby, J. 'The Norman New Town of Hereford', *TWNFC*, 1983

Hornsby, Brian *90 years of Cinema in Hereford,* 1990

Houston, Jenny (ed.) *City of Hereford Official Guide*, 1994

Howse, W.H. *Historic Hereford*, 1951

    'The Coaching Era at Hereford', *TWNFC,* 1946

Hunt. D. *Festival Memories*, 1996

    Elgar and the Three Choirs Festival, 1999

Hurley, Heather *The Old Roads of South Herefordshire*, 1992

Iliffe-Moon, P.H. (ed.) *City of Hereford Official Guide*, 1988

Jakeman & Co. *Hereford Official Guide*, 1930 to 1939

Jancey, E.M. *The Royal Charters of the City of Hereford*, 1973 and 1989

Johnson, Andrew and Punter, Stephen *Aspects of Herefordshire*, 1987

Langford, A.W. 'The History of Hereford General Hospital', *TWNFC*, 1959

Leather, Ella-Mary *Folk-Lore of Herefordshire*, 1912

Leigh, J.W. *Hereford Cathedral: Record of Work done*, 1910

Lloyd, David W. *The Making of English Towns*, 1992

Lobel, M.D. *Historic Towns - Hereford*, 1969

Lysons, Arnott, Williams and Chance, *Origins and Progress of the meeting of the Three Choirs of Gloucester, Worcester and Hereford ...*, 1895

Macky, J. *A journey through England. In Familar Letters*, 1714

Mitchell, D.J. 'Hereford in the Age of Reform, 1832 - 56', *TWNFC*, 1982

Mogg, E. *Paterson's Roads,* 18th Edn.,1829

Morgan, F.C. 'Hereford Presentements, 1611 to 1659', *TWNFC*, 1940

Morris, E.H. 'The Abergavenny and Hereford Tramroads', *TWNFC* 1941 and 1947

Moyes, ed. Bullock *The Herefordshire Golf Club, 1896-1996*, 1996

Nature Conservancy Council *A Nature Conservation Strategy for Hereford City*, 1988

Nuttgens, Patrick *The Home Front*, 1989

O'Donnell, Jean *Education*, (HCC/800 cel.), 1989

    'John Venn and the Hereford Society for Aiding the Industrious', *TWNFC*, 1990

Oppitz, L. *Hereford and Worcester Railways remembered*, 1990

Parrat, Ron *Hereford United — The League Era*, 1998

Pilkington, F.H.H. *Markets,* (HCC Report), 1994

Porter, Roy *The Greatest Benefit to Mankind*, 1997

Price, John *An historical account of the City of Hereford*, 1796

Rackham, Oliver *The History of the Countryside*, 1986

Rammell, T.W. *Inquiry Report to the General Board of Health*, 1853

Raven, Michael *A Guide to Herefordshire*, 1996

Rees, W.J. *The Hereford Guide* 1806, 1827

Renton, Charles *The Story of Herefordshire's Hospitals*, 1999

Roberts, G. (ed.) *City of Hereford Official Guide*, 1969 to 1980

    Three Choirs Country - Hereford Diocese (Festival Programme Book), 1970

    Two hundred and fifty Years of the Three Choirs Festival. Commemoration — Hereford, ed.Still, 1977

Robinson, Son & Pike *Historical, Commercial and Descriptive Hereford*, 1892

Ross, John *Hereford and Cholera - Why did we escape it?*, 1990

    Henry Graves Bull (1818 - 1885): a provincial polymath, 1996

Sandford, Anne *Hereford as it was*, 1984

    (ed.) *Hereford 800 years - a Celebration*, (HCC/800 cel.), 1989

    Herefordshire in Old Photographs, 1992

Scholefield, Bernard *Fifty Years at the Hereford Hospitals, 1920 - 1970*, 1970

Shane, J. *The Last Pub Crawl*, 1976

Shaw, Watkins *The Three Choirs Festival. The Official History of the Meetings of the Three Choirs of Gloucester, Hereford and Worcester, c.1713-1953*, 1954

Shoesmith, Ron *Hereford City Excavations: Vol. 1 - Excavations at Castle Green*, 1963
                                Vol. 2 - Excavations on and close to the defences, 1982
                                Vol. 3 - The Finds, 1985
       Hereford History and Guide, 1992
       The Pubs of Hereford City, 1994, 1998
Simpson, Helen J. *The Day the Trains Came*, 1997
Smith, William H. *Herefordshire Railways*, 1998
Stanford, S.C. *A Hereford Tannery*, 1960
Stockinger, V. (ed.) *The Rivers Wye and Lugg Navigation 1555 -1951*, 1996
Tate, W.E. *The Parish Chest*, 1983
Thomas, A. *One hundred and fifty years of Hereford Choral Society, 1837-1987*, 1987
Thurston, E. (ed.) *Official Guide to Hereford*, 1956 to 1967
Tonkin, J.W. *Early Street Names of Hereford*, TWNFC, 1966
       and Muriel *The Book of Hereford*, 1975
Toulson and Forbes *The Drovers' Roads of Wales II*, 1992
Trevelyan, G.M. (ed.) *English Social History*, 1946
Watkins. A. *Early British Trackways*, 1922
Webb, S. and B. *The Story of the King's Highway*, 1913
West, John *Town Records*, 1983
West, John and Margaret *A History of Herefordshire*, 1985
Welsh Water Authority *Broomy Hill. Hereford's new Waterworks*, 1977
Whitehead, David *Historic Fabric*, (HCC - OG), 1980
       Yesterday's Town: Hereford, 1983
       & J. Eisel (eds.) *A Herefordshire Miscellany*, 2000
Whitehouse, B.J. *A City of Museums; The Public Library Service* (HCC/800 cel.), 1989
Wilkinson, L.P. *Bulmers. A Century of Cidermaking*, 1987
Williams, Chance and Hannam-Clark, *Annals of the Three Choirs of Gloucester, Hereford and Worcester. Continuation of History of Progress from 1895 to 1930*, 1930
Woodham-Smith, C. *Queen Victoria. Her Life and times. Volume One 1819 - 1861*, 1972
Woolhope Naturalists' Field Club *Herefordshire, its Natural History, Archaeology and History*, 1954
Wright, J.P. *A Walk through Hereford*, 1819
Young, Barbara *In Our Dreaming and Singing, The Story of the Three Choirs Festival Chorus*, 2000

OFFICIAL REPORTS ETC.
Department of Transport, A 49 / A 465 Hereford Bypass Environmental Statement, 1990
A 49/A 465 Hereford Bypass - Statement of Case, Department of Transport, 1991
A 49/ A 465 Hereford Bypass - Environmental Statement, Department of Transport/Burrow & Ptnrs., 1990
Hereford and Worcester County Council, Transport Policies and Programme, 1990-1991
Director of Public Health, Health in Herefordshire, 1990
Hereford City Council, including:
       Hereford Livestock Market. Centenary 1856-1956, 1956
       Merton Meadow. Lorry Wash and Car Park, 1968
       Statement of Principles, Central Area Development (with County Council), 1962
       Central Area Redevelopment. Report of Working Party (with County Council), 1964
       Issues and Choices, Central Area (with County Council), 1976
       Preferred Choice, Central Area (with County Council), 1978
       Hereford Local Plan, 1987
       High Town Study (with English Heritage and Hereford Archaeology Committee), 1989
       Population and Housing (Information Note), 1989
       Housing Strategy Statement, 1989/90, 1990/91
       Hereford Local Plan, 1996
Herefordshire County Council:
       County Development Plan. Town map no.1 - Hereford Area. Report of the Survey. Written Statement, 1951
       Housing. Study Report Green Paper - County Structure Plan, 1970
Herefordshire Council:
       Draft Herefordshire Tourism Economic Impact Assessment, 1998/99
       Planning for the New Millennium, 1999

Unitary Development Plan, Development Options; Sustainability appraisal; Summary of responses to the consultation, 1999
Herefordshire Local Transport Plan, 2001/02 - 2005/06
UDP Preferred Proposals for Hereford City, August 2001
& Herefordshire Health Authority, Draft Health Improvement Programme, 2001
Herefordshire Health Authority
Health in Herefordshire. Annual Report of the Director of Public Health, 2000
Herefordshire Nature Trust *et al.*, Biodiversity Action Plan, 2000
The Herefordshire Partnership
The Herefordshire Plan, 2000
Herefordshire Cultural Strategy Summary, 2001
Heart of England Tourist Board, Herefordshire Visitor Survey, 1999
Labour Party, Ambitions for Britain manifesto, 2001
South Herefordshire District Council, District Local Plan - Part 1, 1994

MAPS AND DRAWINGS
Richard of Haldingham and Lafford, Mappa Mundi, *c.*1260
John Speede, Map of Herefordshire,1610
Samuel and Nathaniel Buck, North-east Prospect of the City of Hereford, 1732
Isaac Taylor, Map of Hereford, 1757
H. Price, A Plan of the City of Hereford, 1802 and 1852
G. Cole and J. Roper, Map of Hereford, 1806
Lieut. Robt. Dawson, R.E., Hereford (from the Ordnance Survey), 1831
Timothy Curley, Map of Hereford, 1858
Jos. Jones & Co., Plan of the City of Hereford embracing all the recent Improvements, 1867

DIRECTORIES
Lascelles and Co., Herefordshire Directory and Gazetteer, 1851
Edward Cassey and Co., Herefordshire History, Topography and Directory, 1858
Littlebury, Herefordshire Directory and Gazetteer, 1876
Kelly, Post Office Directory of Herefordshire, 1879
Wells and Martin, Directory of Hereford, Ross and District, 1886
Jakeman and Carver, Directory and Gazetteer of Herefordshire, 1890, 1914
Kent Service Ltd., Hereford and District Directory, 1959

OTHER
Minute Books of the Hereford Town Council, the Paving, Repairing, Cleaning and Lighting Commissioners and the Common Council, 1723 to 1856
Guidebook to the Waterworks Museum, Broomy Hill, 1998
Hereford Times
Hereford Journal
The Morning Post
New Civil Engineer
The Times
Hereford Civic Trust, Newsletters
Hereford Lore. Age to Age, Newsletters
The Friends of Hereford Cathedral (FHC), Annual Reports

Index

Please note, this index has been compiled using various categories of entries, notably: Acts of Parliament; almshouses; architects; churches, chapels and sects; developers; education; health; hospitals; housing (and housing developments); industrial and trading estates and business centres; inns, public houses and hotels; law and order; libraries; manufacturing; markets and fairs; museums and art galleries; public transport; railways; schools and colleges; shops; sport; streets, lanes, passages, squares etc; theatres and cinemas; trades; traffic congestion